The James and Younger Brothers

JESSE JAMES.

From a photograph taken in 1882, at St. Joseph, while passing under the name of Thomas Howard.

The James and Younger Brothers

The Story of One the Most Notorious and Legendary Outlaw Gangs of the American West

J. A. Dacus

The James and Younger Brothers
*The Story of One the Most Notorious and Legendary Outlaw Gangs
of the American West*
by J. A. Dacus

First published under the title
*Illustrated Lives and Adventures of Frank and Jesse James and the Younger Brothers,
the Noted Western Outlaws*

Leonaur is an imprint
of Oakpast Ltd

Copyright in this form © 2017 Oakpast Ltd

ISBN: 978-1-78282-626-2 (hardcover)
ISBN: 978-1-78282-627-9 (softcover)

http://www.leonaur.com

Publisher's Notes

The views expressed in this book are not necessarily
those of the publisher.

Contents

Preface	9
The James Family	11
Frank and Jesse	17
In the Guerrilla Camp	22
Bloody War	25
At the Sack of Lawrence, Kansas	29
A Gory Record	32
Adventures in Separate Fields	42
The Brandenburg, Ky., Tragedy	47
The Liberty Bank Affair	50
Jesse's Sortie Against the Militiamen	52
In the Hands of Friends	55
The Russellville Bank Robbery	58
On the Pacific Slope	63
Were They Driven to Outlawry?	70
The Gallatin Bank Tragedy	73
Attempts to Arrest the Boys	76
Outrage at Columbia, Kentucky	79
Out of Exile	83
The Corydon Raid	89
The Cash Box of the Fair	91
Ste. Genevieve	94
A Railway Train Robbed in Iowa	98
The Gains' Place Stage Robbery	102
Gadshill	107
After Gadshill	112
Whicher's Ride to Death	116
A Night Raid of Detectives	122

Proposed Amnesty	127
The San Antonio-Austin Stage Plundered	131
Farmer Askew's Fate	135
Gold Dust—The Muncie Business	138
Other Exploits	141
Jesse's Wooing and Wedding	145
A Dream of Love	149
Fair Annie Ralston, the Outlaw's Bride	152
A Seventeen Thousand Dollar Haul	156
In Minnesota	163
The Attack at Northfield—Haywood's Death	168
Escape of Frank and Jesse James	176
A Visit to Carmen	180
The Robbers and Their Friends	185
Excursions into Mexico	190
Death to Border Brigands	196
A Golden Harvest Reaped by Outlaws	204
A Visit to Frank James' Home	211
Epistles of Jesse James	218
Glendale	225
Hunting Clues	231
George W. Shepherd	233
Pursuit of the Glendale Robbers	240
Allen Parmer	244
Jesse James Still a Free Rover	247
Changing a Five-Dollar Bill	250
Winstonville	253
After Winstonville	257
Jesse's Last Exploit	261
Gathering Clouds	265
Death of Jesse James	268
Jesse's Last Resting Place	277
The Younger Family	285
With Quantrell	291
The Guerrillas Disband	297
Northfield and Stillwater	302

Strange murmurs fill my tingling ears,
Bristles my hair, my sinews quake,
At this dread tale of reckless deeds.

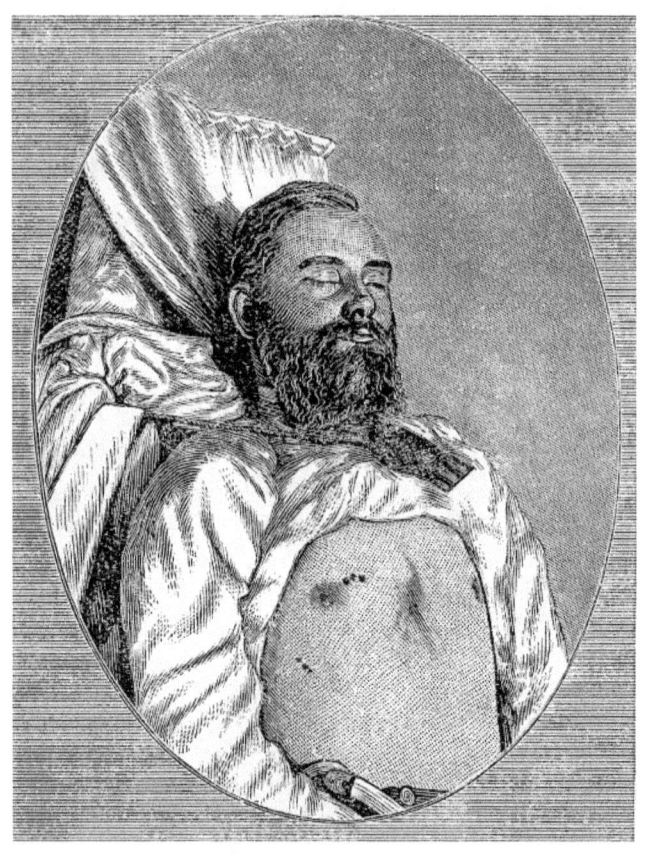

JESSE JAMES AFTER DEATH
Showing scars on right breast, from wounds received during the war.

Preface

The object of this volume is to present the history of Frank and Jesse James in a connected and authentic form. Few persons are aware of the immense labour and difficulties attending such a task, and which are made the secret excuse for those highly imaginative (and even fabricated) accounts with which the public have been repeatedly imposed upon. Convinced, through his experience as an editorial writer for the St. Louis press, of the wide-spread and intense interest attaching to this subject, the author began collecting data three years ago, and has, since then, amassed, collated and weighed a mass of material which it is hardly an exaggeration to call enormous.

Original sources of information have been the author's principal and most trusted guide. Visits of length to the home and neighbourhood of Mrs. Samuel, the mother of Frank and Jesse James, in Clay County, Missouri, have been especially fruitful in this respect, enabling him to establish many otherwise doubtful points, to clear up seeming mysteries, and settle numerous controversies of more or less moment. The information gathered during these visits, the author regards as by far the most valuable which he obtained. It is interwoven into almost every chapter of this book.

It is a strange commentary upon the boasted power of the law that the raids and reprisals of Frank and Jesse James have gone on for twenty years, upon a scale of startling magnitude and boldness. They have been hunted, at different times, by thousands of armed men, stimulated by desperate energy and the promise of large rewards. These rewards aggregate no less than $75,000. They were offered in vain. The outlaws are still at large., (1880).

The remarkable career of Frank and Jesse James has been the outgrowth of circumstances which constitute, when taken together, the most important chapter in American history. Of that history, it is, in fact, a significant part; and it is, besides, a striking illustration of one phase of American life. Recognising the propriety of the demand that it be put on record with accuracy, fullness and candour, the author has conscientiously endeavoured to present the facts as they actually occurred. Conclusions are inevitable and necessary, but it seems the wiser course to leave them for the reader to draw for himself.

Gov. T. T. Crittenden
Who directed the pursuit of Jesse James

Chapter 1

The James Family

He was a godly man,
Gentle and loving.
He sought to save
From mortal shame and eternal death,
Forms laid in the silence of the grave.

The Rev. Robert James, the father of Frank and Jesse, was a native of Kentucky. His parents were quiet, respectable people, belonging to the middle class of society. Their desire was to raise up their children "in the nurture and admonition of the Lord." Being themselves persons of intelligence and culture, far above the average of their neighbours in those days, the parents of Rev. Robert James resolved to give him as good an education as the facilities accessible to them would permit. Accordingly, Robert was early placed in a neighbouring school, and made such progress as to gladden the hearts of his parents, and call forth auguries of future distinction from the friends and neighbours of the family.

Robert James was a moral, studious youth, much given to reflection on subjects of a religious character. Before he had attained his eighteenth year, he had made an open profession of faith in the Christian religion, and united himself with a Baptist church, of which his parents were members. After passing through the various grades of an academic course, young James entered as a student of Georgetown College, Kentucky. Resolving to follow the profession of a minister, he commenced the study of Theology, was licensed to preach, and began his ministry in his twentieth year. Even then he was regarded as a youth of decided culture and more than ordinary ability.

While yet a young man, Rev. Mr. James decided to remove to the

FRANK JAMES. JESSE JAMES.

AT THE CLOSE OF THE WAR

then new State of Missouri. He settled on a farm in Clay County, and commenced in earnest the onerous duties of a pioneer preacher. His labours were not unrewarded. He soon had the satisfaction of garnering the harvest of his sowing. A congregation was gathered and a church organised in Clay County, called New Hope, which is still in existence. For some years, the Rev. Mr. James ministered to the people who had been gathered by his exertions, with great acceptance. Nor were his labours confined to the spiritual welfare of the people of New Hope. He visited many distant churches, and preached with great acceptance in many places.

Old citizens of Clay County still entertain pleasant recollections of the earnest. God-fearing pastor, who went about only to do good, by cheering the despondent, consoling the sorrowful, assisting the needy, upholding the weak, confirming the hesitating, and pointing the way of salvation to the penitent. Everywhere, in that region of country, he was held in the very highest esteem. So, the years of his early manhood passed away while he was engaged in the commendable effort to better the condition, by purifying the moral nature of his friends and neighbours.

In 1850, following in the footsteps of hundreds of others, Rev. Robert James bade *adieu* to his family, friends and neighbours, and set out for "the golden land" of California, on a prospecting tour. We do not know what motives actuated him in making this move, nor is it pertinent to this relation. He went away, and was destined to return no more. Not long after his arrival in California, whither he had been preceded by a brother, Rev. Mr. James was stricken by a mortal disease which terminated his life in a short time. Far away from home, where the tall sequoias rear their lofty branches above the plain, on a gentle slope which catches the last beams of the setting sun, they laid the minister to rest, in a soil unhallowed by the dust of kinsmen, in a grave unbedewed by the tears of loved ones left behind.

When yet a young man. Rev. Mr. James was united in marriage to Miss Zerelda Cole, a native of Scott County, Kentucky. Mrs. James is a lady of great determination of mind, and a masculine force of character. Those who knew the couple in the old days seem to think that the minister and his wife were an ill-assorted pair. He was gentle and amiable, while, on the contrary, his wife was strong in passion, and of a very bitter, unrelenting temper—traits of character prominently developed in her sons, Frank and Jesse. It is said that the home-life of the minister was not as smooth as it might have been, had he been united with a companion of a less passionate and exacting temper. With his domestic life, however, we have nothing to do, except in so far as the home influences thrown around his children gave direction to their character, and tinged their mental disposition. Whatever home-cares he might have had, the public has little cause to inquire now. He went down to death with a stainless name long years before his sons entered upon a career of crime, and made their names a terror to those who care to obey the dictates of justice, love and mercy.

Mrs. Zerelda James was left a widow, having the responsible charge of a family of four small children. She was not left unprovided for, as Mr. James was a prudent, careful man of business, and had already established a comfortable home. With that courage and determination which is so prominently manifested in her character, Mrs. James commenced the battle of life as the head of the family. With all the favouring circumstances, the task assumed by her was not a light one. But she was equal to the performance of any required service.

The years went by, and Frank and Jesse and their sisters were advancing toward manhood and womanhood. The mother was not neglectful of their mental training, and the children were very regular in their attendance at a neighbouring district school.

So, passed away six years of Mrs. Zerelda James' widowhood, and life became lonely; the children were growing up, and her cares and responsibilities seemed to increase as they advanced in age and stature. Though not of a romantic disposition, the widow James was yet young enough in years and comely enough in person to attract to her side more than one substantial citizen on matrimony intent.

Among the number of those who sought to produce a favourable impression on the widow's susceptible heart, was Dr. Reuben Samuels, who, like herself, was a native of Kentucky. To him she was not indifferent. She listened to his plea, and in 1857 they were united in marriage, near Kearney, Clay County, Missouri. Dr. Samuels at once undertook to perform the duty of a parent toward her children.

Thus, the career of the noted outlaws, the James Boys, was commenced, under auspices fully as favourable as fell to the fortune of any of the Boys of their own age, in their country home. And so the years rolled on, and the Boys were approaching the estate of manhood; while fate was shaping them to perform a part in those troublous times, of which they dreamed not in the days of boyhood.

One of the sisters of Frank and Jesse died just as she was approaching the estate of womanhood. She is represented as having been a

yours respectfully
Zerelda Samuel.

(Formerly Mrs. James,) Mother of Frank and Jesse James.

Dr. REUBEN SAMUEL.
Step-father of Frank and Jesse James.

beautiful and amiable child, who was called away from the world while life was still beautiful and all the promises of the future bright. Miss Susan James was arrested with her mother in the early part of the war and confined in the jail at St. Joseph for several months. Afterward she went to Nebraska and remained there for more than a year. She married a gentleman named Parmer, several years ago, and with her husband, resided for a time in Sherman, Texas. From that place she removed to Henriette, and was living there in 1879.

Mrs. Samuels had an eight year old son killed in January, 1875, when the detectives attacked the Samuels' house. A daughter, a half-sister of Frank and Jesse, remains unmarried, and resides, (1880), with Dr. and Mrs. Samuels,

Mrs. SUSAN L. PARMER.   (Formerly Susie James.)

Chapter 2

Frank and Jesse

There will be storms
In causeless, strange abuse, and the strong breath
Of busy mouths will blow upon our course.

Of prophecy, many have a doubt. And yet there are prophecies from simple lips, and warnings from babes and sucklings, which if we could but interpret aright, might assist us to change the whole currents of life in a fellow being.

Deeper than fear or doubting men are thrown into the great vortex of the world's thought and actions. What fortune or fate shall come to them, no one can tell. Every billow in that maelstrom seeks its own wild independence; and the shores of that tumultuous deep—which we call human society—are strewn along with the dull wrecks of what were once glorious schemes—the bright day dreams—once borne buoyantly upon the topmost waves. These, and myriads of other schemes and hopes, are at last remanded to lie under the dark waters of the Sea of Fate, hidden so completely that no thought of man shall ever again recall them to memory.

It is perhaps best so. It would be equivalent to the expulsion of all the joys of life to have opened before us the book of the future, wherein is recorded the deeds which must be performed, and the sorrows which shall fall, dark and impenetrable—extinguishing every scintillation of joyous hope.

It was best for Robert James, the minister, that he was called home before the shadows fell, before the prophet's voice gave warning of the things which should come to pass. It was well he was spared the revelation, so that when the summons came, in peace he drew around him the drapery of his couch, and while the brilliant sun of an undimmed faith shone full upon him, he laid aside the load of life, and went into the presence of the Deity, satisfied with a career which had more of love toward mankind than displeasure at the conduct of the world.

When their father was laid away in a far-off grave, Frank was but a "wee boy," and Jesse still an infant. From him they had received few lessons to guide them through the thorny ways of life. Their widowed mother became their counsellor and teacher. From her they had inherited their most pronounced traits of character—strong-willed, courageous, self-assertive, and unrelenting toward those who had given cause of offense.

Those who knew them during the days of their childhood and youth, differ widely in opinion concerning the character of the promise they gave of their future course in life. Some say they were "nice, well behaved boys," others that "they were about like other boys," and yet another class say that they were "bad boys, very bad boys from the beginning." There is no doubt that they were sometimes "a little wild," as their best friends admit. We have accounts of some of their childish actions which indicate that even in early life they manifested a decided inclination to be malicious, not to say heartless and cruel.

The stepfather of the boys seems to be a man of amiable disposition, and his government over the children was far from being after the order of the traditional stepfather. The consequence was Frank and Jesse advanced to the years of maturity without any of those healthful, restraining influences which moralists assure us are essential to the proper development of the higher qualities of manhood. Be that as it may, we have been assured by persons of the highest respectability, who were acquainted with them long before the commencement of the war between the States, that "they were their own masters" at a very early age, save only when their strong-willed mother asserted her prerogative to dominate over them, which, by the way, she seldom did. Among the boys of the neighbourhood they were not without friends. But among them, they were leaders. Aside from a willingness on the part of other boys to accept such leadership, the Jameses were exceedingly disagreeable, and generally attempted to enforce a due recognition of their superiority. Such were the great outlaws as boys.

It is related of them, that when Frank was thirteen, and Jesse eleven years of age respectively, they met a boy with whom at some previous time they had engaged in a childish wrangle. The lad who had incurred their ill-will was thirteen years old, well developed, and possessed of courage and determination. Bat he was not able to engage successfully in a contest with the brothers. It was in the spring time. The streams were full and deep. The boys met in a large forest. The Jameses attacked their neighbour, and succeeded in administering to him a severe beating. Not content with this, they procured thongs of tough bark, bound their victim securely and threw him into a deep pool in a neighbouring stream. Several times was this ducking process repeated, to the great terror of the boy, and the infinite satisfaction of his tormentors.

After satiating their vengeance in this way, until thoroughly wearied, the young tyrants drew him out and tied him securely to a tree in the midst of the gloomy forest. It was in the morning when they left him there, and he was not released until nearly dusk, when a neighbour, who was out in pursuit of squirrels, heard his cries and went to his assistance. The boy had suffered so much, that he was thrown into a fever, from which he did not recover in many weeks. These tyrant Boys were the predecessors of the guerrillas and the outlaws.

It was an early ambition of Frank and Jesse to have and use firearms. Dr. Samuels presented each of them with a small double-barrel shotgun, and the accompanying accoutrements of the sportsman. The day the gift was received was a proud and happy one to the Boys. They soon learned to use them, and in a brief time they were expert shots, and many feathered songsters ceased to sing forever before their unerring aim. Rabbits, squirrels and other small game were their prey.

The Boys with their New Shot Guns.

But shotguns lost their novelty after a while, and they yearned for pistols. They had read or heard of the skill of the adventurers away out on the borders, and they dreamed of rivalling them some day. At last by dint of self-denial and persistent saving, Frank and Jesse were made glad by an opportunity which was offered to procure pistols, on the occasion of a visit to St. Joseph, which they were permitted to make in company with Dr. and Mrs. Samuels.

We may safely conclude that the pistols were not of the pattern which the outlaws of the present day most esteem. But they had pistols, and the neighbours in the vicinity of the Samuels' residence very speedily became painfully aware of the fact, by the perpetual reports of their weapons while they were out "at practice," which was nearly every hour of daylight. This constant practice gave them proficiency in the use of such weapons, and long before they had arrived at manhood's estate they were masters of the art of pistol shooting.

They became noted throughout the neighbourhood for their skill. So accurate had become their aim that they would measure a distance of fifteen paces from a tree standing in an open space, and commence walking around it, firing glancing shots as they walked, and so continuing until they had completely girdled the tree. Later in life they acquired such skill that they would ride at a full gallop around a circle, with a tree in its centre, at a distance of seventy-five paces, firing as they rode, and entirely girdle the tree with revolver bullets, never losing a single shot. Thus, Frank and Jesse had become masters of an art which rendered them dangerous foes when the days of turmoil came.

Girdling a Tree.

So the years passed away, and the lads had already grown to be tall and shapely, when the tocsin of civil war rang throughout the land. They were not then old enough to enter at once upon the duties incumbent upon soldiers. But they were growing apace, and the days of strife and bloodshed were not destined to pass away ere they grew strong enough to ride with the strongest, and bold enough to face danger with the most daring.

We may well suppose that all their dreams at that momentous period were of war, bloodshed, and all the concomitant horrors of warfare. The shadow of Destiny had fallen athwart their pathway when the first gun was fired—the pandemonium of passion, still dormant in their breasts, was ready to be kindled in all its baleful fury.

Chapter 3

In the Guerrilla Camp

Woe, ah, bitter woe!
The suffering mother and the moaning babe.
The aged feeling in their veins the blood
Chilling forever.

At last the war-cloud, which had been hovering for months over our fair land, burst with a fury that was appalling. Cheeks were blanched and hearts were made tremulous in agony. Missouri was destined to realise a season of despair, such as has fallen upon few people in modern times. It was neighbour against neighbour, kinsman against kinsman, brother against brother, and vengeful hate burning up all that was merciful and good in human nature. The night of woe had descended.

The appearance of the renowned Guerrilla chieftain, Quantrell, on the border; the stories which were circulated concerning his achievements; the feverish state of the public mind, and the circumstances in which the people of this State were involved, all contributed to exert a large influence over the minds of the youths and young men just coming upon the stage of life in the Western counties. Cole Younger, who had not then been regarded as "a wild lad," equally with Frank James, who had been so regarded, was attracted to the standard of the daring guerrilla. In the vortex of passion which whirled through the land, all principles, love, justice, mercy and hope were swallowed up. Men were transformed by the baleful influence.

Previous to the departure of Frank James for Quantrell's camp, there is no evidence that Dr. or Mrs. Samuels had been mistreated or in any way insulted by the Federal militia. The Samuels family were intensely attached to the Southern cause, and the very appearance of soldiers in the blue uniform of the United States was not a little galling to the sectional pride and native passion of Mrs. Samuels, who did not hesitate at any time to abuse the cause which they represented. In this pleasant pastime, she was always emphatic and unamiable in expression.

It was early in 1862 that Frank James bid *adieu* to all peaceful pursuits, and rode away in the dim twilight hour to seek the camp of the guerrilla chieftain. He had made a start toward becoming an outlaw. It was in the spring-time. Frank was away with Quantrell's reckless band, and Jesse, who had attained the age of sixteen years, was ploughing in a field on the Samuels estate, near Kearney, when on a bright day, a band of Federal militia approached the homestead. They first encountered Dr. Samuels, and him they laid violent hands upon, bore him away to a convenient tree, adjusted a rope about his neck and hanged him to a projecting branch until life was almost extinct, and so they left him for others to relieve.

Not content with this exhibition of prowess, the valiant warriors proceeded to the field where Jesse followed his plough, and laid hold upon him, and placed a rope around his neck and told him his hour had come, and while they tormented him in this manner, some of them pricked his body with their bayonet-points or their sabres. The reason assigned by the militiamen for this exhibition of violence, was that Jesse James was accustomed to ride fast and far when the shades of night fell upon the earth, to convey intelligence to the guerrilla chieftain of the movements of the militia. When they had chastised him, and warned him that if he rode any more to carry the news they would kill him, they let him go his way.

But Jesse James was not to be intimidated. He rode again and again to the hidden camp. His bad passions were aroused. The boy had become a savage. That same week the militia made a descent upon the farmhouse of Dr. Samuels, and finding Mrs. Samuels and her daughter, Miss Susie James, at home, they were placed under arrest and conveyed to the jail at St. Joseph, at that time a place reeking in filth, where they were detained for a number of weeks, all the while subjected to the coarse jests and cruel jeers of the unfeeling guards.

This last act on the part of the Federal militia determined the future course of Jesse James. While his mother and sister languished in jail, Jesse mounted a horse, fleet of foot, and rode away, nor did he stop until he drew rein in Quantrell's camp. At this time, he was described as not yet sixteen years of age, with a smooth, handsome face, with deep blue eyes, and a complexion as soft, as delicate and fair as a school girl's. But even then, the bright blue eyes were never at rest, and about the mouth were the lines of strong determination, and a certain expression of countenance that indicated cool courage. He, perhaps, had the susceptibility of being merciful, but *his mercy* was a mere whim—a passing fancy and not a quality.

Frank and Jesse had both entered upon their career—a course in life destined to blight all that was noble, or susceptible of becoming noble and grand in character. The old life, with all its promise, and all its dreams and hopes, was past. Henceforth a new life, fraught with danger and sufferings, and crimes which should make their very names a terror, was to animate them. The hard lines were drawn, and the men who might have served well the interests of a peaceful society, had more favourable circumstances surrounded them, cast loose all the restraints of civilized life, and in a day, as it were, returned to that condition of savage existence from which the race had been raised by ages of struggle. They were not long in proving to their comrades that they were worthy to be numbered among their desperate ranks. Their efficiency as daring and dangerous partisans was soon made manifest.

Chapter 4

Bloody War

The presence of soldiers is a wicked thing,
Bounded in time and circumscribed in space.

The presence of armed men wearing the blue uniform of the Federal Army in the counties of Platte, Clinton and Clay, Missouri, was commingled gall and worm-wood to the souls of that portion of the population which was devoted to the Southern cause. These constituted probably more than two-thirds of the inhabitants. The passions of the people on both sides were at a white heat. Neighbour was contending with neighbour, and friends were ready to strike down the friends who opposed, and old associates divided by politics, had become the bitterest of foes. Anarchy prevailed. Society was rent into fragments and the law of hate was triumphant.

Frank and Jesse James were with Quantrell's band, and were selected to go on an expedition with a scout under Captain Scott, to the north side of the Missouri River. The town of Richfield was garrisoned by a company of some thirty men under command of a Captain Sessions, of the Federal State militia. Scott's command consisted of only twelve. Yet with this feeble force he determined to attack Richfield. Frank James was one of the men appointed to lead the attacking party. A desperate fight ensued. Captain Sessions and Lieut. Graffenstien, of the Federal garrison, were killed at the first fire. The guerrillas gained a complete triumph. Ten of the militiamen were killed, while Scott did not lose a man. The survivors of the fray surrendered to the partisan, Captain Scott, and he paroled them.

After the morning fight, Scott moved about twenty miles that day to the house of one Pat McGinnis, in Clay County. It was made the duty of Frank James to scout through the country that night, and he rode away from the camp of the partisan in the black night—rode straightway to the home of his mother. That lady was at home. She had been collecting information for the use of the guerrillas, and was pleased to see her son. To him she opened her budget of intelligence. The movement of Scott on Richfield had startled the Federal militia. The small bands were rapidly concentrating, and were strengthening their position every day. Plattsburg, the county seat of Clinton, had been stripped of its garrison, which had been sent out to hunt for the bold raiders, and was at that very time defenceless. Such was the character of the information gathered by Mrs. Samuels, and imparted to her son, who, in company with a comrade, Mr. Fletcher Taylor, rode hastily back to Scott's camp to report the character of the information which he had gained.

On receiving the information, Scott resolved to make an attempt upon Plattsburg. During the succeeding day, it was ascertained that Captain Rodgers had left Plattsburg to make an effort to discover and capture Scott, taking with him most of the garrison. In the first watch of the second night after the affair at Richfield, Scott's little band silently deserted their camp and rode rapidly toward Plattsburg. Two o'clock in the morning found them within four miles of that place, on

The Moonlight Conference.

Smith's fork of Grand River. Here they halted and slept until daylight. They were in a deep forest, and quite secure from observation.

Until three o'clock in the evening they remained quiet, feeding their horses and resting. Then the scouts brought intelligence concerning the situation at the town, and the guerrillas, mounting, set out to capture it. There were a few men left as a guard at the Court-house, under the command of a lieutenant. The officer had been out in town when the guerrillas charged into the public square. Before he could rejoin his men he was cut off by Frank James, to whom he was compelled to yield himself a prisoner. James at once conducted his captive into the presence of Captain Scott. The militia in the Court-house, though taken by surprise, were not disposed to yield without a struggle. At the time the lieutenant was brought before Scott, they were pouring a severe fire among the guerrillas, and the issue was in doubt.

Pointing to his prisoner, Frank said, "Captain, shoot that man, unless he delivers up the Court-house."

"That I will!" responded Scott, with a terrible oath as he drew his pistol.

The officer besought his men to yield, which under the circumstances they consented to do.

Two hundred muskets were captured and destroyed, and $12,000 in "Union Defence Warrants," of the State of Missouri, were seized and appropriated. The spoils of victory were divided among the band. Frank's share was $1,000. It was his first taste of gain through violent appropriation—an initiative lesson, so to speak. He has become a proficient since that time. The raiders, whose camps were usually to be found in forests, far away from the generally travelled highways, concluded to sup like civilized men that night, hence they ordered supper at the hotel, and had for their guest the late Federal commander of the post.

Frank James is a silent man, having little to say, and that little is brought out in sharp, short sentences. He is not so tall as Jesse, nor so robust in form. He never laughs, and was never known to jest with his comrades. In the early days of the war he was beardless, and the outlines of his features were visible to all. His face is long, with a broad, square forehead, and a strong under jaw and heavy chin. His eyes are dark grey and are restless, and always have a wicked expression about them. In later years Frank James wears a full beard, and on that account, is not so readily recognisable by those who knew him in the old days.

Jesse James, as a youth, had a round jovial face, and rather a pleasant expression of countenance. He was then the reverse of taciturn; had a merry laugh, and was "a fellow of infinite jest" among his comrades. In all his subsequent career, he has been the Aaron to Frank. Jesse always does the talking yet| when they have occasion to communicate with strangers. In later years Jesse, too, has become reserved, not so taciturn as his brother, but still more silent than the average of men. Neither one of the brothers is given to boisterous merriment nowadays, since life's shadows have fallen so darkly around them.

Chapter 5

At the Sack of Lawrence, Kansas

Wherefore this tangle of perplexities,
The trouble or the joys? the weary maze
Of narrow fears and hopes, that may not cease,
A chill falls on us from the skiey ways,
Black with the night-tide where is none to hear
The ancient cry, the wherefore of our days.

The years come and go, and they give birth to bright and tender dreams, as well as to passions dark as Azrael's wing, and fierce as flames of Tophet. Yes, the years give joy and peace to some, and hope buds, as in the spring days the lilacs bloom. Yet time digs deep graves in which to bury our fondest hopes, and obliterates in indistinguishable night every earthly joy. It is better so. If we could draw aside the screen which hides from our ken the things of the future, who of us would enjoy the prospect?

There was a time, perhaps, when Frank and Jesse James would shudder at the thought that they should become not only soldier-slayers of men, but robbers and murderers as well. And yet they were drifting down a rapid tide toward the great black gulf of evil. A few months calls the leaves from their buds, and dresses the forest in green—a few months more and the leaves and flowers wither before the North wind's breath and the beautiful flowers and the gay leaves become loathsome in the dust of decay.

And so too, we imagine, are the changes of mind and the transformation of character. The James Boys were in a school where the gentle law of mercy was never imparted; in a school where the instructors were incarnations of bitterness and hate, and every pupil devoted to the lessons they gave out. So, the months rolled away and it was not long before they could listen unmoved to the last sigh of the dying victim, and send a foe before the aim of their unerring bullets, to challenge the sentinels on the farther shore of the river of death without a thought or tremor of remorse. They were fit now to take part in the most sanguinary warfare ever waged in this country—the guerrilla warfare along the border of Missouri.

It was therefore without any twinges of conscience that they heard the proposition of the revengeful Quantrell, to capture and sack the city of Lawrence and massacre its male inhabitants. They were in the transforming stage; the full-grown desperadoes were just coming along the steps of time from the closet of the future.

It was a night in August—the 16th—1863, when the commander of the fiercest band of guerrillas that ever marauded in the State of Missouri, gave the order, "Saddle up, men!" in his camp on the Blackwater, and unfurling that ominous black banner with the single relief of the word "Quantrell" in white, the bush-warriors rode west toward the Kansas border, intent upon a mission which could neither succeed nor suffer repulse without bringing sorrow to many hearts. On the way three peaceable citizens beyond the Aubrey, were pressed into service as guides to the bloody band. They forced these to lead them until they had reached a part of the country where their knowledge extended no further, and when they came to a grove of timber on the margin of a stream, the three poor inoffensive men were remorselessly shot, Frank James being one of the executioners. They had set out to kill all Kansas men.

On the morning of the 21st, it was as clear and bright a summer morning as ever gladdened the earth. Quantrell's band was in full view of the ill-fated city. There was a charge, women's faces blanched, and shrieks rent the air. Volley after volley broke the stillness of the morning. The people saw the sombre black flag, and knew that the guerrillas were upon them. On they came, a resistless tide. Men sank down without a groan. The very streets ran red in human blood. Women and children, coming before the fatal revolver bullets which streamed along the street, met their fate as they fled for the shelter of homes that were destined for the flames to feed upon.

In this pandemonium of war-fiends, Frank and Jesse James were conspicuous actors. Here, there, everywhere, when opportunity offered, men either armed or unarmed and defenceless were made victims of their skill as pistol shooters, and they felt no more regret than if they had been acting the part of honourable soldiers and *chevaliers*.

The torch was applied, and the terrors of billowy flames were added to the horrors of the scene. How many houses they burned, and how many lives they destroyed that day, they themselves do not know; of the first there were several, of the second there were many.

They returned with Quantrell to Missouri. They had learned well. The lads who are claimed by their friends to have been gentle as cooing doves in the home nest had been singularly transformed into merciless eagles, or vindictive kites, rather. They had proved that human rights and human lives had little to call for their regard, and so the first stage of a notorious career had been attained by these brothers ere yet they had reached their majority.

After Lawrence.

CHAPTER 6

A Gory Record

Oh, the dread of by-gone days!—
A fearful tale they tell,
When rung the woodland echoes round
To warlike shout and yell,
When fiercely met the hostile bands,
And deadly grew the strife,
And wildly, with the clash of arms,
Went up the shriek for life.

The cruel strife of the border can never be forgotten. Those were tragic days, the very remembrance of which comes like a dream of sorrow and desolation of soul. It is well that such terrible times have passed away, for to those who were exposed to the fury of that tidal-wave of passion, which swept over the fair border-land, physical existence must have been a wheel of pain. But the mighty procession of the ages, sweeping by, will soon obliterate the traces of the storm's ravages, and only the dim legends of horrible deeds will remain.

In that dreadful ebullition of human hatreds, Frank and Jesse James played no laggard's part. As boys, they accepted service under Quantrell, and became renowned for caution and daring even in the days of their youth. Members of a partisan organisation, famed even in the early days of the strife for daring deeds and extraordinary activity; a band, every man of which was a *desperado* of great cunning and prowess, these two callow-youths, taken from a country farm, speedily rose to the eminence of leading spirits among the most daring of men. Both sides in the border counties of Missouri and Kansas prosecuted war with a vindictive fury unparalleled in modern history. The scene of the operations of the guerrillas was at first confined to the limits of

Clay, Platte, Jackson, Bates, Henry, Johnson, and Lafayette Counties, in Missouri, and along the Kansas border.

These men rode far and fast in the night time, and fought their foes at early dawn. Living in out-of-the-way neighbourhoods were their friends. When pressed hard they disbanded and scattered, and rendered all pursuit futile.

Frank and Jesse James early discovered those traits of character which have rendered them famous as the greatest outlaws and freebooters of modern times. They became scouts and spies for Quantrell at the beginning of their career, and showed themselves possessors of remarkable capacity for such service. They were cool and brave, fertile in resources, and marvellous in cunning.

After Lawrence came the disbandment, and with the disbandment came that strange training in individual development and personal reliance which have made the boys objects of fear to the people of many regions, and enabled them to plunder at will, baffle pursuit, and defy the civil authorities of great States.

They had hiding places with friends in Clay, Platte, Jackson, Johnson, Cass and Lafayette Counties, and when the guerrilla band to which they belonged scattered in order to evade pursuers, the Boys retired to the dwellings of their friends and rested in peace till the time of re-organising, when an enemy was to be punished.

Perhaps no two individuals ever lived on this continent who have taken so many lives, as the James Boys. Emerging from the seclusion which they could always find in the Hudspeth neighbourhood, in the eastern part of Jackson County, in July, 1863, with Captain George Todd, a redoubtable guerrilla chieftain, with whose command Frank and Jesse often fought, they struck the road leading from Pleasant Hill to Blue Springs. Major Ransom, a Federal officer with a cavalry force, was traveling that road at the time. A collision took place. The fighting was savage. The volleys of revolver bullets fired by the guerrillas proved awfully destructive to their opponents. Jesse and Frank James have been credited with a tremendous destruction of life—Jesse killing seven, and, Frank eight men in the Federal ranks during that encounter.

One night Frank James and five or six of his comrades were detailed to capture and kill the militia men who were accustomed to frequent a *bagnio*, four miles east of Wellington, in Lafayette County. Frank James preceded the little band, and, creeping up under the window, he saw the company inside. There were eleven men in dalliance with the women. James returned to his comrades, reported the result of his observations, and the guerrillas rode to the house. A peremptory summons brought the militiamen to the yard. The guerrillas poured a volley of bullets among them. The ten men fell, pierced by the deadly missiles. But where was the eleventh man? There had been that number in the house when James saw the company, and the man could not have left the place.

A search was instituted. The man could not be found. But there was one woman more in the party than had been seen before. A candle was procured and a search instituted among them. They all appeared to be women. Frank James discovered the man. He was a youth, fair skinned and blue eyed, with long brown hair. His features were handsome, and in the garments of a woman he appeared not unlike a fresh country girl. Of course, he expected to die there. His ten companions presented the spectacle of a ghastly wreck of humanity in the yard as they lay there cold in death. But he plead for his life. He was so young to die.

"Here, Frank, take him," said the leader. "You discovered him; he is yours to deal with." It was a sentence of death, they said. The boy thought so, and hope vanished.

"Come," said Frank, "come along and be shot." The poor youth trembled in every nerve. He could scarcely walk.

His supposed executioner had to assist him down the steps and out through the yard. They passed the ghastly heap of corpses, lying there in the dim starlight. They went away, into the darkness under the sombre trees, down the road. Poor boy, he thought of his mother. Under the wide-spreading branches of an ancient oak they halted. "Here! we are far enough," said Frank James. The poor youth almost fell to the earth from excess of emotion. To die, and so young, and in such a way, too!

"Oh, spare me for the sake of my mother!" he wailed.

"You are free to go! I give you your life. You are outside of the pickets, outside of danger. Go, and be quick about it!" And at that moment Frank James fired a pistol shot upward through the branches of the oak, and the fair-haired boy soldier disappeared in the darkness—spared for the sake of his mother by the youthful *desperado*. Frank James returned to his comrades. They had heard the shot and naturally concluded that it meant one more life ended.

Frank assumed a grave expression.

"Quick work," remarked a comrade.

Frank James Spares a Life.

"Yes," returned the guerrilla, "babies and boys are not hard to kill."

He never spoke of that better deed he performed out there, with only the stars and God as witnesses. And the border strife went on. Frank and Jesse rode with Quantrell, sometimes with Todd and Poole, then again, they fought at unexpected times by the side of John Jarrette, and Bill Anderson, and Arch Clements. One week they would be charging Blunt's Body Guard in South-eastern Kansas; the next they would ambush a moving column of Federal militia in Lafayette, or Jackson County, Missouri. It was fighting—cruel, savage fighting, all the while.

In the bottom lands along the Blue, or among the Sni hills, when hotly pursued, they would find hiding places, from whence they emerged only to deal out destruction and death. Down to Texas, marching with the close of autumn, like migratory birds, they returned to their old haunts with the bright spring days. Deceiving and cutting to pieces Lieut. Nash's small command in the road west of Warrensburg, on a Monday, we hear of their successfully ambushing a column of Union militia on the banks of the Little Blue on the succeeding Wednesday, and a few days afterwards we hear of Frank and Jesse playing "the trumps" of revolver bullets among a squad of rollicking soldier gamesters at Camden; then again they are heard of with Todd, riding down the road from Independence toward Harrisonville, where, seven miles from the former place, they encounter Captain Wagner, of the Second Colorado Cavalry, and engage in a terrible hand-to-hand conflict in which Jesse James takes the life of the captain, and with his deadly aim sends seven of Wagner's men to the bourne of the dead.

On the same occasion, Frank, riding furiously among the Federal cavalrymen, deals death to eight of them. So, the spring and summer of 1864 was passing with these men engaged in deeds of blood. It was in the last days of July of 1864, that Arch Clements and Jesse James were riding along a country road one evening, when they discovered four militiamen in an orchard gathering apples. Two of the men were in one tree and two in another. Without ceremony, the guerrillas shot them as they would have shot squirrels from a forest tree, and jested of the deed as they might have jested over the fall of wild beasts.

It was about this time that Frank James had a thrilling adventure. He had been ordered out on a scout to ascertain the movements of the Federals in Jackson and Cass Counties. It was a period of deep anxiety to the Guerrilla leaders, as it appeared that special efforts were being made by the Federal militia, and several companies of the Second Colorado Cavalry, to capture all the irregular Confederates found in the State of Missouri. Frank had reached the Independence and Harrisonville road at a point about midway between the two towns. As he passed through the country he ascertained that a force of infantry and cavalry were at a house some miles away from the road. How many there were in this detachment he could not learn. But he resolved to investigate.

Taking a neighbourhood path, not much travelled, he rode toward the Federal encampment. On the roadside was a lonely cabin, now uninhabited, as he believed. He examined the indications, and rode on. At the cabin the road made a short turn. When Frank turned around the corner of the old cabin, two militiamen presented their muskets and commanded him to halt. In an instant the ready pistol was snatched from its place by the guerrilla, and even before the militiaman could fire, the bullet from Frank's pistol had penetrated his brain, and he fell in the agonies of death to the earth.

At the very instant of firing, Frank put spurs to his horse and galloped away, turning and firing at the remaining guard as he did so, and wounding him unto death just as he was in the act of firing at the daring rider. The bullet from the militiaman's gun whistled within an inch of Frank James' ear as it sped on its harmless mission. The picket

A Narrow Escape.

post where the firing took place was within a few hundred yards of a camp where a hundred militiamen, and half that number of cavalrymen, who rode good horses, were taking their dinners. Frank, surmising that the two soldiers with whom he had the combat were on guard duty close to camp, and that an alarm and pursuit would follow, rode with all speed toward the guerrilla camp. He was pursued, as he expected, but he easily eluded the Coloradoans.

In August—it was the 12th day of that month, 1864, that Jesse and Frank participated with their comrades, Todd, Anderson and others, in a desperate conflict in Ray county, Missouri. Again, the deadly revolvers, in the hands of the Boys, accomplished fatal results. Between the two, seven fellow-beings were sent to the silent realms of death.

Two days afterward they were at the Flat Rock Ford, on Grand River, and a desperate struggle with some Federal militia and volunteers ensued. During that fight, Jesse was struck by a musket ball which tore through his breast, cut into and through his left lung, and caused him to fall. His comrades carried him away. At length, he was transported to the house of Captain John A. M. Rudd. The wound was a dangerous one, and all expected it would prove fatal. Jesse believed so himself, and took from his finger a ring which he charged his friends to carry to his sister, Miss Susie James, and give her also his dying message, which was:

I have no regret. I've done what I thought was right. I die contented.

This event occurred August 16th, 1874. By the 7th of September he had so far recovered as to be able to ride and fight again.

On the 12th of September Jesse and Frank rode away with Lieutenant George Shepherd, from the guerrilla rendezvous at Judge Gray's, near Bone Hill, Jackson County, for a raid into Clay County. At this time, he visited his mother. On the 16th of September Jesse James killed three militiamen in an encounter near Keytesville, Chariton County, Missouri. He was now so far recovered as to perform the services of a scout.

On the 17th he rode twenty-nine miles in the night time, through a country swarming with militia, to advise Todd concerning the movements of the Federal forces.

On the 20th of September, 1864, occurred the Battle of Fayette, Missouri. The whole of Quantrell's band was concentrated for the purpose of making this attack. All the chieftains were present, Quantrell and Anderson, Poole and Clements. During the assault on the stockade, Lee McMurtry was desperately wounded close up to the enemy's position. Jesse and McMurtry were comrades, and he would not allow his friend to fall into the hands of the Federals if he could help it. He rushed up to where the wounded man lay, and though exposed to a terrible fire, he carried away his wounded friend without receiving any injury. The guerrillas were driven from Fayette.

At this time the various bands seemed to accept the leadership of Bill Anderson, who was then gathering forces for the Centralia expedition. Quantrell separated from him, and returned to a secure place of repose in Howard County.

Todd and Poole and the James Boys, Pringle, the scalper, the two Hills and Clements, indeed, all of the most desperate of the guerrilla gang followed the black banner of the most savage guerrilla that ever trod the soil of Missouri.

The 27th of September, 1864, must ever be a memorable day in the annals of the civil war in Missouri. On that day, with a flag black as the raven's wing, and ominous of the coming night of death. Bill Anderson rode to Centralia, a village in the north-eastern part of Boone County. Mo., on the line of the St. Louis, Kansas City and Northern Railroad. He was not long idle. A train of cars drew up to the depot. There were soldiers and citizens on that train. Very few of the former, however, were armed. Only a few guns, at any rate, were fired. The train and its passengers were completely at the mercy of the guerrillas. The Federal soldiers and citizen passengers were formed in a line. Then a separation of citizens and soldiers took place. Twenty-eight soldiers and four citizens who wore blue blouses were selected, marched out and shot with an atrocious haste that would make even the cruel Kurds shudder. In this bloody tragedy, Frank and Jesse James were prominent actors.

Scarcely had this butchery been consummated, when Major Johnson, in command of about 100 Iowa cavalrymen, came upon the scene. The force of the guerrillas under command of Todd numbered more than two hundred men, and as both were determined, a desperate fight ensued. But the impetuous charge of the guerrillas, led by George Todd, broke the lines of the Iowans, and a panic ensued among them. Major Johnson made gallant effort to rally his men. It was in vain. The furious riders dashed among them and shot them down like so many panic-stricken sheep. Jesse James, mounted on a superb horse, rode directly at Major Johnson. The issue was not doubtful. The deadly aim of the guerrilla soon laid him stark and still on the prairie. It was all over with him, and also for the men he commanded that morning. Appeals for mercy were of no avail. The vanquished Federals were massacred. Frank James was equally active with his brother. He is credited with having taken the lives of eight men that day. It was a day of horror, and the partisan rangers revelled in the carnage.

After Centralia came hard knocks. In one of the fights immediately succeeding the Centralia holocaust, Dick Kinney, a noted guerrilla, received his death wound. He was Frank James' comrade, and he fell heir to the pistol which Kinney had worn. On the handle of this weapon were fifty notches, each notch signifying one. He had killed fifty men. Frank James probably has the pistol yet.

In a corner of Clay County lived an old man named Banes. He was a staunch Union man, and blessed the guerrillas with the same kind of blessing that Balak desired Balaam to bestow upon Israel. Banes was particularly severe in his condemnation of Jesse and Frank James. One night the Boys went to Bane's house under the guise of Colorado troopers. The old man received them gladly, and at once unbosomed himself freely in regard to the guerrillas. In the course of his remarks he animadverted on Mrs. Samuels, the mother of the Boys, in bitter terms. He denounced her as being "the mother of two devils, Jesse and Frank James." The Boys secured his confidence, and then a promise of immediate assistance in hunting up the *desperadoes*. Banes got his gun and pistols and saddled his horse, mounted and rode out to his death, for when the trio had gone about half a mile away from the house, the pretended soldiers announced themselves as the James Boys, and

The Home of Farmer Banes.

gave him no space for repentance. Two pistol shots rang out on the still night, a heavy body fell to the earth, and then the living men rode away, leaving a cold form of mortality out under the stars.

With difficulty, the guerrillas made their way to their haunts on the Blackwater. Fighting was going on constantly. The shadow of death was gathering over many a bold rider of the guerrilla band. Moving out from their camp on the Blackwater, one day, the guerrillas fell into an ambuscade, and several received wounds. Among those thus wounded was Jesse James, who had his horse killed and received a shot through the leg.

Todd was sent out to skirmish with the advance guard of the Federal Army then following the retiring army of General Price. At every creek, there was a battle, and at every encounter there was bloodshed. In one of these fights, when the leaves were all falling on the brown earth, George Todd was killed. In the night time his followers came to pay the last tribute of respect to his remains. There were not many who gathered there in the gloom of the midnight to gaze for the last time on the face of the courageous guerrilla, but among them were Jesse and Frank James, and they pointed their pistols toward the cloud-veiled, teary sky, and swore to avenge his death.

But the old band was broken up. Late in October, 1864, Jesse and Frank parted, the former with Shepherd went to Texas, the latter with Quantrell to Kentucky.

It proved to be the final dissolution of Quantrell's once formidable force of partisans. George Todd, the *paladin* of the command, the leader who was persistent and daring, slept quietly after the fierce turmoil of life's battlefield had ended. John Poole, another hard rider, desperate fighter and dauntless leader, mouldered in a gory grave. John Jarratte and Cole Younger had sometime before separated from the band, and were operating in the far South where the magnolias grow and the moss-bearded live-oaks stand sentinels in the fever-haunted swamps. Fernando Scott was dead. Bill Anderson had fallen in a terrible combat while endeavouring to effect a crossing of the Missouri River in Howard County. As he had lived for some years, grimly fighting, so in the last extremity when the odds were all against him and unseen messengers of death burdened the air with their low-hummed dirges, his life went out while he still fought in the very shades of despair. Kinney was dead, and many more had surrendered life in the hot *simoon* of battle.

And what a band it had been, which was now broken! Its deeds must ever remain a part of the history of Missouri, and the chapter wherein the record is made will always be read with a shudder, and in years to come men will remember the mournful story of devastation and death with feelings of painful regret that human beings could so revel in the miseries and misfortunes of whole communities.

To those who can calmly sit and look down the *vista* of the dead years and recall without prejudice the history of men who were authors of deeds so notable—actions which, performed under other circumstances, would have made heroes of deathless fame, there must come a feeling of regret that such men should have been the victims of a baleful destiny.

The Headquarters on the Blackwater.

CHAPTER 7

Adventures in Separate Fields

The days of guerrilla warfare were drawing to a close. The retreat of Price and Shelby from Missouri left the Federals free to operate against the guerrillas. The old bands were decimated. Death had been busy in their ranks; and for the remnants of a once formidable organisation, no Confederate Army could extend over them sheltering arms. The drama was about completed; the curtain was soon to drop.

Jesse James went with Lieutenant George Shepherd to Texas in the autumn of 1864. During the long march through the Indian Territory, they met with many stirring adventures. On the 22nd day of November, Shepherd's band encountered the band of Union militia, commanded by Captain Emmett Goss, which had acquired an unenviable name on account of the excesses which they had committed. Goss was coming up from a marauding trip into Arkansas, and had reached Cabin Creek, in the Cherokee Nation. Goss was "a fighting man," and a fierce conflict ensued. Jesse James singled out the commander and rode full at him, firing his pistol and receiving the return fire of the other.

The contest was short; the steady aim of the guerrilla secured him a triumph. Goss fell from his horse with one bullet-hole through his head and another through his heart. On this occasion, there was one other to realise the skill of Jesse James with the pistol, if indeed he realised anything after his ineffectual plea for life. The Rev. U. P. Gardiner, chaplain of the Thirteenth Kansas, rode with Captain Goss' band up from toward the South. Jesse James pursued him, and came up with him. The chaplain told his pursuer who he was, and plead for life. The answer he received to this petition was a bullet through the brain. He fell from his horse dead.

Two days afterward, Jesse and a companion were riding over the

Jesse James' Escape from Pin Indians.

prairie, near the bank of a stream. For some cause the comrade of Jesse left him for a time alone. Not far away was a skirt of heavy timber. On a sudden, a wild shout burst from the wood, and a party of Pin Indians—that is, Cherokees, who were friendly to the Union, came scurrying across the prairie, directly toward the guerrilla. His danger was imminent, for the Cherokees were well armed with long range guns, which they knew well how to use.

Safety lay in retreat, and Jesse turned to flee. He was on the open prairie, and could not get to the timber. There was a high and steep bank before him, and the Indians were following close behind. He determined to leap his horse down the precipice. It happened to be where the water was deep, and a slight projection and growth of brush broke the fall. The leap was successfully made, and neither horse nor rider was badly injured. Jesse, following down the creek, made his escape, and soon regained Lieutenant Shepherd's camp.

During the winter of 1864-5 Jesse James remained in Texas, leading quite an inactive life. With the spring, however, that part of the Missouri Guerrillas which went with Shepherd, began to think of Missouri again. In April, they began the return march. The road was beset with dangers. The Pin Indians in the Cherokee Country were extremely hostile, and left no opportunity to strike at them unimproved. By the time the May flowers bloomed, Jesse James had reached Benton County, Missouri. In that county lived a Union militiaman named Harkness, who had made himself exceedingly obnoxious to people of Confederate sympathies. This man was captured by the returning guerrillas, and Jesse James and two comrades held him in a vice-like embrace, while another guerrilla, Arch. Clements, cut his throat from ear to ear.

At Kingsville, Johnson County. Mo., lived an old man named Duncan, who had belonged to the militia, and was very cordially disliked on account of his bad disposition toward the Southern people. Jesse James sought him, found him, and slew him. Duncan was a man of 55 years of age.

The guerrilla career of Jesse James drew to a close. In May, 1865, all the Confederate bands in the State were coming into the Federal posts and surrendering. A considerable number of those who had come up from Texas with Arch. Clements desired to surrender, but several refused to do so. Among these were Jesse James. But the formality of a surrender of the others led them all to Lexington, Mo., under a flag of truce. There were eight unsurrendered guerrillas to bid a last *adieu* to their old comrades. This little band had proceeded into Johnson County, when suddenly they were met by a band of Federal troops returning from a scouting expedition. These fired upon the guerrillas, and a sanguinary struggle ensued.

Jesse James' horse was killed; he was wounded in the leg and retired into the woods pursued by the Federals. He fought with desperation, but received, at last, a shot through the lungs. The wound was a terrible one, but he escaped, and dragged himself to a hiding place near the banks of a small stream. Here, for two days and nights, alone, consumed by a raging fever, the wounded guerrilla lay. Finally, he

Killing of Citizen Harkness.

crawled to a field where a man was ploughing. This man proved to be a friend, and took James in, cared for him, and finally sent him to his friends. The soldier who shot Jesse James that day was John E. Jones, Company E., Second Wisconsin regiment of cavalry. The guerrilla and his antagonist afterward became acquainted, and were warm personal friends. Jesse James joined his mother in Nebraska, and returned with her to Clay County, Missouri.

******

Quantrell gathered up a small band of his old comrades in the Guerrilla warfare, at Wigginton's place, five miles west of the town of Waverly, Lafayette county. Among those who obeyed the summons to this rendezvous was Frank James. The Confederate armies had retreated from Missouri. There was no longer a field in that State for the exercise of his peculiar talents. He resolved to go East, to Maryland, and there open up a Guerrilla warfare. It was on the fourth day of December when Quantrell and Frank James and about thirty others of their old followers and comrades left Wigginton's for Kentucky.

On the first day of January, 1865, the dreaded Quantrell's band effected the passage of the Mississippi River at Charlie Morris' "Pacific Place," sixteen miles above Memphis. Morris rendered Quantrell valuable service, although at that time he was a frequent visitor to Memphis, and on excellent terms with the Federal authorities at that place. After leaving the river they marched through Big Creek, Portersville, Covington, Tabernacle, Brownsville, Bell's, Gadsden, Humboldt, Milan, McKenzie, and on to Paris. Here they had their first difficulty, and were compelled to mount in hot haste and ride away.

From Paris, the guerrillas proceeded to Birmingham, and crossed the Tennessee River. Their route then lay through Canton, Cadiz, and to Hopkinsville. Near this place, they came to a house where there were twelve cavalrymen. Nine of them fled, leaving their horses. The three men who remained fought the whole of Quantrell's band for many hours, until preparations were made to burn the house, and, indeed, until the fire was kindled. They then came out and surrendered. Quantrell, of course, appropriated the twelve fresh horses which were in the stable.

There was one Captain Frank Barnette, who commanded a company of Kentucky militia stationed at Hartford, Ohio County. Quantrell at that time was playing the role of a Federal captain. As such, he induced Barnette to go with him on a hunt for Confederate Guerrillas. Barnette carried with this expedition about thirty of his men. Quantrell resolved to assassinate them all, and a way was found to do so during the day. Frank James was made the executioner of Captain Barnette, and as he rode by him when they entered a stream of water at a ford, as the sun went down behind the western hills, Frank James fired the fatal shot, and Barnette fell dead from his horse, dying the clear waters of the brook red with his blood.

The career of the guerrillas was drawing to a close in Kentucky as well as in Missouri. Quantrell, and Mundy, and Marion were constantly hunted by dashing cavalry officers.

The disguise thrown off, the Federal officers knew that work must be done in order to stop the Guerrillas, and they were not slow in engaging in the undertaking. Major Bridgewater and Captain Terrell were untiring in their pursuit of Mundy, Marion and Quantrell. Frank James visited an uncle, and was not with Quantrell when that chieftain fought his last fight at Wakefield's house, near the little post village of Smiley, Kentucky. That day Quantrell's band was nearly annihilated. Subsequently, Henry Porter gathered up the survivors of the once formidable guerrilla band, and surrendered with them at Samuel's depot, Nelson County, Kentucky, on the 25th of July, 1S65.

Among those who surrendered was Frank James. After the surrender, Frank remained in Kentucky because of a deed which he had performed in Missouri about a year before. There lived in the northeast corner of Clay County a man named Alvas Dailey. He had made himself very obnoxious to the James Boys, and Frank resolved to rid the world of his presence. One night he went to Alvas Dailey's place, and the next morning he was found dead with two bullet holes through his head. Frank James had assassinated him.

Quantrell's Last Fight.

CHAPTER 8

The Brandenburg, Ky., Tragedy

Frank James went down to Wakefield's house, where the noted Guerrilla chieftain, Quantrell, lay wounded unto death. Had the terrible scenes of the hard, cruel Guerrilla warfare through which he had passed, obliterated from the breast of Frank James every tender emotion? It appeared not, when he bent over the white face of the wounded chief with its traces of suffering and anguish. He shed tears like rain. He loved his leader, and did not hesitate to manifest that regard. Knowing that the hand of death was upon him, Quantrell advised his disheartened followers to accept Henry Porter's leadership and surrender themselves to the Federal authorities. It might have been because their dying commander desired it, that such men as Frank James and his companions so readily consented to lay down the weapons of war. At any rate, the formal submission of the guerrillas was made.

In Missouri, the terrible warfare which had been waged had left scars wide and deep and bloody, and they were yet recent when the banners of the contending armies were furled. At any rate, it so appeared to Frank James, and he did not return at once to the State of his nativity. The part he had played had been a conspicuous one, and, on account of Centralia, he was on the list of the proscribed, and when the war ended, so far as actual hostilities were concerned, it had not ended, so far as Frank James was interested, because he was not restored to the peaceful pursuits which he had abandoned when first the war cry arose in the land. He still lingered in Kentucky.

The conduct of Frank James for some time after the surrender indicated a desire on his part to become once more a quiet, peaceable citizen. He was extremely circumspect in behaviour, and demeaned himself in a most unobtrusive way. Such was the promise of the new life after the years of bitter strife in the 'late guerrilla. But he was not proof against the assaults of passion. One day the old flame burst out anew with consuming fury. Frank had started away from the State and stopped at the town of Brandenburg. It was several months after the remnants of the desperate band which Quantrell led into Kentucky had surrendered to the Federal authorities. But the country was still in an unsettled condition.

Bad men who had found occupation in hovering about the verge of battle and plundering the ghastly victims of war ere the last feeble breath had departed from their pale lips, were now idle and had become wandering thugs in the highways of the land. Horse thieves and bestial monsters were to be found prowling about in nearly every community, and more especially in the border States. A large number of people, and those, too, who had served in the Confederate, as well as those who had been soldiers in the Union Armies, looked upon the men who had been with Quantrell, and Mundy, Magruder and Marion, Anderson, Farris, Hickman and other noted Guerrillas, with suspicion. Many persons looked upon them as men of evil antecedents—as thieves.

Horse stealing was carried on at a lively rate all along the border. Kansas, Missouri and Kentucky were particularly afflicted for many months after the surrender by the presence of these enemies of the farming and stock-raising communities.

Just about the time Frank James was passing through from Nelson County to Brandenburg, in Meade county, on the Ohio River, on his way to Missouri, a number of horses were stolen in Larue County. A posse went in pursuit of the thieves. They traced them to Brandenburg. There they found Frank James. There were four of them when they came up with James, and he was alone, sitting in the office of a hotel. By some means they induced him to come out, and then they told him he might consider himself their prisoner on a charge of horse stealing in Larue County.

"By G—d! I consider no such proposition," exclaimed Frank James, as he drew a pistol and commenced firing. In less time than it requires to state the fact, two of the posse lay extended in the embrace of death, and a third was down and writhing in agony. But the fourth man fired a shot into Frank's left hip, and then ran away.

The wounded *desperado* was immediately surrounded by an excited throng. The ball had taken effect at the point of his hip, and the wound produced was not only painful but dangerous. Yet the superb nerve of the man sustained him in the midst of an appalling crisis. A perfect storm of excitement was raging in the town. Threats loud and terrible were made, and Frank James coolly presented his pistols as he stood leaning against a post and ordered the excited crowd to stand back, and they obeyed him.

Somehow it has always happened that the Jameses never wanted for friends wherever they have wandered. It was so on this occasion. Though the great majority of the people of Brandenburg thirsted for the blood of the slayer of two men in their midst, yet that grim young man, though wounded and suffering, had friends at that town, and in the midst of the excitement, these came to his assistance, and he was borne away to a secure place, where the populace could not tell, and nursed by tender hands prompted by affectionate hearts. Attended by a scientific surgeon, the ghastly wound which had brought him to the very brink of the abyss of death, began to heal, and in a few weeks the surgeon who had attended the hidden patient was able to report that he would surely live and might ultimately recover entirely from the dreadful wound.

When Frank had gained some strength, and it was deemed safe to remove him, in a quiet and secret manner he was conveyed in a close vehicle to the house of a staunch friend and relative in Nelson County, where he remained during many months, suffering excruciating pain on account of the horrible wound. He did not entirely recover from the effects of the wound for several years.

CHAPTER 9

The Liberty Bank Affair

Certainly no one could say that Jesse James possessed any of the qualities which would make him
Like one who on a lonely road
Doth walk in fear and dread,
And having once turned round, walks on.
And turns no more his head,
Because he knows a frightful fiend
Doth close behind him tread.

He was constituted of a different element. If he ever felt the sense of dread, no one ever knew it, for certainly none ever saw it exhibited in his conduct. Yet he knew that he was hunted, knew that shrewd, bold men sought to bind him in fetters, to deprive him of liberty, or, failing in that, rob him of life. And yet this knowledge did not alarm him, and the very presence of his foes did not make him afraid, though they numbered "ten strong, brave men." Perhaps Jesse James never knew what fear meant, having never experienced the sensation.

It was in 1866, on St. Valentine's day, February 14th, that an event occurred at Liberty, Missouri, which created intense excitement in that community, and a profound sensation throughout the West. The event alluded to was the plundering of the Commercial Bank of that city of an amount of money said to have been nearly $70,000. The robbery was not effected in the same bold way as characterized the raids into Russellville, Gallatin, Columbia, Corydon and other notable incidents in the career of the James bandits. But inasmuch as the bank was depleted of its funds, and that the robbery was unusually bold and audacious, there were many who secretly believed that Jesse James planned the robbery, if he did not lead the robbers, and that the treasures of the bank had been largely diverted to the individual possession of that noted young man. It will be remembered that the Liberty bank robbery occurred at a time when the James Boys were regarded only in the light of "desperate fighters—perhaps sometimes cruel in their vengeance," but otherwise they were believed to be honest and honourable men. Hence men were cautious in coupling the name of any member of the James family with an act of highway robbery.

But the conviction was strong in the minds of many people, nevertheless, that the funds of the Liberty bank had gone to minister to the wants and satisfy the desires of Jesse James and his friends and confederates. No immediate action was taken against him, but as time passed on, and other acts were committed by Jesse James and his friends, which were not regarded as either right or proper, the belief that they had participated in the robbery, if, indeed, they were not the robbers themselves, became wide-spread in the community. But in justice to Jesse James, it is but right to say that no evidence directly implicating him in that affair has ever been secured.

Cole Younger, when asked by a visitor to the Stillwater penitentiary concerning the Liberty bank robbery, remarked, "I have always had my opinion about that affair. If the truth is ever told, many of the crimes charged to me and my brothers will be located where they belong." Former friends of Jesse James are firm in the belief that he was the instigator of the deed, if not the leader of the brigands who sacked the bank. This belief, at any rate, influenced the public mind to no small extent, and led eventually to an effort to arrest Jesse James a year afterward, which attempt ended in a bloody tragedy, as narrated in the next chapter.

CHAPTER 10

Jesse's Sortie Against the Militiamen

When the war closed, Jesse James was sorely wounded. It was only by the most persistent and sureful nursing that he could expect to recover. When he was able to travel, he was furnished transportation from Lexington to go to Nebraska to join his mother, who was then a fugitive from her home. It does not appear that he lingered very long in Nebraska, since we are assured that before the brown leaves had fallen, Mrs. Samuels had returned to her old home near Kearney, Clay County, Missouri. This point appears to be conceded by all who have written concerning them. Jesse's wounds healed slowly—so slowly that after the lapse of a year he was but just able to ride on horseback a little. During the summer of 1866 Jesse rode around the country, but there was still considerable feeling against him, and he went well armed. Indeed, he always had his pistols "handy to use." Nothing appears to have disturbed the quiet of his life until the night of February 18, 1867.

It was a cold night. The ground was covered with a thick mantle of snow, and the wind blew bitterly cold from the north; the full moon shone brightly on the glittering garments of mother earth. Jesse James was at his mother's home near Kearney, Clay County, tossing under the infliction of a burning fever. His pistols were loaded and rested beneath his pillow. On that night, five well-armed and well-mounted militiamen rode to the home of the James Boys. Dr. Samuels heard the heavy tread of the armed men on the *piazza*, and demanded their business. He was told to open the door. He went up to confer with the sick ex-guerrilla. He asked Jesse what should be done.

The sick man begged his stepfather to assist him to the window so that he might look out upon the crisp snow out in the moonlight. He looked with a deeper interest at the five horses hitched in front of the house. They all had cavalry saddles on their backs. He knew that they were soldiers, and he well understood the object of their coming. It was a moment when decisions must be reached quickly. He had never surrendered, and he never intended to do so. Hastily dressing himself, he descended to the floor below with his pistols in his hands. The militiamen, impatient at the delay of Dr. Samuels in opening the door, had commenced hammering at the shutter with the butts of their muskets, all the while calling to Jesse to come down and surrender himself. They swore they knew he was in the house, and vowed to take him out dead or alive.

Jesse crept softly and close to the door, and listened attentively until, from the voices, he thought he could get an accurate aim. He raised a heavy dragoon pistol, placed the muzzle to within three inches of the upper panel of the door, and fired. There was a stifled cry, and a heavy body dropped with a dull thud to the floor of the *piazza*. His aim had been deadly. Before the militiamen could recover from their surprise, Jesse James had thrown the door wide open, and, standing on the threshold with a pistol in each hand, he commenced a rapid and deadly fire. Another man fell dead, and two more men had received wounds which were painful and dangerous, and surrendered to the outlaw they came to capture. The fifth man, terror-stricken, fled, reached his horse, mounted him, and rode rapidly away in the moonlight.

Thus, was commenced that long strife which has gone on year after year, and the warfare has made Frank and Jesse James the most renowned outlaws who have ever appeared on the American continent. All the skill and ingenuity of the shrewdest detectives have been at various times brought into requisition, but failure has attended all their efforts to capture the Boys.

The scene presented at the Samuels house, after the flight of the only man of the attacking party who remained unhurt, was indeed a sad one. Here, in the cold night wind, extended on the open *piazza*, with faces ghastly and white in the moonbeams, lay the forms of two human beings, who but an hour before, in the prime of life and the full flush of manhood, had ridden to the retreat of the wounded and sick guerrilla. They were still in death now. And the next day friends came weary miles to bear them away.

Helpless upon their sable biers,
They bore them forth with bitter sighs and tears,

With no gay pageantry, they moved along,
Most silent they, amid a silent throng.
And there they left them in that drear abode
Alone with its still tenants and their God.

And there were two more men who had come with brave hearts and steady hands to capture the weary, feverish ex-guerrilla, lying there writhing in agony after the attempt had been made. They had come with the hope of delivering Jesse James over to the law, and thus bind him forever. Now they lay completely helpless, and in the power of the daring outlaw, who had the name of being devoid of the quality of mercy. And yet they were spared by him.

When a large company of armed men arrived at the house of Dr. Samuels, the next day, to take Jesse James dead or alive, that redoubtable adventurer was many miles away. The place that had proved so disastrous to the five militiamen the evening before, was quiet enough now, and the militia ranged through the old farmhouse without molestation. Jesse was not at home!

CHAPTER 11

In the Hands of Friends

Jesse James, soon after the night attack before related, proceeded to Kentucky, where Frank was stopping with friends. He had not recovered from the effects of the terrible wounds which he had received in the breast just after the close of the war. Frank was still unable to ride abroad on account of the bullet wound in his hip received on the day of the Brandenburg tragedy. In the early part of the summer of 1867, Jesse arrived at the house of a friend in Nelson County, Kentucky, near the town of Chaplin. Frank was already there. In this neighbourhood dwelt a large number of people who were either related to them or devoted admirers of the noted guerrillas. They had been the friends and entertainers of Quantrell, Marion, Sue Mundy, and others of the Guerrillas in the closing days of the war.

Soon after his arrival in Chaplin, Jesse, whose condition seemed to grow worse instead of better, concluded to place himself under the surgical care of Dr. Paul F. Eve, of Nashville, Tenn. He proceeded to Nashville, where he remained for several months, and received much benefit to his health.

In the beginning of the year 1868 Jesse and Frank were once more reunited at the house of a relative at Chaplin. From all that can be learned, the life led by the wounded *desperadoes* while with their Kentucky friends was as pleasant as could be expected under the circumstances. There was a large community of people in that section who were intensely Southern in feeling, and mourned the defeat of the cause for which so many noble lives had been sacrificed, with an intense grief. Everyone who had fought for that cause was dear to them, and when the Missouri youths came to the homes of the Samuels, and McClaskeys, and Russels, and Thomases, and Savers, they were sure to receive a warm welcome.

In that part of Kentucky there were scattered about many of the adventurous partisans who had followed Sue Mundy, Magruder, Marion and other Guerrilla chiefs in the days of the war. With some of these Frank James had served in the closing days of Quantrell's career.

The Jameses were feted and feasted by the hospitable Kentuckians, and so tenderly nursed that their wounds had very much improved. Logan County was also the home of many of their friends, and numerous relatives of the Boys, and between these and those residing in Nelson county, they passed to and fro at will, and wherever they might happen to rest, they were honoured guests of families who possessed the pecuniary means to enable them to be hospitable. Fair ladies smiled on them, and gentle hands were ready to serve them in the hour of pain. It seems that they should have been happy, or at least contented.

But the James Boys' career had been stormy; they had an active, restless disposition; they had lost the delicate sensibilities of well organised members of society, and the rough experiences through which they had passed had evidently destroyed, in a measure, whatever of human sympathy had belonged to their nature.

And yet at this time their friends—and they had many—believed them to be honourable and honest, if desperate in conflict. They knew that they had killed many men, but this was excused, because the men killed were enemies, and the killing was done in combats. So it came about that these most noted of outlaws for many years had friends who believed in their integrity, and were ready at all times to engage in the defence of their character.

The times were favourable. There were many desperate young men turned adrift by the events of the war; men ready to engage in any undertaking which promised excitement and gain. Over such, Jesse and Frank James could exercise a large influence, and from among such they drew allies in the commission of crime.

The individual members of organisations which had hovered along the borders, and hung on the verge of the great field of warfare, in character one half soldier and the other half bandit, were just the kind of men from whose ranks recruits for lawless enterprises could be enlisted. In Kentucky and Tennessee, Arkansas and Missouri, there were many such persons—men who, during the great strife, when mighty hosts clashed against each other, and tremendous events were taking place, had occupied an anomalous position which brought upon them the hate of the Federals, and incurred for them the displeasure of the

Confederates, were in a position where a step further could not materially alter their relations to society. The men who had fought with regiments, banded in great armies, whether on the side of the Federals or Confederates, did not look with any great consideration on those who had lingered along the borders of war, as independent companies of scouts and guerrillas.

There were many men in Kentucky at the time of which we speak who had been in organisations of the character above described—that is, guerrilla bands, both Federal and Confederate. The regular soldiers of both armies, whose families had suffered in consequence of the partisan warfare, looked with ill-concealed dislike upon the free riders of the border, and this fact, no doubt, had a large influence in driving many of the guerrillas into downright outlawry when the war had closed. It was in a community of ex-guerrillas that Frank and Jesse found themselves in Kentucky, and among such "friends," no doubt, their first great project of bank robbing had its inception and complete maturity.

CHAPTER 12

The Russellville Bank Robbery

Russellville is a beautiful village—almost grown to a city—in a lovely region of country in Logan county, Kentucky. The people of Russellville are educated and refined. It is the seat of much wealth and boasts its colleges and academies. In general, Russellville is a quiet place, and from year in to year out its quietude is not often broken by any startling incident. But things will occur everywhere, sometime, to create a profound sensation. It happened that this quiet, prim old place should have a great and notable sensation.

It was a bright morning in March. The blue birds had returned and were singing their *matin* songs from the budding branches of the trees. Russellville was as staid and sober as usual. There was not a single thing to indicate that the old town was about to be shaken up as it had never been before. The bank doors stood wide open, and the cashier stood at his desk. An old lady hobbled down the street, and a fresh school-miss paused to gaze at the early spring flowers which adorned a neighbour's garden; a kitchen maid was singing a ditty to her absent swain in the back yard; and a sturdy citizen crossed the street to inquire if a certain bill which he held in his hands was good.

Nothing strange in all this? Of course not. People were simply minding their affairs according to their own inclinations. There was a sudden clatter of hoofs that morning, the 20th of March, 1868. Terrible shouts and fearful oaths, and the sharp reports of pistols accompanied the sound of the horses' hoofs. The old lady suddenly dropped her staff and stood as if petrified; the young miss ran hastily away; the cashier turned pale, and the sturdy citizen hastily retreated back across the street. A dozen horsemen, armed with two pairs of revolvers each, rode furiously about the streets, and with fearful oaths commanded the people to keep in their houses. Two of the men rode to the bank, dismounted and rushed in. One of them presented a pistol at the head of the cashier, and commanded him, under penalty of instant death, to be still and make no noise. The other took out the contents of the safe, amounting to many thousands of dollars; they then remounted and rode away.

In a few minutes the streets of Russellville were comparatively deserted. The brigands had come in, secured their plunder, and had as suddenly disappeared; the citizens scarcely knew what had happened. Surprise prevented immediate pursuit. The bandits had taken the road toward the Mississippi. They were traced to that stream and across to the rugged hills of Southeast Missouri, and then the trail divided up, and all marks of their passage were lost. They found friends, did these bandits, in West Missouri, Who were the bold raiders? Where did they come from and where did they go when they secured the rich booty from the plundered bank?

The good friends of the James Boys declared that it was impossible that they could have participated in that affair. In substantiation of this position they pointed to the fact that Jesse James was at the town of Chaplin, in Nelson County, which is fifty miles or more from Russellville, and that incomparable raider himself wrote a letter for publication in the Nashville (Tennessee) *American*, in which he triumphantly points to the fact that at the very time of the raid on Russellville, he was at the Marshall House, Chaplin, and refers to Mr. Marshall, the proprietor of the hotel, for the truth of the statement, that on a certain day in March, 1868, he was at his house.

But unfortunately, the date of the robbery, and the day which Jesse asserts he spent at Chaplin, were not the same days. It was no uncommon thing for Jesse James to make more than fifty miles on horseback in six hours, in those days when the roads were good. He rode no inferior animals—the best blooded horses. of old Kentucky were bestridden by the daring raider.

Another thing: Jesse James was only seen in Chaplin the day after the robbery, and in the evening at that; even if he had been seen late the same evening after the robbery, it would not have constituted even a presumptive evidence of his innocence, since after the robbery occurred in the morning he could have ridden to Chaplin before nightfall. Just previous to the robbery, Jesse had spent much of his time in Logan county, almost a dozen miles from Russellville, with relatives, of whom he had a number residing in that region. As we have before stated, Frank had been severely wounded while resisting arrest at Brandenburg; but he was then so far recovered that he had no difficulty in riding on horseback. He had made a number of journeys between his usual stopping place at Mr. Sayers' house in Nelson County, and the houses of his kin in Logan County. The statement made by Jesse that Frank was at the house of Mr. Thompson, in San Luis Obispo County, California, at the time of the Russellville bank robbery, is incorrect. Frank had not then visited California.

The friends of the Boys, however, were unable to make a clear defence for them, and they have been generally credited with being not only participators, but leaders of the raiders.

At the time of the robbery, Geo. W. Shepherd, Oliver Shepherd, and several others of "the old Guerrilla guard," as they were called, had their homes or stopping places in Nelson county. Geo. Shepherd had married the widow of the noted Missouri Guerrilla, Dick Maddox, who was a member of the band which Quantrell led out of that State. This redoubtable warrior, who had assisted at Lawrence and Centralia, and had participated in many desperate and bloody affrays, met his fate in a terrible conflict with a Cherokee Indian. Maddox and Shepherd had been friends and comrades in the dark days when they rode with Quantrell, and as Mrs. Maddox was left alone in a strange land, and was yet young in years and comely in features, George Shepherd readily agreed to console the widow in her affliction and perform the duty of a faithful comrade to the memory of his friend by espousing his widow. They were married and settled in Chaplin before the raid on the bank.

The people of Russellville quickly recovered from their surprise by the audacity of the robbers. The officers of the law rallied, and there was mounting in hot haste and an earnest pursuit of the robbers. Oll. Shepherd had suddenly disappeared from Chaplin; several of the old guerrillas had also gone away, and Frank and Jesse James, too, had quietly departed from that region of country.

The Kentucky blood of the pursuers was up, and they followed the trail of the robbers with tireless energy. They were traced west over hills and through valleys. The Cumberland River was crossed, and through the rugged region between that stream and the Tennessee, they were tracked as foxes might have been trailed. But the pursuers were always just too late to come up with the gang. Still they followed on, and finally reached the banks of the Mississippi only to learn that the persons they sought had crossed before their arrival, and plunged into the wilderness regions of Southeast Missouri. Some effort was made to keep on the track of the fugitives through the swamps of Missouri, but the traces became fainter and fainter as the pursuers advanced, until among the rugged hills of the Southeast they faded out altogether, and the Kentuckians were forced to give up the chase and reluctantly returned home after a bootless pursuit.

George Shepherd had married a wife—moreover, he had bought a house at Chaplin—and therefore he did not travel with his comrades to the West. The officers of the law soon found him, and as he was one of the suspected parties, and the bank robbers had taken Shepherd's horses on which to escape, he was arrested and a thorough search was made for evidence to convict him. He was taken to Russellville and placed in jail. The grand jury of Logan County at its next sitting found an indictment against him, and he was in due time arraigned before the Logan County circuit court on a charge of aiding and abetting the robbers. The evidence was deemed conclusive by the jury before which he was tried, and a verdict of guilty was returned and the punishment was fixed at three years in the penitentiary at hard labour.

The other members of the band escaped to Western Missouri. Oll Shepherd, a cousin of George Shepherd, was found in Jackson county by the persistent Kentuckians. They desired to arrest him. A requisition was procured from the Governor of Kentucky, and the executive order of the Chief Magistrate of Missouri, for the arrest of the fugitive. But Oll Shepherd was an old Guerrilla, and he flatly refused to be taken back to Kentucky as a prisoner. The civil officers were deterred from executing the warrant of arrest. In those days, there were vigilance committees in Missouri. To one of these the situation of affairs was reported.

It was at once determined by the vigilantes that Oll Shepherd must either submit to arrest or be killed. The company of vigilantes found him at his home near Lea's Summit. Would he surrender? they demanded of him. "Never! death first," he shouted back to them. Then the bloody work began. But what could one man do against twenty-five? There could be but one result. The one man must die at last, however bold and skilful. So, it resulted in this case. Oll. Shepherd had been an old guerrilla under Quantrell, and had learned how to shoot and how to despise fear. He resisted, and not until he had received seven bullet wounds did he succumb. In fact, he died fighting.

The other members of the gang implicated in the Russellville robbery escaped. The Jameses soon after went to the Pacific Coast, and remained there for quite a while. They were on a tour in search of health. The hard life which they had led and the desperate wounds which they had received had sadly impaired their superb physical systems, and they needed rest and time to recuperate wasted energies and allow their wounds to heal.

Meanwhile, George Shepherd, shut out from the world, toiled on at his unrequited tasks in the penitentiary at Frankfort. He who had been the free rover and wild guerrilla, the dauntless rider and relentless foe, in the garb of a convict did service to the State, and answered not again when ordered to his daily rounds of labour. And he alone of the survivors of that band of freebooters who rode so fearlessly and madly into Russellville that morning, bent on mischief and crime, was made to feel the heavy rod of retributive justice. Oll Shepherd had perished. Nemesis had overtaken some of the old guerrillas.

Death of Oll Shepherd.

CHAPTER 13

On the Pacific Slope

Immediately after the Russellville robbery, Jesse James appeared once more in his old haunts in Missouri. But his physical system had been greatly taxed by the tremendous strain to which it had been subjected. Twice already had he received bullet wounds through the lungs which would have killed any man less extraordinarily endowed with vitality. Scars of twenty wounds were on his person, and yet the man who had gone out from home as a boy; entered into close affiliation with a band of the most daring and desperate men ever organised in America; sustained his part with them, and even surpassed them all in the daring feats they accomplished ere yet the "manly beard had shaded his face," after having passed through more exciting scenes than any living man, and participated in more terrible encounters than most men, yet survived, and though his terrible wounds had weakened his frame, yet his wonderful courage and tremendous reserve of vital forces were such as to insure his final restoration to complete health.

He had travelled on horseback from the little town of Chaplin, on the eastern verge of Nelson County, in Central Kentucky, to the western border of Missouri, in the space of a few days subsequent to the 20th of March, 1869. Jesse James was seen in Clay County, Missouri, in the first days of April of that year, and was seen at Chaplin on the 18th of March. That he was at Russellville the evidence seems to be clear; and that he led a most exciting retreat from that place, through the hill country of Kentucky, until he reached the banks of the Mississippi, is one of the facts of his history. It was his genius which enabled his confederates to escape from a determined pursuit of resolute men.

Once on the west bank of the Mississippi, to use a Westernism, "he was on his own stamping ground." He knew every "trail" across the swamps of South-eastern Missouri, and every pathway in the tangled brakes over the rugged hills of the southern counties of that State, were as familiar to him as the woodlands about the old farm in Clay County. He knew more—that there were scattered through the country from Chaplin to Kearney, a route of more than five hundred miles in length, men with the reputation of respectable members of society, who always had a warm welcome for him and his daring men. Who, then, could pursue and capture him? There is no room for wonder that Jesse James escaped the irate Kentuckians, who followed his trail from Russellville to the banks of the Mississippi, and finally lost it among the rugged hills and vast forests west of the river.

Jesse's extraordinary journeys under such circumstances did not tend to the restoration of his physical system, which had been greatly shattered by the terrible wounds which he had received at the close of the war, in an encounter with a company of Federal soldiers in Lafayette county.

In those days, the friends of the Jameses were numerous in the State of Missouri; for at that time scarcely anyone believed that they had developed into brigands. Among those who advised with Jesse James at that time was his physician and friend, Dr. Joseph Wood, of Kansas City. It was the opinion of this physician that the condition of his patient imperatively demanded a change of scene, and a more genial climate to insure his restoration.

In accordance with this advice, the patient set about his preparations for a voyage by sea, and a sojourn on the Pacific slope.

Toward the close of May, 1869, Jesse James left the home of his mother near Kearney, Missouri, for New York. Here he spent only a few days. On the 8th of June, he embarked on the steamship *Santiago de Cuba*, bound for Aspinwall, crossed the Isthmus to Panama, and there again took a steamer for San Francisco. The spoils of Russellville allowed him means to gratify every desire in the "City of the Golden Gate," and he remained there for some time.

Meanwhile Frank James, who was not deemed able to make the long ride, in the flight before the officers at Russellville, was secluded for a time in the house of a respectable citizen of Nelson County, Kentucky. But it was not deemed best that Frank should linger long in that part of the country. A friend provided a close carriage, and a few weeks after the Russellville robbery Frank James was very quietly driven northward one evening, passing by Bloomfield, through Fairfield, by Smithville, and on through Mount Washington to Louisville. Here he remained a few days, and then took the cars for St. Louis.

Arrived in that city, Frank put up at the Southern Hotel, registering as "F. C. Markland, Kentucky." The name was one he had used before when he did not desire that his real name and character should be known. Here he met two or three of his old comrades, and he spent several days very pleasantly with them. Meanwhile he communicated with his mother and apprised her of his intention to go West across the Rocky Mountains. Mrs. Samuels met her son at the house of a relative in Kansas City, where he remained for two days, and then bidding farewell to those who had always been true to him, he took passage for California, where he arrived some weeks before the arrival of Jesse.

Frank did not remain long in San Francisco, but proceeded very soon to San Luis Obispo County, and paid a visit to his uncle, Mr. D. W. James, who was at that time proprietor of the Paso Robel Hot Sulphur Springs, a much-frequented resort of invalids in that county. The friends of the Boys, and Jesse James himself, in a published letter, claim that Frank went by sea to California, and that he sailed from New York on one of the vessels belonging to the Pacific Mail Steamship Line. But this story was doubtless set afloat to mislead the public concerning the movements of the Boys. The above account we have from a gentleman who was at that time a friend of the Jameses, and who travelled with Frank from Kansas City to San Francisco. He knew the *desperado* well, and had daily conversations with him on the journey.

After spending some time at the Springs, Frank James proceeded to the ranch of Mr. J. D. Thompson, with whom he had a previous acquaintance, gained while that gentleman was visiting in the States. The noted ex-guerrilla remained at the Laponsu ranch for many months, and until after the arrival of Jesse.

The two brothers met at Paso Robel. Here they remained for several months. In the autumn, they went out to the mining districts of Nevada.

It appears, from information in the possession of the writer, that the Boys behaved themselves with much circumspection while they were the guests of their uncle. Their evil propensities were suppressed, and no one who came in contact with the quiet, sedate Frank, and the genial, companionable Jesse, during those days, would have suspected that these brothers were the most daring and dangerous men who had ever yet defied the powers of the State, and disregarded the demands of society. Some quiet weeks had been passed. The weak lungs of Jesse had healed, and the lame hip of Frank was well again. The climate had wrought a wonderful change in their physical systems. Jesse had grown robust, and possessed all the powers of physical endurance which have been since tested and proved incomparable.

The quiet life at Paso Robel began to be irksome to the men whose lives had been passed amid the rudest shocks and the wildest storms of excitement and passion. They would go out among the miners and have a little fun while prospecting there. In Nevada, society was in its rudest stages of development. The country was filled with adventurers from every country under the sun. In the camps of the miners and prospectors were *desperadoes* from all regions, and a visitor to these places who wanted to fight only had to say so, and there was no delay in getting accommodated. It was then flush times in the Bonanza State.

Frank and Jesse went up to the mountains to take a look at the country. They formed some acquaintances among the adventurers, and they found several old acquaintances from Missouri and Kentucky. The rude life of the mining camps was more congenial to the disposition of the men who had rode with Quantrell than the refined society found about a fashionable resort for invalids; and the restless raiders liked well to linger in the tents of the miners among the lofty summits of the Sierras. For a while they passed their time very pleasantly in such associations. They prospected some, and played sportsmen in the intervals of time so spent.

But their pleasant days in the Sierras were doomed to draw to an abrupt close. There was a new camp formed at a place called Battle Mountain. It will be remembered that we are writing of a period when the rich mineral discoveries of Nevada had drawn a miscellaneous population from the four quarters of the globe. Camps and towns sprang up like Jonah's gourd—in a night, and disappeared with the noonday sun of the morrow. Battle Mountain was "a rattling place;" the people who had pitched their tents there had come in search of gold. Many of them were old pioneers, accustomed to hard knocks and sudden surprises. Others were "hard visaged men," who knew how to flee before the avengers of blood—a knowledge gained during years of practical experience. They were quick with the knife, and "lightning shots."

They were inured to scenes of danger, and were not liable to suffer from sudden surprises. Frank and Jesse James, accompanied by two old Missouri acquaintances, concluded to pay a visit to Battle Mountain, "to shake up the encampment," as they said. They found spirits there who were congenial and some who were uncongenial. At last they brought up at a shanty where women, whisky and cards united their attractions to allure the old pioneers and chance visitors. The Jameses do not drink, but they claim to be "handy with the pasteboard." Here they engaged in a game of cards with two notorious roughs and blacklegs; and their companions also found a pair of gamesters, ready and anxious to join them in a "bout of poker."

For a time, the game proceeded without anything occurring to disturb the amicable relations of the players. At last one of the old Missouri friends of the Jameses detected his opponent cheating in the game. He charged him with it, and the other denied the charge and demanded a retraction. Of course, nothing of that sort could happen. The gambler retorted by drawing a knife, and the other snatched a pistol from his belt. Jesse James, who was sitting at a table a little distance away, saw the danger of his friend, and in an instant, just as the gambler was in the act of striking the Missourian, he threw his pistol out and shot the blackleg through the heart.

As he turned, the man who had been sitting opposite to him, engaged in play, had a pistol levelled at his breast. Jesse brought his pistol around with a swing, and another gambler fell without a groan to the earth—dead!—shot through the brain. By this time the utmost confusion prevailed. Lights were overturned, and the place was shrouded in utter darkness in an instant of time. There was a crowd of twenty or thirty men in the shanty when the firing commenced. Every man was armed, and all had their weapons in hand. Jesse cried out:

"Stand aside! Be ready!"

The other three men of the party understood what he meant. It was for them to get out, and they rushed for the door. A pistol would flash and a heavy body would fall with a thud to the ground. When the door had been gained by his companions, Jesse, who had covered their exit, sprang forward to escape from that pandemonium of darkness, suffering and death. Pistols were popping and knives were clashing in a horrid din. The maimed, writhing in agony, mingled their groans and curses in the awful uproar. By the flashing of pistols, Jesse saw that Frank and his two friends had made their exit, and were firing into the crowd as opportunity offered, taking care to not shoot toward him. He determined to leave the shanty, but two burly roughs, with huge knives, stood in the way.

A pistol ball quieted one of them, and almost before the flash of his pistol had faded away, and before the other could think of using his knife, Jesse sprang upon him and dealt him a fearful blow on the head with the butt of his pistol. The gambler sank with a groan to the earth, and with a spring Jesse joined his friends on the outside. By this time a light had been placed on a barrel behind the slab which served for a counter. Three men were seen weltering in their own blood—dead. Four others were lying writhing in pain, and all were gory from the blood which flowed from ghastly wounds.

The crowd saw all this at a glance. The dead and the wounded in the shanty did not include any of the strangers. The crowd yelled for vengeance on the authors of the bloody tragedy. There was a shout that awakened the mountain echoes for miles around, as the infuriated pioneers and gamblers surged out of the shanty.

Meanwhile the Jameses and their friends had retired a short distance from the place to ascertain the extent of the injuries they had received in the melee. It was a cloudless night and the stars shone brightly. The leaders of the mob soon discovered the four Missourians, and ran, yelling, toward them.

"Back, you d—d miscreants! Stand back, I say!" cried Jesse James.

But they rushed forward at the top of their speed.

"Boys, we are in for it," said Jesse, quietly. "All right, be ready." Then he shouted:

"Come on, d—n you! Just come ahead and be killed!" He had no more than ceased speaking when they had approached near enough to open fire.

"Wait, Boys! Steady! Every shot must tell! Now!" And as the sound of the last word died away, there was the report of four pistols, almost simultaneously discharged, and four men fell badly wounded; once more the four deadly pistols were discharged, and two more of the howling mob sank down in their tracks. The others paused. But they gave the Missourians a parting salute as the latter moved rapidly away. That salute seriously wounded one of the friends of the Jameses, and carried away a portion of Jesse's hat brim. But they escaped, aided by the night, and hastily returned to Winnemucca.

Here they learned that intelligence of the terrible dark seance at Battle Mountain had preceded them, and that it was not a safe place. Aided by friends, they remained in seclusion a few days, waiting an opportunity to get away. During these days of retirement, they made up their minds to return to the States east of the mountains, and when they met a favourable opportunity they embraced it, and in another week after their departure they were secure among friends near their old haunts in Missouri, ready to plan still more startling campaigns than any which they had yet undertaken.

Fight in a Gamblers' Den.

CHAPTER 14

Were They Driven to Outlawry?

Those misnamed men
Whom damned custom had brazed so
That they were proof and bulwark against sense.

Were the James Boys driven to outlawry? A strange question, no doubt, many readers will think, in the light of the history of their lives. And yet it is a pertinent question, when we consider the tendency of the human mind and conscience to deteriorate under the pressure of circumstances. Environments have much to do in moulding character. Perhaps there is not as wide a space between the natural characteristics of mind and heart in Boys of eight as is generally supposed. But philosophizing aside. Are there not mitigating circumstances in the case of the James Boys ? We do not undertake to defend them—their course is indefensible; we cannot apologize for them; for outlawry cannot be palliated. But let justice be done even to these renowned outlaws. Though sinners, have they not been sinned against? Though slayers of men, have they had no provocation? Let facts speak.

When the banner, beloved by the Southern people, whether wisely or unwisely, it matters not, was folded away forever at Appomattox, that event brought peace and repose to hundreds, nay, thousands of grim, worn soldiers who had bravely striven to uphold the ensign they loved so well. The war ended for them, never to be commenced again.

But all along the bloody borderland there existed a distinctly different condition of affairs. The warfare was that of community against community, of neighbour against neighbour, and of relative against relative. Cole Younger, the guerrilla, engaged in mortal combat with Charles Younger, the Union militia officer; it was kindred blood that strove. In such a warfare, the common ties of humanity are severed, and fury and hate come in where love and friendship have expired. Such was the situation in Missouri. The dissolution of the Confederate Government did not restore peace in such communities. The quarrel was no longer political, and for principle, but personal, and for vengeance. For others, there might be peace, but for contestants in such a strife there was no peace.

If Jesse James took vengeance on Bond, it must be remembered that in the dreadful days of the bitter border war. Bond had gone with his band of militia to the Samuels' place, taken Dr. Samuels, Jesse's stepfather, out, and hanged him by the neck until they supposed he was dead, and left him there while they went to find Jesse, who was ploughing in the field. He was but a lad then. But they took him, tied him like a felon, and castigated him like a slave with a plough line, until faint from loss of blood and crazed from the agony of the infliction, he fell in a swoon—a mere quivering mass of flesh and blood.

Jesse James was like other youthful human beings. Could he then forget such treatment? Was it not natural that he should seek vengeance? And the hour came; the tormentor fell into his hands; the strong passion overcame the young man, and he slew his enemy. And so, too, with Banes and others who fell victims to his relentless purpose. They met a fate at the hands of the Boys which, perhaps, better men than the Jameses would have connived at under similar circumstances. Thus, during the long, dark struggle, old scores were paid, but at the same time new causes of offense were given.

The regularly organised armies of the late contending sections had been disbanded, and peace ostensibly reigned in the land. But old wounds had not healed along the border. There were malignant stars in the zenith of the guerrillas. Hope animated them for a space. They sought their childhood's homes. Doubtless they loved the scenes familiar to them in the old days, before they had learned to be slayers of men, as well as others of the race do that anchor-spot of memory. But the bright gleam of hope faded; the clouds of anguish overspread their sky. The lurid lightning of the old bitterness flashed athwart their heavens, and the ex-guerrillas were pursued and hunted, like felons, beyond the pale of hope or pardon.

The resources of the James family had been impaired, absorbed, wasted, in the crucial time of strife. But they were not permitted to make a peaceful effort to build up and restore wasted fortunes. Harassed on every hand, these Boys, who were naturally of a strong temperament, and perhaps of revengeful natures, were yet mere Boys who had learned to be self-reliant; impatient of restraint, bold in action, and acquainted with the art of slaughter, turned upon their hunters and revealed the desperate character of the game they pursued. They were not left in peace after the light of peace blessed the land and made glad other hearts; and they would have been more than human not to have undertaken their own protection under such circumstances. If others attempted to murder them, they did not hesitate to slay.

So, their lives have become lurid with slaughter. It must be remembered that we are not attempting to justify such a line of conduct; but there are many things in connection with human affairs that cannot be defended. We look at things as they are, and not as they ought to be. Doubtless, it will be admitted on all hands that the James Boys ought not to have led such a wild career of outlawry; that they ought not to have entered upon such a course of action; and finally it will be urged that it would have been far better for them, and everything and everybody connected with them, to have quietly yielded to the inevitable, and voluntarily exiled themselves forever from the scenes of childhood and all the dear associations of their tenderer and more hopeful youth. Certainly, it would have been best for them. But such a course would have been contrary to the world's experience of human nature.

So when vigilance committees were hanging their comrades who had been with them by the camp fires in the deep forests, and in many a bloody foray; and when armed men, fours and sixes, hunted for them; when repose was banished from their home, and the phantom shadow of death peered out at them from every forest thicket, and from the sombre shades of the silent night, these Boys rose up in rebellion against that society which refused to own them, and that order which organised the cohorts of vengeance.

Jesse W. and Frank James, the terrible guerrillas of the war-time, were henceforth to "become enemies of every man," or at least outlaws from society, and free companions of the highways. It might have been different with them. But the long, lingering fires of hate burned after the lurid days of slaughter, and they were not the persons to refuse the gauntlet when thrown at their feet. Never too good by nature, circumstances have made them desperate, and hence, after concluding their bloody guerrilla record, we proceed with their history as outlaws and highwaymen of the most remarkable character of any known in the annals of history.

CHAPTER 15

The Gallatin Bank Tragedy

The sudden appearance among the people of a peaceful community of a band of armed men, who whoop like savages, fire off pistols, swear fearful oaths, and issue sharp commands, is calculated to produce a feeling of terror, and, for a time at least, to paralyze the energies of men. By pursuing this kind of tactics, the band of robbers which commenced at Russellville, Kentucky, in 1868, and concluded their last exploit at Glendale, in the fall of 1879, have uniformly, with one single exception, been able to accomplish their work and make good their escape.

The 16th day of December, 1869, will not be soon forgotten by the citizens of the flourishing little city of Gallatin, Daviess County, Missouri, because of an incident which created a thrill of excitement that extended all over the land. Daylight bank robberies were not events of frequent occurrence until these later times. The affair at Russellville had taken place many months before, and it was thought altogether unlikely that such another audacious robbery would be soon attempted.

After the Russellville affair, it was known Jesse and Frank James had made a journey to California, and it was not until late in the fall that they returned. It was supposed that only the Youngers and Jameses were capable of doing such deeds, and it was not known that the Boys were at home by any considerable number of people.

Such conclusions as these proved to be fallacious. On the day named—a grey, cold December day—the people of Gallatin were suddenly startled by the presence, in the streets of the place, of a band of armed men, who rode furiously, shouted loudly, and swore fiercely at the people, commanding them, in sharp, decisive tones, to get inside their houses and stay within their own domiciles. While a part of the band remained out in the streets, two of the robbers rushed into the bank. The cashier, Captain John W. Sheets, was behind the counter. He was instantly covered by a pistol, and imperiously commanded to be still. The other robber proceeded to secure the contents of the safe, placed the bank's assets in a sack, and walking to the cashier, he placed the muzzle of a pistol almost against his temple, and fired, the bullet crashing through the brain, and the unfortunate gentleman fell dead at the foot of his slayer. The robbers regained their horses, mounted, and the whole gang rode rapidly away.

The citizens of Gallatin had seen them come and go. They did not remain long. The whole affair was the work of a few moments. They soon realised what had been done, and then there was mounting in hot haste, and almost as quickly as the robbers had come and gone, a well-armed posse was riding after them in hot pursuit.

Captain John W. Sheets, the murdered cashier of the Gallatin bank, served as a captain in the Missouri militia, and had often met parties of guerrillas in combat during the war. He was much esteemed, and his wanton assassination created a profound sensation, and a strong desire to capture his slayers was manifested throughout the community. The whole country was aroused. Daviess county had sent many men to the ranks of the militia, and somehow the impression rapidly went abroad that the robbery had been committed by the James Boys and their old associates among the guerrillas. It stimulated them to greater exertions in the pursuit. The robbers obtained the start, and the men who had ridden with Quantrell never made a reconnaissance on indifferent steeds. Besides, no dashing cavaliers knew better how to ride than they. It was an exciting chase. The people of Gallatin had been taken by surprise. The startling suddenness of the appearance of the robbers; their matter-of-fact attention to the business in hand, and the terrible tragedy which concluded the drama, were well calculated to create surprise, not to say astonishment.

The robbers were trailed directly toward Clay County. The Gallatin posse, after a hot chase, came up with the fleeing bandits. The latter turned upon their pursuers in so determined a way that they were compelled to call a halt, and retreat to meet reinforcements. This gave the robbers time. They continued to retire toward the Clay County line. It was not difficult to trace them into that county. But after they had once penetrated well into the territory of Clay, all traces faded out. No one had seen such a band of men or any other gang like them, and all efforts to discover their retreat proved abortive. They disappeared—like the picture thrown out by the magic lantern when the slide is withdrawn suddenly and broken—at once and forever.

Hearing that they were accused of the robbery, the James Boys, who were then at home, mounted their horses and rode to Kearney to file their protest against the accusation. Their manner convinced the citizens—that it might be dangerous to insist upon the allegation that they were the Gallatin robbers.

It was given out, in extenuation of the shooting of Captain Sheets, that the person who did it believed him to be Lieut. Cox, who, it is said, claimed to have killed Bill Anderson, when that noted guerrilla was attempting to force the passage of the Missouri River in the face of a superior force of Federal troops. The murder of the cashier has yet to be avenged. Not a dollar of the money has been recovered up to this time.

CHAPTER 16

Attempts to Arrest the Boys

The past, we may never forget,
The present, swift its moments fly,
The future, we must trust it yet,
And trusting will not sigh.

After Gallatin, the situation of the Boys became perilous, for although their denials and the affidavits which they were able to procure, served to convince their friends that they were not at Gallatin; still the conviction had grown and deepened that they were concerned in the robbery, and that they had aided and abetted those who committed the crime, even if they were not present in person. Immediately after the perpetration of the outrage, Jesse W. James wrote a letter on behalf of himself and his brother Frank, offering to surrender to the officers of the law and submit to a trial, on condition that the governor should guarantee them against the chances of mob violence and lynch law in Daviess County.

After examining all the papers in the case, and the facts submitted to him, Governor McClurg declared that he did not believe the Boys had anything to do with the robbery, and was fully convinced that they could not have been personally concerned in it. This had the effect of quieting the suspicions of many persons, but there were others who still cherished the opinion that they were the instigators of the robbery, and had aided the perpetrators in concealing themselves, and had doubtless shared with them the booty which they had secured. In subsequent years, this opinion grew into a conviction, and now many believe that it was Frank James' pistol which proved fatal to Captain Sheets.

Be this as it may, the people of Daviess County were aroused, and many of the citizens of Clay County also, indeed all Northwest Missouri was excited. This led to a systematic and persistent attempt to arrest Frank and Jesse James, the generally recognised leaders of the lawless elements of the State.

Among those who firmly believed in the guilt of the James Boys, was Captain John Thomason, of Clay County, Missouri, a citizen well known and highly esteemed by the people of the county. Captain Thomason had served during the war on the Confederate side, and was known as a man of unimpeachable courage. The war over, he returned to his home, and settled down to peaceful pursuits, with an earnest zeal to repair the losses sustained during the war. He had been sheriff of Clay County at one time, and was an outspoken friend of submission to law. He disapproved of the conduct of the James Boys, and believed that they ought to be arrested and tried for their misdeeds.

So believing, he had the courage to act, soon after the Gallatin robbery, Captain Thomason placed himself at the head of a posse of resolute men, and started out to execute his purpose—the arrest of the Jameses. These men have never yet been caught unprepared—they cannot be surprised. They were aware of Thomason's purposes, they knew the feelings which he entertained for them, and they were ready to meet him. That meeting took place near the Samuels residence in Clay County. Thomason demanded their surrender. They laughed at the idea. Then firing commenced. The affray lasted but a few minutes. Several shots were fired, and by one of them Captain Thomason's horse was killed. The other members of the party did not care to press upon men so daring, and Frank and Jesse rode away scathless, and Captain Thomason had to regret the loss of a valuable horse.

But this little episode did not deter the captain from freely expressing his opinion about the Boys and those concerned with them. He had no admiration for the womanly qualities of their mother, and expressed himself in language much more forcible than elegant in regard to her.

Some of his harsh sayings about her came to the hearing of Mrs. Samuels. She was much incensed against him on this account, and concluded to see him about it. It was ten miles from her residence to Captain Thomason's house; but she mounted a horse and rode the distance. She entered the house. The family was dining, and not the slightest attention was paid to her. She went up to where Captain Thomason was seated, and said:

"Captain Thomason, I understand that you have called me a ———!"

"Yes, I did," replied the sturdy farmer, "and I want you to understand that if ever I, or any of mine, are injured by you or yours, in the least thing, I swear before heaven and earth that there shall not be a stone left of your house."

"Indeed!" was all the reply she made.

"If any killing is to be done," pursued the captain, "it will be well for you to kill all my family, and leave none to avenge the injury."

Mrs. Samuels saw that Captain Thomason was in earnest, and that no compromise or apology could be extorted, and she took her departure.

The efforts of Captain Thomason were not all that were made for arresting the James Boys about the time of the Gallatin tragedy. The Daviess County officials hunted them. Detectives from Chicago and St. Louis tracked them and sought an opportunity to entrap them. But these shrewd men were not so to be caught. All attempts to capture them proved abortive.

CHAPTER 17

Outrage at Columbia, Kentucky

Gold begets in brethren hate;
Gold, in families, debate;
Gold does friendship separate;
Gold does civil wars create.

The James Boys were good travellers, and did not confine themselves to narrow limits. One week they might be in Clay County, Missouri, and the next in Nelson, or Logan, or Jessamine County, Kentucky, and then in five days more or less they would be in New York City, and in another week, they might be found in Texas far toward the Mexican border. The Boys understood the advantages of rapid movements. When they had "business" on hand, they never appeared in the vicinity of the scene of their intended operation. Only one or two of their most trusted friends, under any circumstances, were allowed to know anything of their presence in the vicinity. When going to commit a robbery in a strange place, the utmost caution was used to keep down even the suspicion that anything was wrong.

Thus, it was with the band at Russellville, and at Gallatin, Mo. No one had seen them or even heard of any suspicious characters around. In both cases the first intimation the citizens had of the presence of *banditti* in their streets was the reports of firearms and the shouts of the dashing robbers as they thundered along the highways. They appeared as suddenly as a meteor, and departed as quickly as an apparition. Such were their tactics at Northfield, where the Jameses are known to have taken part in the attempt to rob the bank. Precisely the same order was observed on the occasion of the outrage at Columbia, Kentucky, which we shall now proceed to describe.

Columbia is a pleasant village in Adair County, in the middle part of the State of Kentucky. In the region of country in which Adair county is included, there are many of the relatives of the Boys resident, and these were then also friends. Columbia is a quiet village, except during the terms of the courts which meet there, it being the seat of justice of the county. At the time, which we are now considering, the courts were not in session, and no more sedate a town in all Kentucky could be found than Columbia.

It was a lovely afternoon, April 29, 1872. The genial warmth of the sun had decked the earth in a carpet of green, clothed the trees in the forest, and called into being the myriad flowers, whose perfumes scented the breezy air. It was mild, and one of those lazy, dreamy afternoons, when, from very excess of enjoyment of the beauties of reviving nature, men are disposed to fall into sweet reveries.

But the quietude of Columbia was about to be rudely broken in upon, the repose of the beautiful spring day disturbed, and the place swept by a storm of excitement such as Columbia never experienced before. But we will not anticipate.

At the hour of two o'clock, on the afternoon of April 29th, 1872, Mr. R. A. C. Martin, cashier of the Deposit Bank at Columbia, and Mr. Garnett, a citizen, and two friends, were sitting quietly conversing in the bank office. Neither of the gentlemen was armed, and no one could have anticipated danger. Everything in the village was quiet, and the country around was enjoying the blessings of peace.

A half hour later the equanimity of the gentlemen was disturbed by the entrance of three men, well-armed, who, with cocked pistols, ordered the cashier to surrender up the keys of the safe. Another one attempted to shoot Mr. Garnett, but that gentleman saved his life by knocking up the pistol, but was burned slightly by the flame produced by the discharge. All this was the transaction of a moment of time.

"Will you give up the safe-key, d—n you?" shouted one of the robbers, with a cocked pistol presented at Martin's head.

"I will not," was the answer.

"Then, d—n you, will you open the safe? Come, I've no time to wait. If you don't, I will blow your brains out. Come, will you?"

"I will not. I will d—"

The words were cut short. The sentence was never completed. There was a loud report, an involuntary moan from lips that would never speak again, and the lifeless form of R. A. C. Martin, the brave cashier, fell heavily to the floor. The other three gentlemen were guarded by one of the robbers, who kept his pistol cocked and pointed at them, and in view of their dead friend, jested with them about the facility with which he could dispatch all three of them. They had witnessed a demonstration of his skill, and they trembled for their lives.

Having disposed of the cashier, the two robbers who were in the bank commenced gathering up all the money and other valuables which were outside the safe. They tried to open the safe, but the combination was with the dead cashier, and the robbers were baffled.

It was soon known that five men, splendidly mounted, had entered Columbia, at an hour when very few people were abroad. They were armed with heavy dragoon pistols, but as they were divided, two coming in on one road and three on another, the citizens did not take the alarm until they heard the firing at the bank. Two men held the horses of the three who went into the bank, and with pistols fired at every one who appeared on the street; and by their savage yells and fearful oaths they alarmed the people to such an extent that the place soon appeared as if it had been deserted.

Gathering everything they could carry away that had the semblance of money, placing it in a sack, and, one of them throwing it across his horse, the three robbers who had gone inside the building came out, remounted their horses, and with a shout which sent a thrill of terror to the hearts of the citizens of Columbia, they galloped away unmolested.

The suddenness of the raid; the terrible character of the men revealed by the murder of so highly esteemed a citizen as Mr. Martin; the facility with which they shot a vane off a chimney, and their declarations that they would murder every man in the place, which declarations were accompanied by the most terrible oaths, all had a tendency to demoralise the men of Columbia. Surprise and consternation prevented immediate action. But when the cause of their fears no longer remained, they rallied, and then commenced a pursuit which continued until in the mountains of Tennessee, in Fentress County, one of the robbers, who went by the name of Saunders, was wounded and finally captured.

This man was often seen, by their friends, with Frank and Jesse James. This is conclusive of the fact that the Columbia robbery was committed by the same gang, who for some years are known to have aided the James Boys and Younger Brothers in many of their depredations. It has been asserted by some persons, in a position to obtain reliable information, that Frank James was the leader in this raid, and that Bill Longley, the noted Texas *desperado*, formed one of the party.

At any rate, none of the robbers were ever caught, except the Texan, who went by the name of Saunders, and he was so fatally wounded that death closed his existence soon after.

Martin, the murdered cashier, was a gentleman held in high regard by the people of Adair County, and was a member of the Kentucky Legislature at the time of his tragic death. The failure to catch the robbers on this occasion had the effect of creating in the public mind the belief that an organised band of bank breakers existed, and sometimes the names of the Jameses and Youngers were mentioned as leaders of the band.

CHAPTER 18

Out of Exile

As Frank and Jesse James, the celebrated outlaws, live separate and apart from the rest of mankind, they have no confidence in men, and will not receive the confidence of others. Frank is a self-possessed, silent man, who cares little for the society of his fellows. Jesse, on the contrary, under some circumstances, might have become a rollicking, good-humoured citizen, given to "merry jests and healthy laughter." Both have schooled themselves to wariness and a caution which keeps guard over their words at all times. They are temperate to the extent of total abstinence from everything which could intoxicate. In brief, the James Boys are brave as men ever become; they are daring, but not reckless; they are intrepid to a degree perhaps unexcelled in any who have ever lived on this globe; no combination of circumstances or conditions can place them in a position to be surprised.

In the midst of imminent personal danger, they are cool and collected as if they were sitting at a table with a party of friends. They have made human nature a study, and have noted its every manifestation. They expect no mercy from a society which has long ago proscribed them, and they have little emotional regard to waste on that social organisation which spurns them. Brothers in outlawry, separated from the balance of mankind by an impassable gulf which they have created themselves, they have learned to hate the representatives of law and order, and their defiance is not to be despised.

Superadded to physical courage unequalled, they possess cunning and craft never surpassed. With mental gifts, which, properly directed, might have made them renowned as leaders of men in the better walks of life, they are no trifling foes to the vindicators of lawful authority.

These brothers, when under their true names, never even associate together. They do not travel the same road in company, and never travel the same way on the same day. Though never together, they are never far apart. If one needs assistance the other is sure to be near at hand to render it. If one should fall, it is safe to assume that his fall would be terribly avenged by the other. They ride at will over the vast plains of Texas, nearly always alone, unless danger threatens, and neither savage aborigines or wild borderers can make them afraid. They are veritable roving kings of the plains.

In the haunts of civilization, they are no less men to be dreaded and avoided. The quick pistol and the unerring aim cannot be despised. Dead men tell no tales, and the man who would betray will not return to reveal their counsels. Whicher sought them and Whicher died; Askew would surrender them, and he, too, perished on his own threshold. They seem to possess the occult power of reading other men's very thoughts. Such are the characteristics of the James Boys. Bold, shrewd, cool, deliberate men, whom no danger can appal; no sudden surprise can disconcert. They are always ready, and can act instantaneously whatever may be the emergency.

But it must not be supposed that these men, though outlaws, are exiles from the haunts of men. As Jameses they are seldom seen, by even the most intimate of the associates of other days. But they are not always the terrible outlaws to the seeming of men. Nor are they condemned to a lonely life away beyond the borders of civilization among wild herds and roaming savages. They have travelled much, and have carefully studied; they know the ways of the world, and avail themselves of that knowledge to enjoy some of the privileges and pleasures of civilization. Many times, when they were hunted in the out-of-the-way regions of the country, they have been enjoying life as respectable gentlemen among the citizens of our Metropolitan centres. While Pinkerton's men have sought them among the forests of Clay County, Missouri, they have calmly reposed in the Grand Pacific hotel of Chicago; while McDonough's "staff" hunted the outlaws in Western Missouri, they were listening to the soul-stirring strains of Kellogg and Carey in St. Louis.

It must be known that for years they have led a double existence. They have many names, and are capable of assuming any character. The same circumspection in speech and action which enables them to successfully plunder a bank or overhaul an express train is carried with them into social life, and enables them to make friends and secure immunity from annoyance, and disarms all suspicion.

The plundered money of an express train permits them to appear as gentlemen at the Fifth Avenue hotel. New York, and Jesse James as Charles Lawson, of Nottingham, is not regarded as an outlaw in New York society. It must be remembered that the James Boys are not altogether illiterate, nor did they spring from a parentage of uncouth, unlettered rustics. They have made voyages by sea, and have been thrown with persons of culture and refinement. Their father was a man of decided culture, and they have many relatives of education and refinement. An uncle of theirs is a somewhat prominent citizen of California, recognised as a gentleman of intelligence and good breeding. It is, therefore, not so difficult for them to play the role of gentlemen even in refined society.

The Jameses have various names which they assume as occasion requires. Another peculiarity of their method is the respectable character of their friends in their own immediate neighbourhoods. These are respectable farmers and stock-traders, and merchants and what not. Among their neighbours, they are kind and hospitable, and in every transaction scrupulously honest. On Sunday, they are punctually at church service, and are usually liberal contributors to all neighbourhood charities. No one would for a moment suspect that such persons could possibly be in league with the most desperate outlaws who ever lived. Such good neighbours and upright persons surely can do nothing wrong—so the people think. Among these, Frank and Jesse are not known under their own proper names, and if they were it would make no difference. They are circumspect when with such people, and sometimes can assume the piety of Puritans.

It is related of the Boys that on several occasions after a great robbery, as known and respectable citizens, they have joined in the pursuit of the marauders without exciting the least suspicion that they were concerned in the affair. The following story of Jesse has been repeated among their acquaintances:

One day—it was the second after the Corydon bank robbery—he was riding along a not much frequented highway, when he saw two men in pursuit. Confident that they had not seen him, he turned his horse's head toward them and rode up the road to meet them. They were citizens, well mounted and well-armed. Jesse wore Grangers' clothes, and at once assumed a rustic simplicity which comported well with his garb. When he had approached near enough he quietly saluted the robber hunters, and in a simple manner began to converse with them in the following style:

"Well, gentlemen, hev you met anybody up the road ridin' of a hoss an' leadin ov another one, 'cause you see as how I lives down on the Noderway, an' some infernal thief has gone off with my best two hosses. I hearn about two miles furder back at the blacksmith's shop that er man passed there about a hour an' a half ago with two hosses, an' they fits the descripshun of mine to a T. Hev you seen sich?"

"No. Where are you travelling from?"

"Why, Lord, I've come all the way from the Noderway. The infernal thieves are just usin' us up that way. I wish I'd come on the infernal son of a seacook whose taken my hosses. I do, you bet, I'd go fur him with these 'ere irons. I would that!" And Jesse revealed his "weapon" as he called them.

"Did you see anybody on the road ahead?"

"Not for sum miles. I met four ugly lookin' customers this mornin'. They looked like they might 'a been hoss-thieves theirselves. D—n the hossthieves!"

"Thieves are plenty now-a-days. They come into towns and break banks in open daylight. How far did you say the four men were ahead?"

"Well, I didn't say, but it must be more'n two hours since I met 'em, an' they were a ridin' purty fast, an' I've rid my hoss almost down, as you can see."

"What kind of looking men were they?" asked the robber hunters.

"Well, one was a sizable man, with long, red beard, an' a flopped black hat on, a ridin' on a big chesnut sorrel hoss, an' one more was a smallish man, with very black hair and beard, and sharp black eyes, an' he was a ridin' on a roan hoss, an' another was an oldish man, with some grey among his beard, an' he wore a blue huntin' shirt coat, an' he was a ridin' a grey hoss, and the last feller was a little weazle-faced chap, with tallowy complexion, who didn't ware no beard, an' he rode on a dark brown hoss."

The two robber hunters then consulted together.

"That's their description," said one.

"Precisely," said the other.

"Shall we follow?" asked one.

"I would like to," replied the other.

"But there are four of them," was the remark in rejoinder.

"Yes that is bad. If Ed, Dick and Will would just hurry up. Those fellows are no doubt very dangerous men," was the comment of one.

"You bet they are," was the response.

All this time Jesse had listened as an interested party. Now he thought he was privileged to make an inquiry.

"What's up, strangers, anyhow?" Jesse asked.

"You blow it! Don't you know that the Corydon bank, up in Iowa, was robbed yesterday."

Jesse opened his eyes in well-feigned surprise. "You don't say so!" he ejaculated.

"Yes, in broad daylight, and the men you met are the robbers, no doubt. There's a big reward offered to catch them."

"What's this country a comin' to, anyhow? Hoss thieves down on the Nodervvay, an' bank rogues up to Iowa. 'Pears like hard workin' honest folks can't get along much more."

"Could you go back with us?"

"I'd like to, but the cussed hoss thieves will get away. Besides, you see, my hoss is mighty nigh played out hisself. Howsumever, I might ride with you as fur as I can. D—n all thieves, say I, don't you?"

And Jesse actually turned around with the two pursuers of the robbers, in pursuit of another posse of pursuers which Jesse had been enabled to accurately describe by having seen them pass him while lying snug in a dense thicket.

"They might catch the robbers, an' as he'd hev a sheer ov the reward, it would be better'n nothin' at all fur his stolin bosses."

For some miles he kept company with the robber catchers, until his horse becoming lame, and Jesse getting near a railway station, rendered further pursuit of bank robbers distasteful to him, and as his excuse was received as valid, he bid his late traveling companions an enthusiastic *adieu*, boarded a night train, and was in the vicinity of home next morning. Those were Jesse's courting days.

The writer of these pages has been informed by a reputable citizen of St. Louis, that at a time when the detective forces of both St. Louis and Chicago were out in the western part of the State, hunting for the James Boys and Younger Brothers, that he saw and conversed with Jesse James on the corner of Fifth and Chestnut streets, St. Louis, and that on that occasion Jesse attended the opera, Max Strakosch's *troupe* being then in the city. Of course, Jesse James was not the name the people called him by, but he was to all seeming Mr. William Campbell, a most respectable shipper of cattle from Wichita, Kansas.

As Mr. Campbell, he had business relations with many of the citizens, who esteemed him as "a very clever gentleman." At that time, according to the statement of the gentleman upon whose authority this incident is given, Jesse remained in St. Louis a number of days. His associations were excellent, and he was a visitor on 'Change, and ventured even into the Four Courts building, in company with a well-known citizen, who was, of course, ignorant of his true name and character. It is believed that during this trip he made banking arrangements, and that the Boys now carry a heavy bank account in some St. Louis bank. Of course, this business is transacted under assumed names.

CHAPTER 19

The Corydon Raid

Thus far no arrests had been made of the plunderers of the banks at Russellville, Kentucky; Gallatin, Missouri, and Columbia, Kentucky. Boldly the brigands had ridden, and skilfully they had executed their purpose, and, we may almost say, peacefully they rode away when their deeds were done. At first, people knew not what to think of these daring daylight raids. The best detective skill was placed at fault in ferreting out the haunts of the robbers. Russellville and Gallatin are separated by many hundreds of miles. Could the robbers of the former possibly be the raiders into the last-named place? And Gallatin is far removed from Columbia; was it possible that the murderers and robbers at the first-named place were the same persons who astonished the people, murdered the cashier and plundered the bank at Columbia? People asked these questions, and no one was found able to answer them. Scarcely had the people ceased to talk, and the excitement incident to the bold raid on Columbia, with its concomitant horror, died away, ere the country was shaken by the recurrence of a similar daring outrage in another state.

It was the old story repeated. This time a flourishing town in Iowa was selected for the scene of exciting events. In Corydon, there was, and there still is, a bank. In that town, a considerable amount of business is transacted, and it was a season of the year—June 28th, 1873—when much of the capital usually employed in mercantile transactions—it was reasonable to infer—was held in reserve by the bank, and the raiders calculated on a large prize to compensate for the risk taken. Certainly, the men who went to Corydon were trained in the same school in which the Russellville, Gallatin, Columbia and Northfield robbers were at one time pupils.

Riding into town in daylight, when the inhabitants were out and abroad pursuing their usual avocations, the thoroughly armed and well-mounted *desperadoes* proceeded to the bank. Three of them dismounted, drew their pistols, and entered the office. Taken entirely by surprise, the cashier and two other gentlemen who were present, could offer no resistance. In fact, the memory of Gallatin, and the fate of poor Captain Sheets, came back to them with painful distinctness. They were paralyzed before the dark chambers of the huge dragoon pistols, and could not even so much as protest against the proceedings. They yielded to the inevitable.

The horsemen who remained in the street ordered all citizens to retire to their houses, and, with fearful imprecations, threatened to blow the heads off those who manifested the slightest hesitation in obeying their commands. Meanwhile, the bandits on the inside were exercising their pleasure with the assets of the bank. The safe was opened and its contents raked into a sack which the robbers carried along. During the progress of their labours in "taking in" the valuables of the institution, one of them, who seemed to have been deputied to stand guard over the persons found in the place, amused himself by jesting at their distress, and cheerfully asserting his ability to pick the buttons off their coats with pistol bullets.

The robbers remained but a few minutes. The citizens were becoming aware of what was transpiring in their midst, and were recovering from their surprise, and rallying to contest with the robbers. With great oaths, they bade the people in the bank to remain perfectly quiet until they were gone, forced them to the door while they retired, regained and mounted their horses, and, shouting loudly, they rode rapidly away, and were out of town many minutes before anyone was ready to go in pursuit. They were pursued afterward, but none were captured.

CHAPTER 20

The Cash Box of the Fair

Fair time! Kansas City was gay with flags and streamers and banners. It was a holiday season. The streets were thronged and trains from Leavenworth and Sedalia, and St. Joseph and Moberly, and Lawrence and Clinton and regions further removed from Kansas City, brought crowds of men, women and children to see the show. It was a lovely October day. The temperature was mild, and the sun shone through an atmosphere which tinged his rays with gold.

All day the great crowd surged and circled about the grounds and through the textile hall, and the art gallery, and the agricultural exhibition, and among the fat kine and the lazy swine, the sheep and the horses, and the poultry coops. It was a good day, so the "management" thought, one of the very best they had ever had. Shrewd mental arithmeticians declared there was not a soul less than twenty thousand visitors present that day, and an incident of some importance has placed it forever out of the power of anyone to disprove the statement of the mental arithmetician. The management, too, from that day to this, have been unable to count the gate money. Why not we now proceed to tell.

The people visiting the fair were deeply interested in "the speed and bottom" of sundry "blooded horses" which were making time around the race track. The sun was getting low in the west. It was the last "ring" to be exhibited that day. Of course, no one would think of paying their entrance fee and go away without seeing the races.

While the great multitude was so engaged, there was a commotion near the entrance gate. The level beams of the declining sun cast gigantic shadows over the ground. A sudden clattering of horses, hoofs on the beaten road aroused the guardians at the gate. What could it mean? The noise came nearer. The guardians looked up. A strange sight met their gaze. A band of well mounted, well-armed, strange, weird looking men, seven in number, dashed up to the gate. Among some of the spectators it was supposed that these singularly brigandish looking men, were simply actors, that they had been employed by the "management" for the entertainment of the visitors to the fair—that it was, in short, an eruption of the "Cowbellions," or some such mystic order of men. Even the treasurers in their "cuddy boxes" did not comprehend the character of the movement.

But they were not kept in doubt long. Riding directly to the receiver of money, who, like Matthew, of saintly memory, was sitting at the receipt of customs, two of them sprang to the ground, drew their pistols, and rushed up to the cashier. With a fearful threat, they commanded him to remain quiet, and designate the money box. What could he do? Instantly the other robber seized the cash-box. The men who still remained mounted covered the retreat of the two who did the seizing. They remounted, fired a volley as a warning, and dashed away with the receipts of the day, probably $8,000 or $9,000.

There were twenty thousand people, they said, on the ground. And yet in the sight of all these the brigands had done this thing, and were galloping away unmolested. There were hundreds who saw them, and if any old guerrilla comrade was one of them, and recognised Frank and Jesse James, and Cole and Bob Younger, they said nothing about it.

As soon as the "management" of the fair and the police authorities, and sheriffs, and constables, and marshals had time to think and consider the necessity for energetic measures in efforts to capture the brigands, there was mounting in hot haste of police officers, marshals and other enforcers of the law, and pursuit was commenced with great vigour. But the pursuers had little better success than those who went after young Lord Lochinvar when he eloped with the bride of Netherby Hall, whom "they never did see." The pursuers of the robbers of the gate did hear of a man who was riding along a country road in Clay County who looked as if he might have been a robber, but the robbers they never did see.

The fact of the matter is, the robbers rode away about five miles over the hills, until they came to a piece of wild forest country, rode into the woods; came to a sequestered glade; struck a light; emptied the cash out of the box; counted and divided the spoils; remounted their horses, and favoured by the darkness of the night, and their thorough knowledge of the country, they went their way, every man choosing his own route. Jesse and Frank James made a visit to the east part of Jackson County to see some friends, and Cole and Bob

Younger, passing down to the neighbourhood of Monegaw Springs, to visit Mr. Theodoric Snuffer and others of their friends and relatives.

A great many people did not believe that the James Boys and Younger Brothers had anything to do with this robbery, or had ever had anything to do with any robbery at that time. But there is now no longer a doubt that the Boys enjoyed the good in this life which the receipts at the fair ground gate could procure for them.

An incident in connection with the robbery at the fair ground gate is of sufficient interest to bear reproduction here. As we have before related, the robbery took place while the attention of the people was deeply engrossed in the horse races then in progress on the track. That day Mr. Ford, a well-known journalist of Kansas City, was acting treasurer at "the pool stand." There was a sum of money in the box amounting to between $8,000 and $9,000. Mr. Ford was seated upon the box when a couple of strangers came along. One of them approached the treasurer, and entered into a conversation about as follows: The stranger remarked, "You must have considerable money in there?"

"Well, yes," responded Mr. Ford. "There is a considerable amount of cash in here."

"Suppose the James Boys should come and demand it; what would you do?" asked the stranger.

"Well, they would have to fight for it," replied Mr. Ford. "They might kill me, but somebody would have to be killed before they could get this box away, that is certain."

"You would fight for it, eh?" responded the stranger.

"That I would," said Mr. Ford.

"If you knew it was the James Boys who made the demand?" asked the stranger.

"Certainly, I would," replied Mr. Ford.

The stranger gazed sharply at the treasurer of "the pool stand" for an instant, and, turning about, walked away without further remark.

Mr. Ford had met Frank James before, on some occasion, and was convinced that the person who addressed him was no other than Frank James. He recognised him beyond a doubt before he had passed out of sight.

That evening the robbery was consummated. Other respectable parties saw Frank and Jesse James that day about Kansas City, but for a time they were able to beguile the public into the belief that they were not present on that occasion. But time has furnished sufficient evidence to connect them with that daring enterprise.

CHAPTER 21

Ste. Genevieve

Ste. Genevieve! To many it calls up sweet memories, and in many hearts the name is sacred and holy. The very words sound as if full of gentleness, and love, and purity. And yet, in the very midst of the Ste. Genevieve of Missouri, acts of wickedness have been committed which from, their very nature, startled the whole people of the West.

Ste. Genevieve, Missouri, is an old, old town. More than a century ago it was a beacon light of civilization, in the midst of the vast wilderness then called the "far West." And the people of Ste. Genevieve are quiet and sedate, and still preserve, with the traditions of the venerable past, the grand, courtly ways inherited from their ancestors from the banks of the Rhone and the Saone. When springtime comes, Ste. Genevieve is redolent with the perfumes of many flowers, and when the sun climbs higher toward the northern parallel, Ste. Genevieve reposes amid gardens of summer roses. Why should brigands dare place their unhallowed feet on the dust in these ancient streets? If they were not brigands, they would have loved to inhale the perfumed air of the old gardens. But being brigands, they preferred to handle the gold which the fathers of some generations of men commenced to hoard. And for this cause they came to Ste. Genevieve. Brigands are not a sentimental race of beings.

Tuesday morning, May 27th, 1873, was lovely, as such spring days are, when the sun is bright, and the flowers blooming, and the air balmy. Mr. O. D. Harris, cashier of the bank known as the Ste. Genevieve Savings Association, being a gentleman of fine sensibilities, thought so as he sniffed the delicious aroma of the perfume-laden air, when he wended his way to the bank, and so he said to his friends who saluted him by the way. Arriving at the bank—it was just about the hour of opening—he was joined by young Mr. Rozier, a son of

General Firman A. Rozier, then president of the bank.

As Mr. Harris was about to enter the bank office, his attention was momentarily engaged by the appearance of two men who were walking on the street in front of the building, and looking up at it with an intense interest. They were just passing it, when suddenly they turned, and came back as though they intended to enter. They approached the steps and commenced to ascend them, preceded by Mr. Harris, who, having reached the front office, started at once to go behind the counter. He had not progressed half the distance when he was suddenly arrested by a harsh, authoritative command:

"Stop! Surrender, d——n you!"

Of course, Mr. Harris stopped, but could not turn round, because the fellow who had given the command had two pistols, with muzzles against his temple.

The other fellow presented a pistol at the head of young Rozier, and called out:

"You keep still, you d———d little rat, if you don't want to die in an instant."

"I? for what?"

"Not another word, young chap! That's enough! A blabbing tongue can be stopped d———d easy."

Fearing to remain, and impelled by a sudden and overpowering desire to take his departure, young Rozier sprang down the steps, near the landing of which he was standing, and fled swiftly from the place. As he ran away, the fellow fired at him, the bullet cutting its way through his coat on the shoulder, and just grazing his person.

A neighbour across the way saw the robber with his pistols at the cashier's head, and started to get his gun. Just at that moment the other robber fired at Mr. Rozier, and the wife of the neighbour, seeing the predicament of Mr. Harris, dissuaded her husband from attempting to fight them, because she feared resistance would inevitably lead to the shooting of Mr. Harris. Young Rozier, after his escape, gave the alarm to the citizens, who at once began preparations to make an attempt to capture the bold marauders.

Meanwhile Mr. Harris, without arms, was helpless, and could only comply with the demands of the robbers.

"Open that safe!" thundered out one of them.

"Certainly, sir. I cannot do otherwise," said Mr. Harris. The safe was opened.

By this time the other robber, who had pursued young Rozier, joined his comrade in the bank. A money package, containing upwards of $3,600, was secured. Then the thief took the coin box, containing between three and four hundred dollars, principally in gold. By this time the town was aroused, and men began to move toward the bank. The robbers had no time to waste. Turning to Mr. Harris, they emphatically commanded:

"D—n you, come with us!" Mr. Harris obeyed. What else could he do?

When they had gone about fifty yards along the street, they turned to the little knot of women and Boys collecting about the bank building, and shouted:

"Hurrah for Sam Hilderbrand!" and continued to move rapidly away. Two hundred yards from the bank they came to two other men equally well armed, and all having superb horses, who awaited their coming. Here, perceiving that Mr. Harris wore an elegant gold watch, one of the robbers took it from him, and transferred it to his own person.

Then all four of the men started to get on their horses. Just at that time one of the horses got loose and ran off. A German farmer, in a wagon, happened to be passing. Him they compelled, under the most dire threats of immediate extermination, to go after the horse. The German caught the horse and brought him back to where the robbers still held Mr. Harris. Then they all mounted and rode rapidly away, not forgetting to fire a salute at the crowd of citizens who had started in their direction. By this time fully a dozen citizens had armed themselves, and taking horses, were ready for pursuit. They followed the robbers rapidly, and soon came up with them. But it was at once evident that the four men were *desperadoes*, who would not submit to arrest. They fired at the pursuing posse, and compelled them to fall back. Then the whole population turned out, and went in pursuit. But they never came up with them, and soon lost even the trail which they followed.

Some miles from Ste. Genevieve the robbers met a farmer going toward the town. They informed him that he would find something valuable, which belonged to the bank, in the road ahead of him. In accordance with their statement, the farmer found the empty coin box and a lot of papers scattered about. The robbers had taken away a number of valuable papers belonging to the sheriff and others, for which they had no use, and these they had considerately thrown away.

This was one of the boldest robberies which had ever taken place at that time in the West. The "Ste. Genevieve Savings Association" building was situated in the most populous part of the town of Ste, Genevieve, with a population of about three thousand souls. The street through which they passed to reach the bank was the most travelled thoroughfare in that part of the country. It happened in broad daylight, when all the people of the village were engaged about their ordinary concerns.

Of course, a deed like this was calculated to create a sensation. The citizens of Ste. Genevieve pursued the bandits, but lost them, and even all traces of the route which they had taken. What could be done? That was the question.

Mr. Harris went up to St. Louis on the 28th of May to see the police authorities in that city. General Rozier, at that time a State Senator, and on duty at Jefferson City, as a member of the State Board of Equalization, was advised of the robbery, and went down to St. Louis to confer with Mr. Harris and the Chief of Police. Then the hunt was commenced, and prosecuted with a great show of vigour for a time. Theories as to who the robbers were appeared in the public journals almost every day. Some said it was Sam Hilderbrand—who was not known to be dead then—and his gang of *desperadoes*; some said that it was Cullen Baker's crowd from Arkansas; others thought it might possibly be the James Boys and Younger Brothers who "put up the job," but were far from satisfied that they "were the lads who did it."

In those days there were a vast number of very respectable people who, while admitting that Frank and Jesse James, and Coleman and James Younger, were dangerous men, so far as taking the life of fellow-beings was concerned, would at the same time repel any insinuations that they might possibly raid a bank or flag a train. No, they were too honourable and honest for that sort of business. While the people were discussing these questions, the band, of which the James Boys were the leading spirits, was enjoying life on the spoils of Ste. Genevieve.

CHAPTER 22

A Railway Train Robbed in Iowa

"Robin Hood and his merry men," of Sherwood Forest fame, have left a name indelibly written on the pages of history. In the days of our youth we have heard or read about Claude Duval and Jack Shepherd, and their wonderful exploits in old England; and we have a faint recollection of one John A. Murrell, who obtained great distinction as an outlaw in the Southern section of our own country. The Harps who infested the passes of the mountains of East Tennessee were celebrated robbers in their days. And that shrewd mongrel of the commingled blood of old Castile and a red daughter of the western wilds, Agatone, the terror of the Rio Grande border, made no little noise in his day as a daring brigand. But neither these nor the celebrated Fra Diavola were like the brigands we are speaking about.

William de la Marck, the outlawed nobleman of the low countries, and known in history as "The Wild Boar of Ardennes," plundered by the wholesale. There was nothing little or mean in his methods. He would scorn to pounce upon a lonely traveller and demand his purse. He sacked villages and plundered caravans. In this our Missouri outlaws resemble "The Wild Boar of Ardennes." They do not wait in gloomy places to catch a single wayfarer; they do not meet a weary traveller on the highway and cry out to him, "Your money or your life!" They would despise such petty meanness.

After Ste. Genevieve they rested. But their season of repose was not long. A new campaign was planned. Hitherto they had depredated on the banks. But they were about to commence another line of business. The whole question was, no doubt, discussed with profound interest in their secret conclave. Such a thing as plundering a railway train was something new. The public mind had not become accustomed to read accounts of the arrest of railway trains and the robbery of the passengers by a band of armed robbers. The Missouri bandits thought to create a sensation.

In the early part of July, 1873, Frank James, Cole Younger, Robert Moore, a desperado from the Indian Territory, Jesse James and Jim Younger, held a conference in Jackson county, Missouri, when a scheme was broached to overhaul and rob a railway train. The first suggestion was to rob a train on the Hannibal & St. Joe. railway, or some other road in the state of Missouri. But that was rejected after due deliberation. The plan of going into Iowa was suggested and met with favour. The plans were matured before the gang separated. About the 14th of the month the robbers met at the house of a friend in Clay County, and the final arrangements were made; a place of rendezvous was appointed, and the gang then separated into couples. As usual, Frank and Jesse James took the same route; Cole Younger and Bob Moore another, and Jim Younger and a Texas desperado who went by the name of Commanche Tony, followed another route. The robbers leisurely pursued their journey, and on the 20th of July they were near the line of the Chicago, Rock Island & Pacific railway, about fourteen miles east of the city of Council Bluffs.

At the appointed place of rendezvous, they all meet after dark, on the night of the twentieth. During that day, Jesse James and Cole Younger made a reconnaissance, and selected the exact spot to carry out the enterprise in which they were engaged. It was agreed that they would "throw" the morning train bound east from Council Bluffs, as it was supposed to carry a large amount of specie *en route* east from the Pacific slope. The robbers didn't care much for silver, but they were willing to accept all the gold bricks that might fall into their hands. The place selected was about three miles from the rendezvous, in the edge of a belt of timber, and where the road bed was in an excavation about four feet deep. The train was due at that point about three o'clock in the morning.

With deliberate purpose the robbers took their station in the underbrush near the track. Several cross ties were placed in a position to be immediately utilised when the time came. Three or four rails were loosened from the ties, and in silence the bandits waited for the approach of the train.

In due time the train was descried by the watcher at the upper end of the curve—the road was very straight for a long distance to the west of the place selected. At that point there is a rather sharp curve and an obstruction placed on the track could not be seen by the engineer until he was within sixty yards of it. As soon as the train was seen coming down the long straight track, the robbers suddenly awoke into life and activity. The loosened rails were thrown apart, and half a dozen cross ties were thrown across the tracks just above.

The engineer saw the danger when too late. He reversed his engine, but the momentum was too great. The ponderous locomotive plunged on, struck the obstruction, and careened on the side of the track. The shock was terrific. The engineer was killed and the fireman seriously injured. But the train stood still. The aroused passengers had no time to inquire the cause of the sudden stoppage. They knew full soon. The presence of armed men—strange, weird, desperate—appearing on the platforms of the coaches informed them concerning the situation.

The train passed into the hands of bandits. The passengers were ordered in a peremptory manner to keep still. The command was accompanied by dreadful threats of instant annihilation on the least evidence of disobedience. Surprised and unnerved by the suddenness of the attack, the passengers obeyed. Then three of the band proceeded through the train and commanded the passengers to surrender up their money and their jewellery. They made a searching examination of each person in the cars. It is understood that several thousand dollars were obtained in this way. The express and mail car were searched and rifled. The spoils of the examination were put into a sack, and the robbers sought their horses, and mounting, speedily galloped away.

Of course, the intelligence of such an occurrence was telegraphed far and wide. A most determined pursuit of the robbers was at once organised and set on foot. The sheriff of the county in which the rob-

Scene of the Chicago, Rock Island and Pacific
R. R. Robbery.

bery was committed summoned a large posse of men and started in pursuit. His theory was that they were Missouri outlaws. He got on the trail of the robbers, and tracked them through western Missouri as far as St. Clair County. Here he lost their trail, and efforts to find the outlaws proved unavailing. The sheriff finally gave up the chase and returned home.

It is proper to add that friends of Cole Younger denied that he could possibly have had anything to do with this robbery. They assert that he was at the Monegaw hotel, St. Clair, on Sunday morning, the 20th of July, and therefore could not have been in Iowa the next morning. But there is no doubt that the Youngers—at least Bob and Jim—were present with the Jameses on that occasion. At any rate, the bandits escaped with their booty.

CHAPTER 23

The Gains' Place Stage Robbery

Their cruel bandits you would climb
The rungs of the world! oh, curse sublime
tears and laughters for all time.

They used to say that the James Boys and the Younger Brothers might kill men who attempted to impose upon them, but they would not rob or steal. Those who rob men of life must be the greatest criminals, and the lesser crimes are included in the greater. The career they had chosen required the service which money alone can render. These men had need for money which their legitimate resources were inadequate to supply. Those who have taken many lives will not hesitate long to take a few dollars when their necessities require it. Such are the laws which govern human actions.

Long before many of the very respectable citizens of Clay, Clinton and Jackson counties believed it, the sons of the excellent minister whom they had known were the most unscrupulous and daring highwaymen who had ever followed the roads on this continent. The Jameses early became the most dangerous outlaws of which history gives us any account. They were bold, but cautious; skilled in the school of cunning; trained in the art of killing; shrewd in planning, and swift in the execution of their designs.

They seldom attempted a robbery except in out-of-the-way places where the presence of robbers was not expected. Nor did they ever attempt robberies a second time at the same place. Their plan was to strike unexpected blows. This week they would rob a train at Gad's Hill, next week at Muncie, Kansas; again, they would arrest a stage on the Malvern and Hot Springs road, and then again, they would flag a train at Big Springs, Wyoming Territory, a thousand miles from the scene of their last exploit.

It was a grey, raw day in January, 1874, when the regular stage running from Malvern, on the St. Louis, Iron Mountain & Southern Railway, to Hot Springs, pulled out from the little town. Two ambulances for the accommodation of the afflicted pilgrims bound for that Mecca of relief, accompanied the stage on the road. This cavalcade had reached the romantic vale of the Gulpha, near the old Gains' mansion. This is a narrow dell, shut in by abrupt hills, clad with a dense forest of pine and tangled underbrush and evergreen vines. At this particular place the valley widens, and there is a beautiful farm and lovely grounds bordering the roadside on the east and north side of the stream. West and south the deep, tangled forest crowns the hills, which rise to a great height. Here is a favourite halting place for travellers along that way. The clear waters of the Gulpha afford refreshing draughts to the wearied teams.

We have said it was a grey, raw morning in January. The long drive from Malvern over the stony roads inclined the passengers, as well as the horses, to rest. That particular Thursday morning the drivers had stopped, as usual, directly opposite the Gains residence, which is about two hundred yards from the road, toward the northeast. The spot is about five miles southeast from Hot Springs. A little beyond the stopping place the road crosses the stream at a ford. Beyond the creek, the country is very rugged, and covered with forest trees. And in those trees a band of robbers were crouched, waiting the approach of the stage and ambulances. The unsuspecting pilgrims were soon moving on, inwardly congratulating themselves on the near termination of their fatiguing journey.

The stage and ambulances had proceeded well into the wood on the Hot Springs side of the Gulpha, perhaps half a mile from "the watering place," when a strong, emphatic voice called out from the borders of the brush: "Stop! d—n you, or I'll blow your head off!"

Thus commanded, of course the driver of the stage brought his team to a standstill. The passengers naturally threw aside the flaps of the vehicles and thrust out their heads to ascertain what the strange proceedings meant. They saw at once. Cocked revolvers yawned before them, and stern, harsh voices exclaimed in chorus, "D—n you, tumble out!"

"Certainly, under the circumstances, we will do so with alacrity," replied one of the passengers, a Mr. Charles Moore.

"Raise your hands, you d—d ——."

Of course, every passenger promptly obeyed the order. One passenger, a rheumatic invalid, alone, was left undisturbed. Then the leader cried out:

"Come! be quick, form a circle here!"

The order was obeyed. Then two of the robbers, one of whom was armed with a double-barrel shotgun and the other with a navy repeater, mounted guard over the prisoners, and made many sinister remarks, doubtless intended to be jocose, but which kept the prisoners in a tremor of apprehension all the while.

Then two of the brigands proceeded to examine the effects and pockets of the passengers.

When the affable gentlemen of the road had completed their undertaking, they proceeded in the coolest manner imaginable to cast up their accounts. They had lost in cash—nothing; in jewellery—naught; in conscience—well, it happened they didn't have any to lose. They had gained from sundry passengers as follows:

Ex-Gov. Burbank, of Dakotah, cash,	$850 00
" " " diamond pin,	350 00
" " " gold watch,	250 00
Passenger from Syracuse, N.Y.,	160 00
William Taylor, Esq., Lowell, Mass.,	650 00
John Dietrich, Esq., Little Rock, Ark.,	200 00
Charles Moore, Esq., " "	70 00
E. A. Peebles, Hot Springs, " "	20 00
Three country farmers, " "	45 00
Southern Express Company, " "	450.00
Geo. R. Crump, Memphis, Tenn., "	45 00
Total,	$3,090 00

It was a very good morning's work, and the bandits were so well pleased that they were inclined to indulge in a sort of grim facetiousness. One of them unharnessed the best stage horse, saddled him and mounted him, and after trying his gait by riding up and down the road a few times, called out:

"Boys, I reckon he'll do!"

Another one of the band went to each passenger as he stood in the circle. John Dietrich was the first to pass through the ordeal of cross-examination.

"Where are you from?"

"Little Rock," replied Dietrich.

"Ah, ha!"

"Yes, have a boot and shoe store there," remarked Dietrich.

"You'd better be there attending to it," was the observation of the chief of the bandits.

"Are there any Southern men here?"

"I am," replied Mr. Crump and three others.

"Any who served in the army?"

"I did," said Crump.

The leader then asked him what regiment he belonged to, and what part of the country he had served in. The answers were satisfactory, and then the robber handed Crump his watch and money, remarking as he did so;

"Well, you look like an honest fellow. I guess you're all right. We don't want to rob Confederate soldiers. But the d——d Yankees have driven us all into outlawry, and we will make them pay for it yet."

Mr. Taylor, of Lowell, Mass., was examined.

"Where are you from?"

"St. Louis."

"Yes, and d——n your soul, you are a reporter for the St. Louis *Democrat*, the vilest sheet in the land. Go to Hot Springs and send the dirty concern a telegram about this affair, and give them my compliments, will you?"

Then Governor Burbank felt encouraged to ask a favour of them.

"Will you please return me my papers?" asked the governor. "They are valuable to me, but I am sure you can make no use of them."

"We'll see," said the leader, sententiously, and took the packet and kneeled down to examine them.

In a few moments, he took up a paper with an official seal, that excited his ire, and before he paused to examine it sufficiently to enable him to determine its character, he reached the conclusion that the bearer was a detective, a class which he held in the utmost hatred.

"Boys, I believe he's a detective—shoot him, at once!" was the sententious command. In an instant Governor Burbank was covered by three ready cocked dragoon pistols. The ex-governor was on the border of time.

"Stop!" cried the robber, "I reckon it's all right. Here, take your papers."

And the ex-governor felt that a mighty load had suddenly been lifted from him, and that a dark cloud, which but a moment before had enshrouded the world in the deepest gloom of midnight, had drifted away, allowing the bright sun to shine out on the scenes of time.

The passenger from Syracuse asked for the return of $5, to enable him to telegraph home for assistance.

The chief looked at him rather sternly for a few moments, and said:

"So, you have no friends nor money. You had better go and die. Your death would be no loss to yourself or the country. You'll get nothing back, at any rate."

All this while one of the robbers, said to have been James Younger, held a double-barrel shot-gun cocked in his hand, which he pointed ever and *anon* at Mr. Taylor, the supposed *Democrat* reporter, making such cheerful remarks as these: "Boys, I'll bet a hundred dollar bill I can shoot his hat off his head and not touch a hair on it." And the others would respond with a banter of a very uncomfortable character, while the facetious bandit went on: "Now, wouldn't that button on his coat make a good mark. I'll bet a dollar I can clip it off and not cut the coat!" With such grim jests, did he amuse himself and torment the captive.

Having thoroughly accomplished their work, the bandits made the drivers hitch up their teams and drive away. The whole transaction was completed in less than ten minutes. The robbers did not linger. In a few minutes, they scattered through the brush. Some "struck out," as they expressed it, for the Nation, another for Texas, and one for Louisiana.

Of course, denials of complicity on the part of the Jameses in this affair were at once entered by their friends. But it has since been ascertained that the party who did the deed consisted of Frank and Jesse James, Coleman and James Younger, and Clell Miller, one of the associates of the daring outlaws.

Chapter 24

Gadshill

During the morning of January 31, at the hour of 9:30 o'clock, the St. Louis and Texas express train, with a goodly number of passengers, and the mails and valuable express freight, departed from the Plum street depot m St. Louis, bound for Texas, via the St. Louis, Iron Mountain and Southern railroad. Mr. C. A. Alford was the conductor in charge of the train when it departed, and when the event which we are about to describe occurred.

Gadshill, a name rich in historical associations, is a lonely wayside station on the road, situated in the northeast corner of Wayne county, Missouri, about seven miles from Piedmont, which is the nearest telegraph station.

The 31st of January, 1874, was a dreary, winter day. The cold grey clouds veiled the sky, and no ray of sunlight filtered through the wintry pall.

The day wore away, wearily enough, with the passengers on Mr. Alford's train. They had not yet been together a sufficient length of time to assimilate, and each one was left to his, or her, own device for amusement or entertainment. Slowly the hours passed away. The landscape was cold, dreary and forbidding; the winds came blowing from the north with a chill in their breath that made the passengers think longingly of "sweet home." Iron Mountain, and Pilot Knob, and Shepherd's Mountain, and the beautiful valley of Arcadia, in their winter dress, wore anything but a pleasing aspect. In fact, it was a comfortless sort of day, which made the passengers feel anything but merry.

Nightfall was approaching. Already the thick atmosphere was becoming sombre in hue, and it was evident the curtains of darkness were falling over the earth.

By this time, it was about 5:30 o'clock in the afternoon. The train was approaching the little station dignified by the name of Gadshill, in honour of the locality where Sir John Falstaff so valiantly met the Buckramite host, an event graphically delineated by the historian and poet of all climes and times. As the train drew near, the engineer saw the red flag displayed, and whistled "down brakes."

Before proceeding to relate what happened to the train and the passengers on it, we shall state what had happened at Gadshill before the train came.

About half-past three o'clock that afternoon, a party of seven men, splendidly mounted and armed to the teeth, rode to the station, secured the agent, then took in a blacksmith, and afterwards all the citizens and two or three countrymen, and one lad, who were waiting for the arrival of the train. Among the persons so detained was the son of Dr. Rock, at that time Representative in the Legislature from Wayne County. The captives were taken to the little station-house and confined there, under the surveillance of one of the armed robbers. Then the bandits set about completing their arrangements for executing the work which they had come to perform. The signal flag was displayed on the track and the lower end of the switch was opened, so that the train would be ditched if it attempted to pass. Then the bandits waited for their prey.

In due time the train came dashing down the road. The engineer saw the flag and gave the signal for stopping. Mr. Alford, the conductor, was ready to step upon the little platform as soon as the train came alongside. The robbers did not show themselves until the cars were at the station. No sooner had the train come to a full halt than Mr. Alford stepped off to the platform. He was instantly confronted by the muzzle of a pistol and greeted with the salutation:

"Give me your money and your watch, d—n your soul! quick!"

Nearing Gadshill.

Mr. Alford had no alternative. He gave up his pocket-book containing fifty dollars in money, and an elegant gold watch.

"Get in there!" they commanded, and Mr. Alford obeyed.

While this was going on, one of the brigands had covered the engineer with a revolver, and compelled him to leave his cab. Meanwhile, part of the band occupied the platforms at the ends of the passenger coaches, while two of them went through the train with a revolver in one hand and commanded the passengers to give up their money. Of course, the defenceless travellers yielded their change to the uttermost farthing into the hands of the robbers.

Mr. John H. Morley, chief engineer of the St. Louis, Iron Mountain & Southern Railroad, was among the passengers, and was plundered along with the rest of them. The robbers made a clean sweep, taking money, watches and jewellery from all. Among the passengers robbed, were Silas Ferry, C. D. Henry, Geo. G. Dent, Mr. Scott, Sr., Mr. Scott, Jr., Mr. Lincoln, Mr. Meriam, O. S. Newell and A. McLain. After having effectually stripped the passengers of worldly wealth, the robbers proceeded to the express car, broke open the safe, and secured the contents. The mail bags were next cut open and their contents rifled of everything of value. The whole amount of money secured by the robbers was somewhere between eight and ten thousand dollars. After completing their work the bandits went to Mr. Alford and remarked that as he was conductor he needed a watch, and they gave him back his timekeeper.

When they had satisfied themselves that there was no more plunder to be gained, they released the conductor and engineer, and told them to draw out at once.

As the robbers, whose part of the business it was to relieve the passengers of their spare cash, passed through the cars, they asked each one of the gentlemen passengers his name. One of the victims, a Mr. Newell, asked the brigands,

"What do you want to know that for?"

"D—n you, out with your name, and ask questions afterward!" was the profane reply.

"Well, my name is Newell, and here's my money, and now I want to know why you ask me for my name?" said Mr. Newell, with an attempt at pleasantry, fortified by a sort of grim smile.'

"You seem to be a sort of jolly coon, anyhow," said the robber, "and I'll gratify you. That old scoundrel, Pinkerton, is on this train, or was to have been on it, and we want to get him, so that we can cut out his heart and roast it."

During the time, they were in the cars among the passengers, they mentioned the name of Pinkerton many times, and exhibited the most intense hatred of the distinguished detective. It was very fortunate for Mr. Allan Pinkerton that he was not a passenger on the train that lumbered up to the dreary station of Gadshill that winter day.

This circumstance is confirmatory of the evidence that Jesse and Frank James were leaders in the Gadshill affair. They, for years, have cherished the most bitter animosity toward the detective, and the very mention of his name was sufficient to render them almost frantic with rage.

The citizens were released, and the robbers mounted their horses and rode away in the gathering darkness, over the forest-crowned hills to the west.

Some of the features of this bold robbery were ludicrous in the extreme. The trepidation of the passengers made the job a quick one, because they were ready on demand to give up everything to the freebooters. One passenger complained at the hardship, and the following dialogue ensued:

"Give me your money, watch and jewellery, you blamed cur! quick!"

"Now, please, I—"

"Dry up, d—n you, and shell out!" And the robber thrust a pistol against his temple.

"Oh, yes! Excuse m-m-me, p-p-p-please, d-don't shoot. Here's a-all I've g-got in t-t-the world." And the poor fellow, all tremblingly, handed up his wealth.

"I'm a good mind to shoot you, anyhow," remarked the robber, "for being so white livered."

At this the alarmed traveller crouched down behind a seat.

It was nightfall when the robbers rode away. Gadshill is in the midst of a wilderness country. There are but few settlements among the hills, and it was impossible to organise an effective posse at once for pursuit. At Piedmont, on the arrival of the train, the news was telegraphed to St. Louis and Little Rock. The citizens of that vicinity were aroused, and before midnight a well-armed posse of a dozen men were riding over the hills westward in pursuit.

But the robbers, who were all mounted on blooded horses, rode swiftly away. Before the dawn of day they were sixty miles from the scene of the crime. They called at the residence of a widow lady named Cook, one mile above Carpentersville, on the Current River, to obtain a breakfast. There were but five of them in the party, and these were each armed with a pair of pistols and a repeating rifle. They continued on, and passed Mr. Payne's on the Big Piney, in Texas County, and went to the house of the Hon. Mr. Mason, then a member of the State Legislature, and who was at that time absent attending its session, and demanded food and lodging from Mrs. Mason. They remained there all night, and proceeded westward in the morning. The same day that the five men took breakfast with Mrs. Cook, a dozen pursuers from Gadshill and Piedmont arrived at the same place, having tracked them sixty miles.

CHAPTER 25

After Gadshill

The bold act of brigandage at Gadshill aroused the whole country. The outlaws had become formidable. Missouri and Arkansas were alike interested, and the citizens of both states were ready to make personal sacrifices to aid in the capture of such daring brigands. But who were the robbers? A question not easy to answer with any assurance of correctness. Some said at once that it was the Jameses and the Youngers and their associates. Geo. W. Shepherd, one of Quantrell's most daring Guerrillas in Missouri, and one of those who separated from him when he went to Kentucky, was an intimate friend of the Jameses in the old Guerrilla times. After the war, Shepherd emigrated to Kentucky and married at Chaplin, Nelson County, where he settled down.

After Russellville, circumstances pointed to him as one of the persons implicated in the robbery. He was arrested, carried to Logan county and tried. The proof was of such a character that he was found guilty of aiding and abetting the robbers, and was sentenced to the penitentiary for a term of three years. At the expiration of his sentence he returned to Chaplin and learned that during his incarceration his wife had obtained a divorce and married another man. Shepherd had paid $600 on the house and lot which he found his ex-wife and husband occupying. But he left them there and took his departure from Kentucky. At the time of the Gadshill affair he was somewhere in Missouri. But there is not a particle of evidence to connect him with the robbery.

Bradley Collins was a noted *desperado* in those days, who figured in Texas and the Indian Territory as one of the worst outlaws in the business. He also rode at times with the Jameses and the Youngers. John Chunk was another daring outlaw who infested Texas and the Indian Territory, and often came into Missouri and co-operated with the brigands of that state.

Sid Wallace, afterwards hanged at Clarksville, Arkansas, was another noted outlaw between the years 1866 and 1874. He, too, was a "friend" of the Jameses. Cal Carter, Jim Reed, John Wes. Hardin, Sam Bass, Bill Longley, Tom Taylor and Jim Clark, all notorious in Texas and the Nation, often joined the Missouri outlaws and hunted with them. Indeed, it appears that there was a regularly organised band of brigands ramifying through the states of Missouri, Kansas, Colorado, Arkansas, the Indian Territory and Texas. This *banditti* was composed of the most desperate and daring men who had ever placed themselves beyond the pale of the law in this country.

Whatever doubts might once have existed concerning the personality of the bandits of Gadshill, they have all vanished in the light of subsequent events. Jesse and Frank James, some of the Youngers and their associates, were undoubtedly the men who rode to Gadshill. The fellows seemed to have had a bit of classical humour in their composition in selecting a place so named as the scene of such an exploit.

It seemed to have created a conviction in the minds of those in authority, also, that the Jameses were the leaders. Governor Woodson, of Missouri, offered a reward to the full extent of the law's provisions. Governor Baxter, of Arkansas, communicated to Governor Woodson his desire to aid in the capture of the outlaws, and also offered a reward. The express company offered a heavy reward for the capture of the bandits, and the United States authorities took an active interest in the movement set on foot to break up the formidable *banditti*. Stimulated by the prospect of gain, the detectives all over the country became active in the pursuit. The citizens, too, were on the move, and it seemed that the auguries all pointed to a speedy annihilation of this formidable gang which infested the West.

Meanwhile another outrage was committed almost on the line of retreat from Gadshill, which still further agitated the public mind.

During the afternoon of the 11th of February, 1874, five men, splendidly mounted and well-armed, rode into the town of Bentonville, Benton County, Arkansas. Their entrance was quiet. They rode to the store of Craig & Son; dismounted and entered the store; made prisoners of the proprietors and clerks at the muzzle of pistols, and proceeded to rifle the cash box. Fortunately for the firm of Craig & Son, they had made a deposit that day and the robbers only obtained about one hundred and fifty dollars in money. They helped themselves to about one hundred dollars' worth of goods; warned the proprietors and clerks not to give the alarm until they had passed out of town; went out; mounted their horses and rode away in the most nonchalant manner. In a saloon, adjacent, there were more than twenty men who were uninformed as to what was taking place in the store of Messrs. Craig & Son, until after the robbers had departed. Pursuit was made, but the bandits escaped.

The weeks following the Gadshill outrage were busy ones with the detectives. A carefully planned campaign against the marauders was at once instituted and prosecuted with great vigour. Allan Pinkerton, the American Vidocq, was employed by the express company to hunt the robbers down. The United States Government ordered the Secret Service force into the field, and the police and constabulary forces of Missouri and Arkansas, under orders from the Governors of the respective states, were acting in concert with the forces of detectives called into service by the General Government and the express company.

The brigands were successfully tracked through the wilds of southern Missouri, and their trail led into the hill country of St. Clair county, and across Jackson county on beyond the Missouri river. No doubt was left upon the minds of the man-hunters as to the personality of the Gadshill robbers. The James Boys and some of the Youngers were certainly engaged in it. The Youngers, at least John and Jim, had returned to Roscoe, St. Clair County, "flush with cash." The detectives were on their tracks. To the force was added Ed. B. Daniels, a courageous young man of Osceola, who was thoroughly acquainted with the country. The detective force in St. Clair County was under the direction of one of Allan Pinkerton's picked men. Captain W. J. Allen, whose real name was Lull. With him was a St. Louis "fly cop," well known, and distinguished for his shrewdness and daring, who for the time had assumed the name of Wright. Daniels was extremely serviceable as a guide.

One morning, when near the residence of Theodoric Snuffer, a short distance from Roscoe, these three men were suddenly surprised by John and James Younger, who rode up behind them in the road. They were at Snuffer's house, and saw the detectives pass, and started out with the avowed purpose of capturing them. Approaching the three men in the rear, they raised their double-barrel shotguns, and with an oath commanded them to hold up their hands and drop their pistols. Taken thus, at a disadvantage, the detectives complied, and dropped their belts of pistols in the road.

James Younger dismounted to secure them, while John remained on horseback with a double-barrel gun covering them. For a moment, he lowered his gun. That moment was fatal. Captain Lull drew a concealed Smith & Wesson revolver from his bosom, and fired. The ball took effect in John Younger's neck, severing the left jugular vein. In the very agonies of death, as he fell from his horse to die, John Younger raised a pistol and fired, the ball taking effect in the left arm and side of Captain Lull. Two more shots were fired, probably by James Younger, before Allen, or rather Lull, fell. James Younger then commenced firing at Ed. B. Daniels. That gentleman also had a concealed pistol, returned the fire and inflicted a slight flesh wound on the person of James Younger. But his fate was sealed. A fatal bullet crashed through the left side of the neck, and Daniels fell, and soon afterward expired. This tragedy excited and alarmed the whole country. It was no longer possible for James Younger to remain in the country. He took the pistols which his dead brother, John, had worn, and departed for the house of a friend in Boone county, Arkansas, where he was soon joined by Cole and Bob.

Wright, who was riding a short distance in advance of Captain Lull and Ed. Daniels, hearing the summons of the Younger Brothers, turned, and at a glance saw the situation, and, putting spurs to his horse, dashed away. Although he was fired upon and pursued a short distance by James Younger, he managed to escape unharmed, aided as he was by a very fleet horse.

The hunters for the Jameses met with no better luck. One of the darkest tragedies which ever disgraced the state of Missouri followed the efforts of the detectives to capture the shrewdest and most daring outlaws who have yet appeared in this country. There is an air of mystery about this terrible episode which makes it all the more thrilling. The full details of this crime are reserved for another chapter.

Theodoric Snuffer's Residence.

CHAPTER 26

Whicher's Ride to Death

The James Boys were believed to have been the projectors and leaders of the Gadshill enterprise. Soon after that event they returned to Clay County. Traces of their trail through Southern Missouri were soon discovered. The description given of two of the five travellers who took breakfast at Mrs. Cook's on Current River, and lodged at Mr. Mason's house in Texas County, answered well for Frank and Jesse James. The detectives caught at every clue. The James Boys were at Gadshill beyond a doubt. And so, the brigand hunters passed into Clay County.

Meanwhile the James Boys and other members of the gang were resting in the vicinity of Kearney, in Clay County, at the residence of Dr. Samuels. Among those known to have been there were Jim Cummings and Clell Miller, Jim Anderson, a brother of Bill Anderson, of Centralia notoriety, and Bradley Collins, a Texas *desperado*. The sheriff of Clay County thought Arthur McCoy was probably at that time with the Jameses. On the 9th day of March, Jesse James spent a portion of the day in Kearney. The gang had several horses shod a few days before at a country blacksmith shop in that vicinity.

Wednesday, March 10, 1874, arrived at Liberty, the county seat of Clay County, Missouri, J. W. Whicher, from what place it mattered not to the citizens of Liberty. This man was in the very vigour of a matured manhood. He was just twenty-six years of age, lately married to an estimable and accomplished young lady, a resident of Iowa City.

Whicher was intelligent, shrewd and daring. He was selected by his chief, Allan Pinkerton, who is acknowledged as a consummate judge of human nature, as the fittest instrument to execute the most dangerous enterprise which he had ever yet undertaken.

Immediately on arriving at Liberty, Whicher called at the Commercial Savings Bank to see Mr. Adkins, its president. To him he made known his errand into that section. At the same time, he deposited in the bank some money and papers. Mr. Adkins was not able to give Whicher all the information which he desired, and sent him to Col. O. P. Moss, ex-sheriff of Clay County, for further information.

When he opened his plans to Moss, that gentleman advised him not to go. He gave him a terrible account of the prowess of the *desperadoes*; told him of their shrewdness and of their merciless nature when excited by the presence of an enemy, and warned him that he need not hope to secure such wary men by stratagem. Col. Moss was earnest in his efforts to dissuade Whicher from making the rash attempt.

But it was of no avail. Whicher had received what he regarded as positive evidence that the Jameses were the leaders of the Gadshill bandits, and, further, that they were now at home, near Kearney. Stimulated by the hope of "catching his game," and securing the large rewards, Whicher, who seems to have been destitute of any sense of fear, made his arrangements to go that very evening to the Jameses' place of retreat. Disguised in the garb of a farm labourer, with an old carpet bag swung on a stick, Whicher took the evening train for Kearney, and there made inquiries for work on a farm. He did not tarry long at the station, but soon started out toward the Samuels place.

Poor Whicher! he little thought that his fate was already determined upon by those whose destiny he was seeking to determine. But so it was.

There was a friend of the Jameses in Liberty that day—a fellow named Jim Latche, who had been expelled from Texas on account of his worthless qualities as a citizen and dangerous attributes as a criminal. Latche had met the James Boys, and had made a raid with them, on one occasion, down in Texas. He had been resting at their retreat for a few days, and was probably on a scout for them that day. At any rate, he was in Liberty when Whicher arrived. He observed his movements, because Whicher was a stranger; saw him go to the bank and make a deposit; waited while he conferred with Mr. Adkins, and then tracked him to Col. Moss' office. He came to the conclusion that Whicher was a detective; and when afterward he saw that the detective had changed his clothes, he was convinced that he was right. Latche hastened away to give a report of what he had heard and observed.

When Whicher arrived at Kearney the Jameses knew of it, and suspected the truth concerning his mission. It was in the evening.

Jim Anderson, Jesse James and Bradley Collins were in waiting on the roadside, about half a mile from the Samuels residence. Soon after Whicher came along. He was carrying a carpet-sack. Jesse James came out of their concealment alone, and met Whicher in the road.

"Good evening, sir," said Whicher.

"Where in h——ll are you going?" responded the other.

"Well, it's a rude response, but I will not answer as rudely again. I am seeking work. Can you tell me where I can get some work on a farm?"

"No, not much, you don't want any, either, you d———d thief. Old Pinkerton has already given you a job that will last you as long as you live, I reckon."

And Jesse laughed a cold, hard laugh that meant death. Of course, Whicher was helpless, for the other had him under cover of a pistol from the moment he came in sight. But Whicher was dauntless and wary, and, without exhibiting the least trepidation, he said:

"Who do you take me to be? What have I to do with Pinkerton or his business? I am a stranger in the country and want something to do. I don't see why you should keep that pistol pointed at me. I don't know you, and have never done you any wrong."

"Oh, d——n it, you are the kind of a dog that sneaks up and bites, are you? You will carry in the James Boys, will you? You are a nice sneaking cur, ain't you? Want work, do you? What say you, my sneak? Eh?"

The tantalising manner of Jesse James did not disconcert the detective. He answered these taunts with perfect coolness:

"I don't understand you, sir. I am no cur, and know nothing of the James Boys. I addressed you politely, and you did not return the same. I said I wanted some employment, and you taunt me for it. I must bid you good evening."

With this, Whicher made a step forward. His progress was arrested by the harsh voice of Jesse James.

"You shall die if you move out of your tracks! Keep up your hands!"

Whicher realised by this time that his chance of escape was small, for he knew that Jesse James stood before him, and he had quickly made up his mind that he would sell his life dearly. He was cool, active and expert with the pistol; his right hand was almost involuntarily seeking to grasp his weapon. But Jesse James evidently had him at a great disadvantage. Instantly realising this, he changed his purpose.

"Well, this is a singular adventure, I declare. Now, why you should make such a mistake concerning me is more than I can imagine. You are surely making sport of me. I tell you I know nothing of the persons of whom you speak, and why should you interrupt me? Let me go on, for I must find a place to stop tonight, anyhow."

Jesse James laughed outright. "What," said he, "were you doing at Liberty today? Why did you deposit money in the bank? What business did you have with Adkins and Moss? Where are the clothes you wore? Plotting to capture the James Boys, eh?" and Jesse laughed aloud, and Jim Anderson and Fox, another confederate of the Boys, came from their concealment, with pistols in hand. Poor Whicher saw this, and for the first time he fully realised the helplessness of his position.

"Betrayed," he thought, almost said.

Jesse James said, in a cold, dry tone: "Young man, we want to hear no more from you. We know you. Move but a finger and you die now. Boys," he said, addressing Anderson and Fox, "I don't think it best to do the job here. It wouldn't take long, but for certain reasons I don't think this is the place. Shall we cross the river tonight?" The others answered they would, if it was his pleasure.

All this time Whicher had stood still; not a muscle moved, and not a single wave of pallor had covered his features. He knew what they meant by "the job," and made up his mind to improve any incident, however slight, to have revenge on his murderers.

But there were no favourable incidents for him. He had been tried and condemned in a court from which he could not appeal. At what time the sentence would be executed he could not tell.

"Boys, relieve him of his burden and weapons," said Jesse James.

Quick as thought, Whicher's hand was thrust into the bosom of his coat. It was too late. Fox and Anderson sprang upon him, while Jesse James placed the muzzle of his pistol against his temple. To struggle was useless. He was compelled to yield, for just then Brad Collins and Jim Latche joined the others. The case of the detective was hopeless. In an instant, they had disarmed him; he had brought only one Smith & Wesson pistol. Then the *desperadoes* felt of his hands, and laughed at his pretensions as a farm-labourer.

Confident in the belief that he had been betrayed by one of the two gentlemen to whom he had applied at Liberty, Whicher made up his mind that he would make no whining petition to the murderers. If he had known the exact state of the case he would not have gone to Kearney, and if he had gone he would have been better prepared to encounter the Boys. But fate had ordained it otherwise, and another

Whicher Meets his Fate.

victim to the long, long catalogue of names which Jesse James had written in blood was the outcome of it all.

Darkness had fallen upon the fair scenes of nature while these things were happening. The cool March winds whistled dismally through the yet naked forest trees. The stars came out and looked coldly from the empyrean, but there was purity in their beams, and no blood marks on their twinkling discs. It was meet that the tragedy which was about to take place should be enacted in the hours of gloomy night, and at a time when all without was comfortless and dreary.

Whicher was bound securely, and a gag was placed in his mouth that he might call for no aid or deliverance. The *desperadoes* placed him upon a horse, in the still hours of the night, and rode away. His legs were tied securely under the horse's belly, and his arms were pinioned with strong ropes. Jesse James, Bradley Collins and Jim Anderson were the executioners. In silence himself, Whicher, during that long, lonely ride heard the three discussing their bloody deeds with a thrill of horror, for they had told him what his fate was to be.

About three o'clock on the morning of the 11th of March, the drowsy ferryman at Blue Mills, on the Missouri River, was roused to wakefulness by the shouts of men on the north side, who signified their desire to cross over.

"Be in a hurry," cried the belated travellers. "We are after horse thieves and must cross quick if we catch them."

Thus appealed to the ferryman crossed the river to the northeastern shore, where the horse thief hunters awaited him.

When they came down to the boat, they said to the ferryman:

"We have caught the thief, and if you want to keep your head on your shoulders you had better put us across the river very quick."

So persuaded, the ferryman obeyed. They were soon on the south side of the river. The ferryman observed that one of the men was bound and gagged. It was poor Whicher on his way to his execution. The very stars shone piteously through a veil of mist, and the winds sighed sadly as the strange group moved off on the Independence road. But neither the helpless condition of their victim, nor the sad aspect of nature in the solemnity of the hours of darkness could evoke a spark of pity in the seared hearts of Whicher's executioners.

They rode away in the darkness. Just how the executed their purpose only the red-handed outlaws and the merciful God knows.

The next morning an early traveller on the road from Independence to Blue Mills, about halfway between the places, in a lonely spot, saw a ghastly corpse with a bullet-hole through the forehead and another through the heart. It was all that remained of Whicher.

CHAPTER 27

A Night Raid of Detectives

After Whicher's melancholy fate, Allan Pinkerton had motives aside from those of gain for pursuing to the death the celebrated border bandits, Frank and Jesse James. In one year, three of the most courageous and trusted men in the employ of the distinguished detective had been sent out after the Missouri outlaws, and were carried back cold in death, after conflicts with the desperadoes. Whicher and Lull and Daniels were asleep in gory beds. And yet Frank and Jesse James, and their followers and allies, were free as the winds that blow, to come and go as interest or caprice might dictate to them. While this condition of affairs continued, Pinkerton must have felt that his reputation as a skilful entrapper of criminals suffered.

About the first of the year 1875, the great detective commenced a campaign against the renowned brigands which was meant to be finally effective. The most elaborate and careful preparations were made. Nothing was left undone which could in any way contribute to the success of the undertaking. The utmost secrecy was observed in every movement.

Several circumstances seemed to favour the detectives. Many of the most respectable citizens of Clay County had grown weary of the presence in their midst of persons of the evil reputation of the Jameses, and entered with alacrity and zeal into the scheme inaugurated for the capture of the Boys. Among those of the citizens most prominent in the movement which had for its design the annihilation of the band of which Jesse James was supposed to be the chief leader, were several of the old neighbours and acquaintances of the James and Samuels families.

With these citizens, Mr. William Pinkerton, who had gone from Chicago to Kansas City, to direct the movements of the detective forces, opened communication. A system of cipher signals was adopted, and communications constantly passed between the different persons engaged in the undertaking. The citizens in the neighbourhood of Kearney were watchful, and keenly observed every movement in the vicinity of the residence of Dr. Samuels, and daily transmitted the results to their chief, who had established temporary headquarters at Kansas City.

It was known to some of the immediate neighbours of Dr. Samuels that Frank and Jesse James were at home. They had been seen occasionally at the little railway station of Kearney, which is three miles distant from the residence which had been, and was still claimed, as the home of the outlaws. Near neighbours, in casually passing, had seen them about the barnyards. All these things had been faithfully reported to the chief detective at Kansas City.

At length, the opportune time for striking a decisive blow was deemed to have arrived. Dispatches in cipher were sent to Chicago for reinforcements, and specific orders touching their movements after their arrival near the objective point, were given. The Kansas City division of the forces was held in readiness to co-operate with the force from the East. The citizens of Clay County, who had so zealously aided the detectives, received final instructions as to the part they were to take in the grand *coup*, by which their county was to be forever relieved of the presence of the dangerous outlaws.

Extraordinary precautions had been taken to maintain a profound secrecy as to the movements and purposes of the detectives. No strange men had been seen loitering about Kearney. Everything which could possibly be done to allay suspicion on the part of the outlaws had been done. But the Jameses had friends everywhere in Western Missouri keen, shrewd, vigilant men, who noted everything,

and whose suspicions were aroused by the slightest circumstance. The very quiet which prevailed was ominous of approaching danger. Somehow, too, they had learned of the sending and receiving of cipher messages by a Clay County man, at Liberty. This made them doubly watchful.

The extensive preparations which had been made, and the necessity imposed upon them of waiting for a suitable opportunity to strike, had occupied much time, and it was not until the night of the 25th of January, that the detectives made the final attack.

Jesse and Frank had been seen near the Samuels place that very evening, and no doubt was entertained that they were at home.

The detective forces destined for the attack on what was facetiously termed "Castle James," were divided into small squads, and began to arrive in Clay County on the afternoon of the 24th, from the East. Coming after night, they were met by citizens of Clay County and conducted to places of shelter in the most quiet and secret manner. After nightfall on the evening of the 25th, a special train came up by Kearney, and on it came another detachment from Kansas City. These were met by citizens well acquainted, and conducted to the place of rendezvous.

Secretly as these movements had been conducted, the ever-vigilant Jesse had his suspicions aroused by some trivial circumstance, which would have escaped the attention of almost any other man. Convinced that some formidable movement was going on, designed to consummate his destruction, Jesse James, his brother, and another member of the band rode away from the Samuels house after nightfall that very evening, and at the hour when the detectives arrived in the vicinity of the place where they expected to capture them, the Jameses were riding in the cold, well on their way to the house of a friend, miles away.

The detectives had no intimation that their intended victims had taken the alarm and departed from the place. They were assured that the outlaws had been seen in the vicinity of their home at a late hour in the afternoon, and it was believed that they were there still.

The night was cold and dark. It was late—perhaps near midnight, when the detective force arrived at the farm-house. There were nine men selected from Pinkerton's force because of their shrewdness and courage, and several citizens of the vicinity who, like the detectives, were fully armed. The assailing forces took up their stations completely surrounding the house. Some balls of tow thoroughly saturated with kerosene oil and turpentine had been prepared, and the detectives carried with them some formidable hand-grenades to be used in the assault. Two of the assailants approached a window at the rear of the house. The slight noise made in opening the shutters and raising the sash aroused a negro woman, an old family servant, who was sleeping in the apartment. She at once set up a shout of alarm which speedily brought to the room Mrs. Samuels, her husband, and several members of the family, some of them young children.

Just then a lighted ball of tow and oil was thrown into the room. The place was instantly brilliantly illuminated. The inmates of course, having just been aroused from slumber, were greatly agitated at this unexpected assault. The situation was truly appalling. Another lighted ball was hurled into the room. The younger members of the family cried out piteously as they fled aghast from the lurid flames that shot toward the ceiling. Mrs. Samuels quickly recovered her presence of mind, and began to give directions and personally to exert herself in the work of subduing the flames.

She was permitted only a moment to engage in this employment. There was a sudden crash as a great iron ball struck the floor, followed in an instant by a terrific explosion. Instantly the room was filled by a dense cloud of smoke, through which the white flames of the fireballs gleamed with a lurid red hue as if tinged with blood. There was a wail of agony from within that pandemonium of midnight horrors which might well have called emotion to a heart of stone. The piteous moans of childhood in dying throes, were mingled with the deeper groans of suffering age, and the shriller cries of terrified youth.

The work of the assailants in that particular line of attack was complete. And yet the noted outlaws did not appear. It was at once concluded that they were not present or they would have shown themselves under such circumstances. The attacking force did not wait to ascertain the result of the explosion of their terrible missile. They realised only that the game they sought had escaped them, and they retired from the place without caring to learn anything more about the consequences of their effort. They had failed, and that was all they felt interested in ascertaining.

When the smoke had cleared away and the fires which had been kindled about the house were extinguished, the extent of the execution done by the explosion was fully revealed. The spectacle presented was awful beyond any power of our pen to describe. There, lying on the floor, in a pool of blood, poured out from his own young veins, was the mangled form of an eight-year old son of Mrs. Samuels, in the very throes of death; Mrs. Samuels' right arm hung helpless by her side, having been almost completely torn off above the elbow. Dr. Samuels was cut and bruised; the aged coloured woman was wounded in several places; in fact, every member of the household was more or less injured. Blood was everywhere. Death was in the room; and pain and grief combined smote upon every soul in that stricken home.

Whatever the crimes of the Boys of ill-favoured reputation, they afforded no justification for this terrible assault in which innocent childhood was made the victim for the deeds of others. And the people of the state, without any exceptions, condemned the deed as wholly unjustifiable. The detectives made haste to leave the country, and the citizens who had assisted them returned to their homes and kept counsel with themselves.

The dead boy was taken away, and in his little grave under the snow they left him lying, the sinless victim of sin, over whose untimely fate many hearts have swelled with emotions too big for utterance.

Night Attack on the Samuels Residence.

CHAPTER 28

Proposed Amnesty

There can be no doubt that there was a heavy undercurrent of popular opinion in favour of the James Boys, generated by a conviction that they were the victims of cruel and uncalled-for persecution, brought upon themselves by their adhesion to a cause which was dear to the hearts of many thousands of the citizens of Missouri. Their later deeds were forgotten, while their former acts were remembered with admiration. Though the evidence seemed clear, which connected the Jameses and Youngers with innumerable daring robberies, yet many hundreds of good people refused to credit the reports, and offered their sympathy to the men whom they believed to be victims of vile slanders and unwarrantable persecutions.

The sympathy openly manifested for the Boys came not from the reckless and vicious elements, but from influential persons all over the state. As late as 1875, there were thousands of respectable people in Missouri who had no sympathy with the movements set on foot by the legal authorities for the apprehension of the desperadoes, simply because they did not believe them to be robbers, and that the killing done by them was a justifiable punishment inflicted on ancient enemies who richly deserved their fate.

The effect of the raid on the residence of Mrs. Samuels, the mother of Frank and Jesse James, was to create a diversion in favour of the Boys. The tragedy of that event was of so horrible a nature, that public sentiment set in strongly against any further attempt to capture the Boys by force. There was a strong sentiment in many quarters of the state in favour of trying a policy of conciliation toward the desperadoes. The reasons advanced in favour of this policy were numerous, and some of them possessed some weight.

It was alleged that the state had already suffered the loss of considerable sums in pursuing them; that it was extremely doubtful whether their capture could ever be effected; that in consequence the good name of the state must be tarnished; that while the Jameses and Youngers were declared to be, and treated as outlaws, other bad men would commit crimes and shift the responsibility to the outlawed men; that the course pursued toward the Jameses and Youngers was a species of persecution, and finally it was plead that all this persistent hunting of these men was stimulated by the animosities of enemies, dating from the war time, and inasmuch as the United States Government had granted amnesty to its enemies for acts committed during the continuance of hostilities, that it was not right the state of Missouri should pursue with vindictive persecution any of its citizens for acts committed during the war, and their friends contended that the outlawry of these men grew out of their course in the period between 1861 and 1865.

These views and opinions in respect to the Jameses and Youngers assumed a formal shape in the early part of March, 1875, by the introduction in the Legislature of Missouri by the late General Jeff. Jones, then a member of the House of Representatives from Callaway County, of a bill, or preambles and resolution, offering amnesty for all past offenses to Jesse W. James, Thomas Coleman Younger, Frank James, Robert Younger and James Younger, on the condition that they should return to their homes and quietly submit to such proceedings as might be instituted against them for acts alleged to have been committed by them since the war.

The preambles and resolution offered by General Jones received the approval of Attorney-General John A. Hockaday, and of many other lawyers of acknowledged ability. General Jones supported the measure with great zeal and earnestness, and no little ability and eloquence.

As this measure was one of great importance to the subjects of this volume, we deem it necessary to give the essential parts of the document, as follows:

> Whereas, By the 4th section of the 11th Article of the Constitution of Missouri, all persons in the military service of the United States, or who acted under the authority thereof in this state, are relieved from all civil liability and all criminal punishment for all acts done by them since the 1st day of January, A. D., 1861; and,

Whereas, By the 12th section of the said 11th Article of said Constitution, provision is made by which, under certain circumstances, may be seized, transported to, indicted, tried and punished in distant counties, any Confederate under ban of despotic displeasure, thereby contravening the Constitution of the United States and every principle of enlightened humanity; and,

Whereas, Such discrimination evinces a want of manly generosity and statesmanship on the part of the party imposing, and of courage and manhood on the part of the party submitting tamely thereto; and,

Whereas, Under the outlawry pronounced against Jesse W. James, Frank James, Coleman Younger, Robert Younger and others, who gallantly periled their lives and their all in the defence of their principles, they are of necessity made desperate, driven as they are from the fields of honest industry, from their friends, their families, their homes and their country, they can know no law but the law of self-preservation, nor can have no respect for and feel no allegiance to a government which forces them to the very acts it professes to deprecate, and then offers a bounty for their apprehension, and arms foreign mercenaries with power to capture and kill them; and,

Whereas, Believing these men too brave to be mean, too generous to be revengeful, and too gallant and honourable to betray a friend or break a promise; and believing further that most, if not all the offences with which they are charged have been committed by others, and perhaps by those pretending to hunt them, or by their confederates; that their names are and have been used to divert suspicion from and thereby relieve the actual perpetrators; that the return of these men to their homes and friends would have the effect of greatly lessening crime in our state by turning public attention to the real criminals, and that common justice, sound policy and true statesmanship alike demand that amnesty should be extended to all alike of both parties for all acts done or charged to have been done during the war; therefore, be it

Resolved by the House of Representatives, the Senate concurring therein:

That the Governor of the State be, and he is hereby requested to issue his proclamation notifying the said Jesse W. James, Frank

James, Coleman Younger, Robert Younger and James Younger, and others, that full and complete amnesty and pardon will be granted them for all acts charged or committed by them during the late civil war, and inviting them peaceably to return to their respective homes in this state and there quietly to remain, submitting themselves to such proceedings as may be instituted against them by the courts for all offenses charged to have been committed since said war, promising and guaranteeing to them and each of them full protection and a fair trial therein, and that full protection shall be given them from the time of their entrance into the state and his notice thereof under said proclamation and invitation.

The above bill was introduced about the first of March, 1875, and was referred to the Committee on Criminal Jurisprudence, of which its author was a leading member. The bill was fully discussed in committee, and finally, through the influence of its author, a majority of the committee agreed to make a favourable report on the measure to the House of Representatives. Sometime towards the close of the session of the 28th General Assembly, the bill came up for its third reading in the House. General Jones made an earnest speech in advocacy of the measure.

A member aroused a strong opposition to the measure from the very side of the house from which General Jones had hoped to obtain assistance in carrying it through. The member simply read a portion of a message transmitted by Governor Silas Woodson to the 27th General Assembly denouncing these same outlaws; and the Democratic Legislature of Missouri refused to pass the bill. Thus, the stigma of outlawry remained upon them, and their hands were turned against every man.

CHAPTER 29

The San Antonio-Austin Stage Plundered

It had been a lovely day. Nature had put on her richest habiliments of bloom and beauty. The sun shone with a genial warmth, and the air was soft and perfume-laden from the thousands of wild flowers exhaling the rich aroma from the wide prairies. It was an eminently respectable party who travelled from San Antonio on the stage that day. There were in the company the Right Rev. Bishop Gregg, of the Protestant Episcopal Diocese of Texas, and Mr. Breckenridge, president of the First National Bank of San Antonio; three ladies, and six other gentlemen, merchants of San Antonio—in all, eleven travellers, well provided with the means to get through the world without fear of famishing.

The stage was the regular four-horse. United States mail coach, running in the line between San Antonio and Austin, Texas.

The respectable party of eleven travellers had as pleasant a time as the crowded condition of the stage and the monotonous nature of the scenery could be expected to afford them. Of course, the bright sunlight made the scenery appear at least cheerful.

The stage was bowling along the well-beaten highway, drawn by four fresh horses, which had been hitched to it about half an hour before sundown. They had gone from "the stand" perhaps as much as four miles, and it was getting quite dusky—daylight fading away in the west. The stage had reached a point about twenty-five miles west from Austin.

In the gathering gloom, the driver beheld what appeared to be six rancheros, wearing sombreros, approaching the road just before him. Such incidents were not infrequent on that part of the route, and the appearance of the six men did not at first create any feeling of disquiet in the mind of the *Jehu*. But as the party drew nearer, and he discovered that they were mounted on splendid "American horses," and not "mustangs," he thought it very singular, to say the least of it. He was an old stager on the plains, and not inclined to be "panicky," but he muttered, "I'll sware, them's queer fellers, anyhow."

He did not have time to think very much about them, for in another moment two of the horsemen rode alongside the stage, with revolvers cocked, and commanded, with a great oath, "Halt!" Of course, there was no alternative, for two more of the robbers had galloped in front of the foremost span of horses and checked the further progress of the stage team. The other two robbers had taken up a position on both sides of the stage—one at each post, and were pointing pistols at the passengers, and with horrible oaths telling them to "tumble out" at once, or die. The astonished passengers—not even the Reverend Bishop—were just then ready to adopt the latter alternative, and very gracefully descended from the stage.

The passengers were formed into a group, which included the driver, and two of the bandits, with drawn revolvers, stood guard over them. The two horsemen in front dismounted and detached the lead-span of horses, and with the other two commenced their search for booty.

The trunks of the passengers were broken open, and every valuable thing which could be easily carried away was appropriated. The United States mail bags were then cut and the letters torn open. In this part of the stage-load they were quite successful, securing a large amount of bills in registered packages. One of the mail-bags was appropriated as a receptacle for the plunder. Having gone through the baggage and mail matter, the bandits turned their attention to the passengers. There was an animated dialogue carried on for a time, in the following style:

"Well, gentlemen and ladies, allow us to trouble you for the money and jewellery which you may have about you."

"Do you mean to rob us?" asked the bishop.

"Oh, no! Don't use such ugly language. We just want to relieve you of a burden—that's all, old sock."

"You don't call that robbery?" asked the bishop.

"Come, now, old coon! Dry up, or you'll not have an opportunity to ask any more nonsensical questions. Hand out your money!"

The bishop reluctantly complied.

"Now that watch of yours!" they further commanded.

"What! Will you not allow me to keep my watch. It is a gift and dearly prized. You would not rob an humble minister of Christ of his timepiece, would you?" queried the bishop.

"So, ho! You are a parson then, judging from the cut of your buckskins—or a priest—it makes no difference. Well, Christ didn't have any watch, and he didn't ride in stages either. He walked about to do his Father's will, and wasn't arrayed in fine clothes, and didn't fare sumptuously every day. What use has a preacher for a watch? Go and travel like the Master. Out with that watch! No more words—not one, mind you! We are not Christians, we are Philistines."

The bishop was constrained to give up his watch—a valuable and much prized one.

"Anything more? Out with it."

The bishop protested that he had nothing more of value about his person. They, however, made a personal examination before they were satisfied, one of them remarking:

"You can't depend on many of these long-faced canters, anyhow."

Then the robbers searched Mr. Breckenridge, and from him they obtained a plethoric pocketbook, containing one thousand dollars, and an elegant gold watch, and a very valuable diamond pin.

So, they went from one to another of the passengers, until the eight gentlemen of the respectable party of travellers had been politely plundered. Then the turn of the ladies came.

"Hand out your pocket-book," said the leader to the first lady approached.

"Yes, sir, here it is," replied the frightened lady, handing him her money.

The robber took it, opened it, and examined the contents by the light of the stage lantern. Then he came back to the lady, and asked if that was all the money she had. She replied that it was. He then inquired where she was going. She told him to Houston.

"Here, madam, take your money. We regret the trouble we have given you."

So they went to the other two ladies, and from one they got a watch, some jewellery, and about one hundred dollars in cash. From another they received some valuable jewellery, and a considerable sum of money.

Their work was now completed. During the two hours, they held the passengers under guard, they sometimes made jesting remarks, and at other times threatening ones. The least want of alacrity in obeying their orders was sure to subject the passengers to the direst threats. The robbers took with them the lead-span of horses when they rode away.

The whole amount of cash taken from the passengers exceeded three thousand dollars, besides several gold watches, and considerable jewellery of value. The amount taken from the mail bags was several hundred dollars.

Who were the robbers? This question was inferentially answered sometime afterward, when, in a conflict with a Texas official, Jim Reed, a member of the gang, was mortally wounded, and confessed that he was one of the party, and that his associates were men from Missouri, noted as "brave Boys." Who were so noted on the 7th day of April, 1874, at which time the stage robbery took place, but Frank and Jesse James, and the Younger Brothers? It is now the settled conviction of all who are acquainted with the facts, that the James Boys were there and "bossed the job."

Death of Farmer Askew.

CHAPTER 30

Farmer Askew's Fate

During the time General Jones' amnesty measure was pending in the Legislature of Missouri, Jesse and Frank James remained very quiet. They even opened up communication with Governor Charles H. Hardin and Attorney-General John A. Hockaday, through Sheriff Groome, of Clay County. From all the evidence at present available, we are forced to believe that at this time Jesse and Frank James were sincerely anxious that the measure should be adopted, and were in earnest in the desire to conclude a peace with society with which they had been at war for ten long years.

For a time, their vengeance slumbered. It was known to them that certain neighbours of theirs in Clay County had taken an active interest in the efforts which had been put forth to accomplish their arrest, and everyone expected that a bloody retaliation would follow. Their conduct had made for them many enemies in the community of which their father had been an honoured member. Some of these were open and outspoken in denunciation of their course, while others were restrained in expressions of hostility by their knowledge of the desperate and vengeful character of the men.

But the Jameses knew when to restrain themselves, and carefully abstained from any act that might lose to them the effect of the slight revulsion in public opinion in their favour caused by the tragic results of the night raid. But they had marked their men—vengeance was only delayed. Possibly, if General Jones' amnesty measure had succeeded, they would have withheld the hand of destruction, and their intended victims, instead of mouldering in gory graves, might today be alive. It is impossible to even conjecture what might have been the effect on the future life of the daring *desperado*, Jesse James. He might have turned away from the evil way which he had travelled so long, and atoned by an upright life for all the past. But it was not to be. For to them—

> The die now cast, their station known.
> Fond expectation past;
> The thorns which former days had sown,
> To crops of late repentance grown,
> Through which they toil'd at last;
> While every care's a driving harm,
> That helped to bear them down;
> Which faded smiles no more could charm,
> But every tear a winter storm,
> And every look a frown.

They were outlaws still. Hunted as enemies of their kind, they turned viciously to avenge what they, no doubt, earnestly believed their wrongs.

Among those who had expressed in strong terms his disapproval of the conduct of the James Boys, was Mr. Daniel H. Askew, a well-to-do farmer, and somewhat prominent citizen of Clay County, whose farm and residence was near the home of the Jameses. The outspoken opinion of Mr. Askew had given great offense to the Jameses and their friends, and when the night raid was made in January they at once suspected that Askew had been partly instrumental in bringing it about. This belief was strengthened by some of the scouts in the interest of the Jameses finding a couple of blankets, and evidences of the late presence of men among Mr. Askew's haystacks. To still further confirm them in the belief that Askew assisted the detectives in the attack on the Samuels' house, a young man known as Jack Ladd, who had been in Askew's employ as a farmer, departed from the country on the night of the assault.

It is but justice to the memory of Mr. Askew, to state in this place that he frequently and earnestly disclaimed having any knowledge whatever of the movements of the detectives in the employ of Mr. Pinkerton. But his denials had no weight with the vengeful Jameses. They and their friends continued to believe that the attacking party were sheltered and led by farmer Daniel H. Askew, and they resolved to execute dire vengeance upon him.

On the night of April 12th, 1875, Mr. Askew went with a bucket to a spring some distance from his residence, and returned to the house with the bucket filled with water. He had sat the bucket on a bench and was standing on his back porch, not having yet entered the house after returning from the spring. Just in the rear of the house, and within ten paces of the edge of the porch on which Mr. Askew was standing, there was a heap of firewood reaching perhaps to the height of five or six feet. Behind this wood-heap the assassins found a convenient hiding place. Whoever they may have been, they had ridden to the rear of a field, hitched their horses, and walked through the field to their place of concealment.

Suddenly the report of a pistol, followed instantaneously by the report of two shots, rang out on the night air, and Mr. Askew fell upon the floor of the porch and immediately expired. Some members of the family, in a great state of alarm, rushed out to his assistance, but found him already dead. Three shots, evidently fired from heavy revolvers, had taken effect in the head of the poor farmer, and one had crashed through his brain.

The murderers had run back across the field, mounted their horses and departed before the grief-stricken and astonished family could make any movements toward discovering their identity.

That night at a late hour some men on horseback rode by the house of Mr. Henry Sears, and summoned him to the door. He saw three men in the road. One of them called to him and said, "We have killed Dan Askew tonight, and if anyone wants to know who did it, say detectives."

Having thus delivered their terrible message, the men rode away in the dark. And the friends and neighbours gathered to the Askew farmhouse to console his bereaved and stricken family, and the coroner came next day, "due inquisition to make into the causes which led to Daniel H. Askew's death." But from that day to this no one knows to a certainty who took the farmer's life. The general belief at the time was, that he had fallen a victim to the vengeance of the James Boys. The years that have elapsed have only served to strengthen that belief and deepen the convictions of those who believed that Askew died at the hands of the vengeful outlaws. Who can tell? Only Him who knoweth all things, and the assassins, if still alive, hold the dreadful secret.

CHAPTER 31

Gold Dust—The Muncie Business

Scores may be found whose errant-time
Know not one hour of rest;
Their lives one course of faithless crime,
Their every deed—unrest.

Muncie is a little wayside station on the Kansas Pacific Railroad, not many miles from Kansas City, in Wyandotte county, Kansas. The situation, surroundings and small importance of the place in other respects, were not calculated to give it a widespread fame; and yet Muncie has become a place of historic renown, as the scene of one of the most daring exploits of the most renowned outlaws of modern times.

It happened one dreary December evening in the year 1875. On that occasion the programme which had served at Gadshill was carried out at Muncie. A band of armed men, well mounted, and keen and alert, had waited until the east-bound passenger train on the great thoroughfare between the rich mines of the West and the centres of commerce in the East arrived near their chosen lair. The topography of the region, and other favourable circumstances, rendered the task one of easy accomplishment, though it involved an exhibition of daring which few men care to manifest.

In some way, the bandits, of which Frank and Jesse James were chiefs, had information that a large amount of silver and gold was in charge of the express messenger on that train. It has been said that this information was transmitted to them by Jackson Bishop, who had been a noted Guerrilla in Quantrell's command, and who, subsequent to the cessation of hostilities, had journeyed to the "Far West," and entered into business as a mining operator in Colorado. Be that as it may, one thing is certain, the knights of the road had information that the express company had treasures in trust that trip, and these they were ready to appropriate.

In due time the train approached Muncie. There was no sign of warning, and when the engine came to a standstill at the wayside station, in obedience to a signal, it was immediately taken possession of by seven men. The engineer and fireman were carefully guarded. The passengers were admonished and intimidated by the presence of armed men on the platforms of the cars, whose formidable pistols seemed to be pointed at each individual passenger, and the harsh commands of those men were obeyed with alacrity by the surprised passengers. But the robbers were generous that evening. The treasure in the express car was what they sought. Individual possessions were as "the small dust" compared to that.

The express messenger was immediately confronted. Demands were made upon him with which he was compelled to comply. The safe was opened, and then the robbers proceeded to examine the contents of that treasure box at their leisure. The gain was worth the daring. Their reward was *thirty thousand dollars in gold dust*. The contents of the car were further examined, and a large amount of silver and other valuables were secured.

On this occasion the bandits were content with the spoils of the express car, which, it is said, amounted to about *fifty-five thousand dollars*. The passengers were, therefore, not subjected to the manipulations of the robbers.

Pursuit by U. S. Soldiers, after the Muncie Robbery.

As usual, the news of this fresh outrage by bandits was flashed far and wide. The country was aroused, and in an incredibly short space of time many bands of men were abroad in all directions, hunting the robbers. All their efforts proved vain. The shrewd raiders escaped with their booty.

A few days after the great train robbery at Muncie, a police officer at Kansas City, in the discharge of his duty, arrested one Bill McDaniels, charged with being drunk on the street. When he was brought to the station and searched, articles on his person were identified as having been taken from the express car at Muncie. Every possible effort was made to induce Bill McDaniels to designate his confederates in the train robbery. But to every proposition he was deaf, and finally, in attempting to escape, he was shot dead, dying without revealing the name of his confederates. The bandits escaped.

Chapter 32

Other Exploits

Where I am injured, there I'll sue redress,
Look to it, everyone who bars my access;
I have a heart to feel the injury,
A hand to right myself, and by my honour,
That hand shall grasp what grey beard Law denies me.

The James Boys have always claimed that they were driven into outlawry by the very instrumentality which organised society has employed to subserve the ends of justice and afford protection to the rights and liberties of all—namely, the government. This claim, made by them, has been partly conceded by a large class of persons, irrespective of all political affiliations and social relations. So, their wild career was commenced, and so it has proceeded through many years.

That the Jameses have been accused of crimes which they did not commit, there is scarcely room for doubt. One of the deeds which has been laid to their charge was the robbery committed at Corinth, Alcorn County, Mississippi. This event happened the same day that the train was robbed at Muncie, Kansas. The two places are many hundred miles apart, and of course the Jameses could not have been at both places at the same time. It is possible, indeed probable, that the robbery at Corinth, which stripped the bank at that place of a very large sum of money, was the handiwork of some of the members of the desperate band of men, of which the Jameses were the acknowledged leaders.

The same tactics which had been so successfully employed at Ste. Genevieve, Russellville, Corydon, Gallatin, and other points, characterized the raid on the funds of the bank of Corinth. The spoils obtained were exceedingly valuable, and although energetic pursuit was made, the robbers succeeded in making their escape. Their trail, however, was followed into Missouri, and several circumstances indicate that the successful bandits were members of the same organisation with the James Boys and Younger Brothers. After this there was a season of quiet.

In the spring of 1876 the robbers renewed the campaign for spoils. The incidents of the past year had begun to become memories, and the success which had attended the gang during the past years had given them confidence in their ability to plunder at will wherever they might select a field for the exhibition of their prowess and skill. The trees had assumed their green habiliments, and the early spring flowers exhaled their choicest perfumes, scenting the balmy breezes as they blew over hills and through valleys. The schemers had planned another raid. This time they selected an objective point remote from the scenes of their former deeds. It was a romantic expedition away into the mountain regions of Eastern Kentucky and the state of West Virginia. The spring-birds sang cheery lays as the brigands marched on to their destined halting place.

Huntington, West Virginia, is a beautiful town of about 3,000 inhabitants, situated on the Ohio River, in Cabell County, and is on the line of the Chesapeake & Ohio Railroad. In 1876, the advent of the steam cars had given an impetus to trade, and the old town had taken a new growth. The bold bandits had selected Huntington as the scene of a most sensational event. The tactics which had served so well on many other occasions were once more adopted.

On a bright April day, four men made their appearance at the bank. They had come through the streets without exciting any suspicion. When they had arrived at the front of the bank, two of them dismounted, drew their pistols, rushed into the bank, where they found Mr. Oney, the cashier, and another gentleman. These they at once covered with their pistols, and proceeded to overpower the cashier. They then emptied the contents of the safe into a sack, and leaving Oney and his friend securely bound, they proceeded to remount their horses.

While the two robbers were engaged inside, the other two, who had remained in the street, very effectually overawed the citizens who came that way, by displaying their pistols and occasionally firing a shot. The whole operation was completed within less than half an hour from the time the robbers made their appearance in Huntington. There were not many persons who knew what had happened until after the marauders had left the place. When the people awakened to a realisation of the true nature of the morning occurrence, there was at once a storm of excitement raised. Officers of the law and citizens of Huntington, without official relations, vied with each other in the alacrity with which they prepared to pursue the robbers.

As soon as the two robbers who had taken the treasure were mounted, the whole party galloped away, intimidating the citizens as they went by firing off their pistols.

A vigorous pursuit was at once commenced. The robbers were a long way from their base; and the road before them was rugged and difficult. For days, the pursuit was unabated. Bligh, the well-known detective of Louisville, sent his best men on the road to track the fugitives. The chase became exciting. Diverted from their intended line of retreat, the marauders sought refuge among the mountains of Eastern Kentucky and Tennessee. The horses of the robbers failed and were abandoned.

Finally, the pursuers came up with the fugitives. A fight ensued, and one of the robbers was killed before they had left the borders of Kentucky. This person was identified afterward as Thomason McDaniels, a brother of Bill, who was killed while attempting to escape from the officers in Kansas City, after the affair at Muncie. The pursuit was continued. In the hills of Fentress County, Tennessee, the officers came up with the robbers again. This time they succeeded in capturing Jack Kean, another *desperado*, known in Western Missouri and Kentucky. The others escaped, and finally made their way into Missouri.

Kean was taken back and lodged in jail at Cabell. The grand jury

A Narrow Escape—After the Huntington Robbery.

of Cabell county returned a true bill against him, and in due time he was placed on trial, convicted, and received a long sentence in the penitentiary of West Virginia. The presence of McDaniels and Kean, both well-known *desperadoes* of Missouri, at once suggested the James Boys as leaders in the Huntington robbery. Detective Bligh at first heralded to the world that Jesse James was captured when Kean was taken. Statements subsequently made by the convicted robber left no doubt that certainly Jesse James, and probably Frank, were parties to the robbery of the bank at Huntington.

It matters not who were the robbers in name. The deed was undoubtedly committed by members of the organisation of which the James Boys were the most noted leaders. The destiny which seems to have led them continued to favour them. The leaders of the Huntington raid escaped, and carried the bulk of the Huntington bank's funds with them.

Chapter 33

Jesse's Wooing and Wedding

Oh, say not that my heart is cold
To aught that once could warm it;
That Beauty's form, so clear of old,
No more has power to charm it;
Or that the ungenerous world can chill
One glow of fond emotion,
For those who made it dearer still
And shared my wild devotion.

Jesse James, the bold raider and dashing outlaw, in love? Preposterous! And yet why not? Those who have studied the ways of human nature with most attention, find nothing singular in the fact that Jesse might prove an ardent lover, or wonderful in the assumption that he might be beloved in turn. Love is the grand passion after all, and few persons have lived who did not at some time in the course of their lives feel the deep chords of their hearts touched, and realise the tender spell that enchained them. Why should not Jesse James, the man of splendid physique, the very embodiment of strong passions, yield to the powerful influence which so universally sways the human heart? Rather, we might ask, why should Jesse James not "fall in love," as the expression goes? It was perfectly natural that he should at some time, somewhere, find someone endowed with the capability of awakening in him the tender passion. Was he not human? Were his emotions and constitution so different from the rest of the children of time? What if he was outlawed? Had he not eyes to see and ears to hear? Had all tender feelings found a grave in his heart?

It is true that the nature of his employment and the circumstances which surrounded him, rendered his life an isolated one to a certain extent. He was not thrown into the great whirlpool which the world calls society, and this very isolation of his position would very naturally prompt him to seek the companionship of one who could hold a nearer and dearer place in his heart than even his brother. He might yet retrieve some of the disasters of the past, and wipe out some of the stains which blurred his character, if led by the sweet, gentle influence of a true woman.

Who can ever know what hopes animated him; what bright dreams of a better life cheered him, when he thought of her who would not—perhaps could not join in the general execration of his name? It may be that at such times a vision rose before him, of a quiet home with peace after the strife, where love dwelt, and where the bitter curses of the past might never come; it may be that he looked forward to the rest which would come to his tempest-riven breast, when the storm had passed and the serene sun lighted his pathway through a quiet land. And at such times it was but natural that he should seek the presence of the beloved one, and plead with her—

> *Oh linger yet a moment!*
> *Is it a sin that I have loved thee so,*
> *And worshiped thy bright image? If it be,*
> *Let grief and suffering atone for that,*
> *Long as this heart can know the power of pain,—*
> *But let me look on thee and hear thee still.*

And what woman ever listened unmoved to such appeals? "The brave deserve the fair," and the history of the race shows that when the heart is enlisted, when the tender bloom of love sheds its perfume around her, woman is careless of the world's opinion, and brave in daring its frowns.

Jesse had a fair cousin—a handsome young lady, possessed of an amiable disposition, and a mind well stored with knowledge. This destined bride of the distinguished outlaw is the daughter of a sister of the Rev. Robert James, who was married in the days of her youth to a Mr. Mimms. Miss Zee Mimms was deprived of a mother's love and guidance at a time when she was just entering the estate of womanhood. She had a sister older than herself who was united in marriage with Mr. Charles McBride, a respectable carpenter and builder in Kansas City, about the year 1869. For several years, Miss Mimms resided with her relatives in Kansas City, and gained the respect and esteem of a large circle of acquaintances. In the days of her childhood she had known her cousin Jesse, and his bright blue eyes and soft, peach-like complexion, and the smile that used to ripple over his countenance, and his cheery words, may even then have drawn the little girl toward her cousin. As time went by, Zee had grown to the condition of womanhood, and Jesse had become celebrated as a daring soldier, and afterwards a reckless outlaw. But somehow Miss Zee could never believe her cousin Jesse to be so bad as he was represented, and when they met—which they frequently did—she always had a word of gentle affection for cousin Jesse, who was ever kind in his behaviour toward her.

Many times, Jesse James was seen in Kansas City, when to be there was an exposure to imminent peril. When the wild winds swept across the frozen river, and screamed over the hills, Jesse was accustomed to dare the fury of the tempest, brave the chill of the temperature, and seek the cosy fireside which became a shrine, when blessed by the presence of his fair cousin.

And when it was summer time and the forest pathways were gloomy in the shadows of night; and the stars in the deep azure vault of heaven alone lent their feeble rays to illuminate the dark world, then the outlaw would take his lonely way across the wide prairies, through the deep-tangled forests where the owls hide by day and hoot by night, and the wild tenants of the woodlands make their lair; by lonely streams, murmuring as their waters go on the way to mingle with the far-wandering tide of the mighty Missouri, to seek the side of her whose smile was always brighter at his coming. What mattered it to him if the streets of the city were deserted by all, save the guardians of the law, who, in the deep shadowed recesses waited and watched for him? His courage owned no limitations under ordinary circumstances. What might it become if stimulated by the all-intoxicating influence of love? If the watchers saw him under the gaslight in the streets of the slumbering city, they let him go, and so Jesse's courting days passed away.

The outlaw's wooing proceeded, and was completed. Who knows what thoughts were his in those days? Who can ever tell by what processes of reasoning, or influence of love. Miss Zee Mimms reciprocated the outlaw's passion? Who knows what earnest councils she held with her own mind and the processes which ended in the triumph of the affections, and a perfect yielding to him, and the development of a devotion which smiled at contumely and consented to sacrifice all things which had before been pleasing to her, at the shrine of love? His presence became necessary to her happiness, and her smile was sunlight poured into the otherwise dark recesses of the outlaw's heart.

So, it came about one pleasant evening in 1874, that Jesse James and Miss Zee Mimms repaired to the house of Dr. Denham, a mutual friend, near Kearney, Clay County, Missouri, where they were met by the Rev. William James, of the M. E. Church, South, an uncle of Jesse, who proceeded to unite the lovers in the holy bonds of matrimony. The ceremony was performed in the presence of the doctor's family and one or two intimate friends. Jesse James had won a wife, and Miss Zee Mimms had consented in her devotion to become an outlaw's bride.

Ostracised by society, proscribed by the law, and hunted by enemies and the officers of justice, Jesse James took his bride, and they journeyed away. Across plains, through valleys, over streams toward "the clime of the sun," the outlaw and his bride sought a place where they could rest, and in each other's society,

Like some vision olden
Of far other time,
When the age was golden,
In the young world's prime.
Of the future dreaming.
Weary of the past,
For the present scheming,
Happy they, at last.

What cared they for the cold world's scorn? Jesse had provided a cosy home far away on the borders of civilization, where the names of mountains, vales, and springs, and streams, are softened in the musical' language of old Castile. But we have heard that even in that distant land the life of the outlaw's wife is not isolated, but, on the contrary, under a name which their conduct has made respectable, they have friends, and she her associates, who are ignorant of the history of the outlaw, and hold her in esteem. A little child, born sometime in 1876, has come to bless their union by its childish prattle, and the daring outlaw has been seen with the innocent little one mounted on his shoulder engaged in racing about his ranch. It maybe that there are episodes in the life of Jesse James which are like the green oasis in the sun-beaten desert—bright moments when the demon is temporarily vanquished, and the spirit of goodness illuminates the world about him. The man who can love cannot be wholly the slave of vengeance and hate, and even Jesse James may possess traits of mind and qualities of the heart, which point to something higher and better than what is known of him.

Chapter 34

A Dream of Love

Fancies, bright as flowers of Eden,
Often to his spirit come,
Winging through the mind's brief sunlight,
Glad as swallows flying home.
Love is the true heart's religion!
Let us not its power deny.
But love on as flowers love sunshine,
Or the happy birds the sky.

Frank James was an outlaw. The smooth-faced, beardless youth who came from the school where he had pondered over the thoughts of Euripides, who had all Greece for a monument, to unite his fortune and venture his fate with Quantrell's band, had become a man, bearded and strong, daring and dangerous to his fellow-men. And the sprightly intellect that had enabled him to lead his class, and the youthful ardour which had conjured up classic forms among "the sacred relics of Almighty Rome," as his mental vision was turned back through the vista of many departed centuries, were now floundering in the muddy pools, and revelling in plots and schemes, sordid and debasing.

He was not old in years, and yet he was ripe in experience. Year after year had chased each other down the steeps of time since Frank James became a soldier of the highways, a participant in the well-planned ambushment, and an executioner in the sudden surprise and fatal catastrophe to the enemy who came into the well-planned ambuscade, and he had witnessed unmoved the agony of victims when shaken by the throes of death.

Could this man, whose hands were red with the crimson stains left there by the blood of victims; whose mind was made harsh and hard by years of struggle against organised society; whose conscience must have become seared by the long contact with the rude, rough elements inhuman nature; whose heart must have become callous by reason of the cruel scenes through which he had passed—could such a one have tender dreams of love? And yet we might ask, why not? The tender affinities of affection which sprang from psychological causes is one of the most beneficent schemes of God's benevolence, which traverses all space in its flights, and lives the visible token of man's divinity on earth and his hope in heaven. The hand that would thwart them would interrupt the course of laws based on eternal verities.

The fact is, neither time, space, conditions, nor the recognised canons of social life, can induce or hinder the inception, growth, or maturity of a passion, which is acknowledged to be the most potent of all to which man is subject. Why, then, should Frank James not be smitten? In his wanderings he had met many fair ones. And beauty had smiled on him. But he knew that they were unacquainted with his name and antecedents, and so he refused to be led captive by these, whose love might turn to hate when they knew all.

It is said by those who know Frank James, that he is endowed with a very superior mind; that his education is very good; that he is able to read the classics, and can converse fluently in both the German and Spanish languages. With these accomplishments, he possesses a handsome person and agreeable features. In conversation, he speaks in a soft, low tone of voice, and in private life, among his friends, his manners are pleasing, and well calculated to produce a favourable impression. Frank has been about the world a great deal, and has mingled in refined society not a little. It is his custom to visit New York almost every season, and sometimes he goes to Saratoga, Newport and Long Branch. Friends of Frank assume that he is in many respects a superior man to Jesse; that he has more principle, and that there is far less of the desperado in his composition. He is cool, cautious, shrewd, and more manly than the other, and is not so reckless nor so revengeful in disposition.

Frank James was susceptible to the blandishments of the fair sex in the days of his youth. In Kentucky, he came near being caught in the silken meshes spread by a beautiful young lady of the "Blue Grass" country, who had come to regard him as a hero, whose adventurous career she longed to share.

But fate interposed for her sake, or against him. Frank found it for his interest to take his departure from Kentucky, and it was not convenient for him to return for two whole years. In the interim, another gallant was attracted to her side, and eventually won her affections, and the young lady was married.

A story is told, by persons who claim to know much of Frank James' private affairs, about a love affair between that redoubtable outlaw and an heiress in New York. She was beautiful and accomplished, and when she met the handsome and gentlemanly outlaw, who was not known in that character to her, she conceived an admiration for him which was fast ripening into affection. They rode together through the parks, and were soothed by the music of the waves, when the twilight and shadows fell, as together they strolled along the lonely shore. But circumstances over which she had no control summoned her away from the side of the Western adventurer, and they never met again.

So, the years passed away, and Frank James found one being long ago who inspired his heart with tenderer dreams of love than any which had ever come to him before. For years, the fair face, with its shadings of glossy brown hair, and eyes of deepest azure, glancing from beneath their long silken lashes, was imprinted on his mind and shrined in his heart. Frank James had met her many times, and no more touching story of woman's devotion has yet been told, than that of the attachment of pretty Annie Ralston for Frank James, the bold border bandit. In time to come, the writers of the romance of the period covered by the career of the James Boys, will recall the name of the fair girl who became the outlaw's bride, and weave around it the choicest flowers of literature.

CHAPTER 35

Fair Annie Ralston, the Outlaw's Bride

The loves and hopes of youthful hours,
Though buried in oblivion deep,
Like hidden threads in woven flowers,
Upon life's web will start from sleep.
And one loved face we sometimes find
Pictured there with memories rife—
A part of that mysterious mind
Which forms the endless warp of life.

There are many people about the old town of Independence who cherish pleasant memories of fair Annie Ralston. There are many who knew and loved her long ago, who will not soon forget the beautiful face of the outlaw's bride. And long after those who knew her in the halcyon days of her innocent girlhood shall have passed to the quiet repose beneath the sod in "the silent cities of the dead," her story will be repeated. Many a romance has been based on incidents in lives far less dramatic than has fallen to the fortune or the fate of Annie Ralston. The years which have rolled their cycles round to swell the measure of the greedy past, have not been so many that they have swallowed up the memories which cluster around the name of the gentle Annie, and bring sighs to the lips of those who but a few short winters ago conned with her the lessons of the sages from the dreary pages of text books when they were schoolmates.

People are not all ossified—brain, sense and heart, because God's Commentary on his written Revelation was given first—was handed down from a thousand Sinais, and strewed in green and golden shadowy lines through all the ages. It yet lives, and is, from under His own hand, above, around, beneath us; and by it we may understand that holy mystery—how God is Love, and Love is God-like. And we feel, and know, that never again to us from out the shade of the years, can ministers of grace or glad ideals come, except through such sweet enchantment.

Who, then, will condemn gentle Annie Ralston, the pet of the class, the warm friend, the glad-hearted girl, if she proved at last to be—like all her sisters—human? What circumstances conspired to induce her to become an outlaw's bride? If we could answer all the questions which might be asked concerning the emotions of the heart, the freaks of the mind, and other phenomena of human nature, and the structure of society, then might we be able to answer why fair Annie Ralston became the wife of Frank James, the proscribed enemy of society. But we cannot engage in such an undertaking. Her story is brief, but full of interest.

Before the period of blighting war, which swept like a destructive tornado over the fairest portions of Western Missouri, Annie's father, Mr. Ralston, was a wealthy man. and his home was one of the most pleasant to be found in the vicinity of Independence. He was a gentleman of culture and refinement, and his wealth gave him leisure to cultivate all the social graces. His hospitality was unbounded, and no man was more esteemed than Samuel Ralston.

Annie was a "wee girl" when the thunder peal of war burst in all its lurid terrors all around and about her. It was no period of sentimental dreaming, and she was early accustomed to see and hear of bloodshed and devastation. She must necessarily have grown familiar with scenes which, under ordinary circumstances, would have excited her terror, and she had learned to look unmoved on the bloody corpse of the battle's victim. But no storm can continue forever; after the convulsion comes quiet; after the night dawns the day—so, at last, the war-cloud rolled away. Then commenced the work of collecting fragments of wrecked fortunes and rebuilding waste places. But some wrecks were complete, and no fragments remained. In a large measure this was the case with the life-barque in which Mr. Ralston sailed down the river of time.

Annie grew with the passing years, and stood, as it were, "with reluctant feet on the boundary where childhood and womanhood meet." The residence of Mr. Ralston was convenient to the Independence Female College, and Annie became a student in that institution.

She possessed excellent intellectual gifts, and in her course of study she led her classes. In due time the prescribed course of mental training was completed, and "at commencement," fair Annie carried away the highest honours of her class. She was now a young lady, accomplished in "all the learning of the school." She sang delightfully, and could touch and cause to thrill with deepest harmony, the chords of the harp and other instruments. She was a favourite in society at once.

And Annie Ralston was handsome—almost beautiful. Her complexion was fair and soft, her features regular and pleasing, her eyes were large and azure blue, and these soulful orbs looked out from curtains of long silken lashes of deep brown, that lent a charm to their expression, and her long brown tresses well completed this charming picture. And she possessed a symmetry of form and a gracefulness of carriage which might well attract the admiration of those who knew her.

But there came a time when a shadow fell athwart her pathway, and eclipsed this star in the social firmament. Annie's father had been ardent in his attachment to the Southern cause, and all who had contended in behalf of that cause were ever welcome to the hospitality of his home. He had suffered much from the consequences of the war, and perhaps more from the genial convivialities in which he indulged, and which had extended beyond the bounds of propriety. Frank and Jesse James, with their confederates, became frequent visitors at the Ralston home. People saw them there often, and it was whispered softly at first, but shouted aloud later, that pretty Annie Ralston was an attraction for the outlaws, and received from them, without rebuke, their openly-expressed admiration, and then her social star paled, and finally went out.

Frank James became to her a hero worthy of her love—nay, her heart's deep adoration. She waited with impatience his coming, and when he was away, and she thought of the hazards which he might make, and the destruction which might overtake him, she grew faint through apprehension. To her, he was assiduous and gentle and kind, whatever might be his disposition toward others, and she gave her heart to him long before an opportunity was presented to her to yield to him her hand.

One bright day, in 1875, some friends who had known pretty Annie Ralston from the days of her childhood, met her at the Union Depot, Kansas City, with many valises and travelling bags in charge. "Would she go up in town? Could they render her any service?"

were questions which were asked. No, at another time she would go up town, there was nothing they could do for her. Soon she was joined by her outlawed lover. Together they look a train and proceeded to Leavenworth, Kansas, where the vows which they had made to each other were renewed and sealed by legal authority, and fair Annie Ralston became the outlaw's bride, and with him she journeyed toward the yellow Southern sea, where the sunlight is warm and the breezes balmy.

It was a sacrifice to thus banish herself from that society in which she was so well fitted to shine as one of its brightest ornaments; it was a trial to surrender up the friends and associates of her girlhood; to bid *adieu* to those who were near and dear to her; it was heroic to cast herself upon the care of the man she loved. On the altar of her affection, therefore, she placed all the idols of her youth; and in her devotion, she proceeded to dig a wide, deep grave in which to bury forever the images which she had cherished. And so, Annie Ralston became an outlaw's wife.

The Home and Girlhood of Annie Ralston, who became the Wife of Frank James.

CHAPTER 36

A Seventeen Thousand Dollar Haul

It had been some weeks since the people of the West had enjoyed a sensation growing out of the robbery of a train, or the plundering of a bank. Frank and Jesse James, and Cole, and Jim, and Bob Younger, with their merry companions, had been unusually quiet for quite a long season for these restless rovers and adroit plunderers. The gang was increasing in numbers, and was now really formidable. Others as daring had joined themselves to the noted outlaws—the Jameses and the Youngers. Cal Carter from Texas, and Clell Miller, and Bill Chadwell, Charles Pitts, and Sam Bass, and Bill Longley, and the Hardins and the Moores of the Indian Territory and Texas divisions of the clan were frequently with Frank and Jesse James and the Younger Brothers. In the gang, but apparently merely as a subaltern, whose principal employment was to hold the horses of the chief robbers when business required them to dismount, was a young fellow who went by the name of Hobbs Kerry.

Before Otterville, the protestations and denials of the Jameses and the Youngers were accepted by many good citizens, and there were numbers of very honourable persons who believed sincerely that these men were sadly slandered. The express robbery at Rocky Cut, near Otterville, served to remove the scales from the eyes of numbers of these good people, and Frank and Jesse James, and the three Youngers were revealed before the public as most dangerous highwaymen.

The principals in the Otterville affair were Frank James, his brother Jesse, Cole Younger, and his brother Bob, Clell Miller, Charlie Pitts, Bill Chadwell and Hobbs Kerry. These men concerted the project in Southwest Missouri, in the lead mining districts. Frequent interviews took place between Frank and Jesse James, and Cole and Bob Younger in regard to the feasibility of the undertaking. The Jameses were the original suggesters of the enterprise, and from what information we have been able to gather, the Youngers did not at first entertain the suggestion favourably; indeed, it was some time before it was finally agreed that the attempt should be made. Then the bandits discussed the route to be taken, and the place to be selected for the scene of this notable robbery, on the iron-highway. All these were settled in due time, and everything was ready to carry out their well-matured plan.

Jesse James was the leader, the others merely acting in concert with him, and taking their places in accordance with his suggestions.

The expedition left the scene of their plotting about the first day of July, 1876.

Before leaving, the band separated into two parties, Jesse and Frank James, Bill Chadwell and Bob Younger, composed one, and Cole Younger, Charlie Pitts, Clell Miller and Hobbs Kerry, made up the other. The journey through the country was made leisurely enough. The two parties travelled by different routes, and had no difficulty in securing lodging places. Sometimes they travelled in the night to make the distance to the house of a friend in good time the next day.

On Sunday, July 3rd, there were four of the bandits at Duval's house. Tuesday a part of the band were in California, and after lingering about the place for a part of the day, they mounted their horses and rode to a house four miles north of the town, where four others of the robbers were stopping. A heavy rain came on that night, and so the robbers stayed nearly all of the day on the 5th, and remained during the night. There is no evidence that the people where they stayed had any knowledge of the character of the persons whom they received under their roof. However, Jesse James and Cole Younger were acquainted with the gentleman, but not under their names.

On the morning of the 6th, the raiders mounted their horses and rode west in pairs. The James Boys travelled together, Clell Miller and Hobbs Kerry rode by each other, Charlie Pitts and Coleman Younger formed a pair, and Bill Chadwell and Bob Younger followed another route in company. These all travelled different roads.

The place of meeting previously agreed upon was a spot about two miles east from the bridge, across the Lamine River, and the time appointed was at 3 o'clock Friday evening, July 8th. There were designated stopping places on all the roads. The Jameses under assumed names were acquainted personally with a number of very respectable people along the route travelled by them, and therefore had no difficulty in obtaining comfortable quarters and receiving a hospitable welcome. And so of the others of that band—"on mischief bent"—they all had good quarters on Thursday night, and as only two travelled together on a road, no suspicion was aroused on account of their presence.

The robbers came by pairs to the rendezvous. They had all assembled by 4 o'clock in the evening. Some of them went without their dinners that day. Here the whole band remained until sundown on the evening of the 8th.

The place selected was at a deep cut known as Rocky Cut, about four miles east of Otterville, in Pettis County, Missouri, on the line of the Missouri Pacific railroad. Three of the band. Bob Younger, Clell Miller and Charlie Pitts, were detailed to capture the watchman at the bridge. Bill Chadwell and Hobbs Kerry, it appears, were assigned the duty of taking care of the horses. A dense piece of timber land adjacent to a field was selected as the place of concealment. The express train bound east was due at that spot about 11 o'clock at night. The robbers did not arrive at the designated rendezvous until sometime after the curtains of night had been drawn over the scene. At a little after 9 o'clock, Younger, Miller and Pitts went down to the bridge, and were hailed by the watchman. They were close upon him, and with drawn revolvers and fearful oaths they commanded him to surrender. The helpless watchman could not do otherwise. They took him in charge and secured his signal lanterns.

"What are you going to do with me?" asked the astonished watchman.

"You keep still," was the reply.

"But you ain't going to hurt me?" he inquired.

"What do we want to hurt you for? We want that money on the train, that's all we care for," was the reply he received.

The whole party walked up the track to the mouth of the cut. It was about half past ten o'clock. A heap of rocks and a number of old cross ties were piled across the rails. Then the cunning brigands sat down quietly in the darkness to await the coming of the train. The horses of the robbers were about fifty yards away ready to be bestridden, and fresh enough to make a long journey if that should be necessary. Crouched there, they were silent as the broken fragments of rocks which lay scattered around them. They had not long to wait. A distant rumbling was heard, like the first low mutterings of thunder before the storm cloud appears. Then it grew louder and shriller like the raging wind. It was the train.

The robbers were not asleep. Charlie Pitts had been detailed to display the red lantern—the danger signal—as the train came thundering around the curve into the cut. He performed his part of the programme well. Precisely at the right spot the train came to a standstill. The engineer had reversed his engine and put on the air brakes.

Instantly the train was boarded by a number of masked men, said to have been twelve at least, all heavily armed. Guards were placed at each end of the cars, and the leader boarded the express car, compelled the messenger under threats of immediate death to open his safe, and then the contents were emptied out into a sack, and the car was thoroughly searched for valuable packages. The result was about $17,000 were secured and carried away for the use and behoof of the robbers.

The whole transaction was completed in less than an hour. The passengers were greatly alarmed during the time of the detention. The robbers stationed at the ends of the cars kept their revolvers bearing upon the passengers, and would not allow them to stir a finger under threats of death. Every moment they expected their turn to be robbed would come. But the robbers appeared to be satisfied with the amount realised from the plundering of the express car, and when they had accomplished that job thoroughly, they released the train, sought their horses and rode away. Several shots were fired during the time the train was standing, for the purpose of keeping the passengers in a state of alarm.

The news was telegraphed from the next station to St. Louis, Sedalia, Kansas City and other points. By this event the whole country was thoroughly excited. The detective forces of St. Louis, Kansas City, Chicago, and even the cities of the Atlantic seaboard were taken by surprise, and aroused to make efforts to capture them. The railroad and express companies offered large rewards, and the governor of the state took measures to aid in the pursuit of the brigands.

Meanwhile, the men who had created all this furore of excitement rode through the darkness with their treasure bag. When "the first faint blush of dawn streaked the east," the plunderers of the express car at Rocky Cut were twenty miles away and just turning off the main highway into the dim recesses of a large forest.

After travelling more than a mile in the woods, the brigands came to an open space. Here they dismounted. Jesse James had the treasure bag. During the journey, Frank James, Cole Younger and Charlie Pitts had relieved each other alternately in carrying the precious burden. Now they had reached a safe place, and the spoils of the adventure were about to be divided. Frank James acted as master of ceremonies on that occasion. Whether "the divide "was an equal one we are not advised, and perhaps we shall never know. The envelopes were torn from the express packages and the money divided into separate heaps, one of which was given to each of the men who had participated in the exploit.

The ceremony of dividing the money having been gone through with, and Jesse James, Cole Younger, Frank James and Charlie Pitts having parcelled out the captured jewellery among themselves, the robbers remounted and separated into pairs, each pair selecting the route which pleased them best. In the daytime, they rode in the woods and along by-paths; in the night, they returned to the highways, and were soon secure from pursuit because they went at once among friends who, if they were acquainted with the character of their guests, "never gave away anything."

An outrage of so daring a character was not slow in producing effects. The news had been flashed afar on the lightning's track. The Chief of Police of St. Louis, the marshals and constables, and county sheriffs were aroused to unusual activity. The people everywhere were excited by an event of so sensational a character. A keen pursuit was inaugurated. Watchful eyes and open ears were in every town and hamlet throughout Missouri, and even in adjacent states. This time, it appeared, the robbers would be surely compelled to remain hidden far from the habitations of man.

But secure in their retreats, the shrewd leaders of the raid, Jesse and Frank James, and Cole and Bob Younger and Charlie Pitts, laughed at the efforts of the officers of the law to capture them. They enjoyed reading the newspapers containing accounts of their daring feat, and made merry at what they were pleased to term "the stupid work of the d——d detectives."

The robbers had one single thing on their minds which gave them some concern. The "cub" robber, Hobbs Kerry, was scarcely shrewd enough to evade capture, and, they feared, not brave enough to withstand the pressure which they knew would be brought to bear upon him to "make him squeal on his associates." What if Kerry should fall into the hands of the hunters? And was it not extremely probable that he would? These were questions which they asked themselves, and in time they framed an answer in the form of another question, "What if he does? We don't know the fellow?"

We have said the passengers and trainmen were passive witnesses of the proceedings of the robbers. But there was one person on the train who was not afraid to resist. That individual was the train newsboy. Johnny, as he was called, had a small pistol, of a cheap grade, with which to defend himself against all enemies, and robbers in particular. Now the opportunity had come to display the latent heroism which he knew he possessed. Johnny did not believe in being plundered, and, though his weapon was not very dangerous, he believed he could do some execution with it; at any rate, he could try. From the car window, where he had taken a position, he opened fire on the marauders. His first shot was ineffective, and the bandits derisively encouraged him to try again, when they discovered the youthful appearance and diminutive size of their assailant. Johnny took them at their word, and blazed away again. The robbers were well satisfied and good humoured, and they laughed and jeered at the little hero who had exhibited so much courage. They told him he would do for a train-robber himself when he was a little older. Johnny insisted for a time that he knew he had shot one of the robbers badly.

Charlie Pitts, Bill Chadwell and Hobbs Kerry made a forced march to Southwest Missouri. Late Saturday night they forded Grand River. After going a little distance from the river, the three robbers dismounted, threw themselves on the ground, and slept soundly until morning. Here Kerry's horse which was well broken down, was abandoned. The saddle he hid in the brush in the Grand River bottom. Kerry at this point separated from Pitts and Chadwell, they remaining in the Grand River forests, while he proceeded to Montrose station, on the M. K. & T. railway.

He had not long been there when a train bound south came along. He stepped on the car and went down to Fort Scott, Kansas. Finding a clothing store open, he purchased a good suit of clothes, which he donned at once. With valise in hand, he boldly entered a hotel, called for supper, which he partook of, and then proceeded on the train to Parsons, took lodgings there, where he remained until 4 o'clock next morning. From Vinita, to which he went from Parsons, he proceeded to Granby, where he had "a good time with the Boys." From Granby to Joplin, and from that place to Granby again, and then away down in the Indian Territory Hobbs Kerry went, without remaining very long at one place. Wherever he went he drank, and whenever he drank whisky he talked, and showed his money and boasted. He was liberal with the Boys, had money for the faro dealer, and was for the time "a hale fellow well met" with all. But the eyes that were looking, and the ears that were listening, putting this and that together by an act of cogitation, concluded that Hobbs Kerry knew about the Rocky Cut business.

It was not a mistake. The detectives "pulled" Kerry, and when he had time to reflect, he unfolded his mind, and told of his friends and their ride at night. He proved to be "a good peacher," as the police say, and whatever may be the slight inconsistencies of his narrative of the Otterville affair, the events at Northfield, Minnesota, a few months later, confirm the truthfulness of Hobbs Kerry's story in all the main particulars.

Of course, the James Boys and their friends were swift to denounce Hobbs Kerry as a fraud, and his stories of the midnight ride and the flaring of the "danger signal" before the train, as pure fabrications of a diseased or wicked brain.

Meanwhile, the Jameses and Youngers had not gone far away. The former found friends and a safe retreat in the eastern part of Jackson County, and the latter retired to St. Clair County, where they rested in contentment for a season. The Jameses have friends yet in a certain neighbourhood in that section of Jackson County—men and women—who, despite their known character, and the edict of outlawry against them, would receive them into their houses and treat them not only with ordinary hospitality, but with marked consideration.

Chapter 37

In Minnesota

Hitherto the brigands, led by the Jameses and the Youngers, had only committed outrages in those countries with the physical features of which they were well acquainted. They had ridden through Missouri, Arkansas, Texas and Kentucky, and Iowa was not so far away from their haunts in Clay County that they could not reasonably hope to retreat to their hiding places. The list of outrages already committed by them was extravagantly long. Commencing at Russellville, Kentucky, they had ransacked bank safes at Gallatin, Corydon, Iowa, Columbia, Kentucky, Ste. Genevieve, Mo., Huntington, West Virginia, and a section of the band had paid a visit to, and plundered the bank at Corinth, Mississippi. They had stopped trains in Kansas, Wyoming, Iowa and Missouri, and they had plundered stages in Arkansas, Texas and Kansas. But over the whole territory intervening between the widely-separated scenes of their depredations, they had often travelled and were perfectly familiar with the topography of the country, and had friends in many places.

Having achieved such remarkable success in their nefarious calling, the brigand chiefs were emboldened to enter upon new enterprises, and seek new fields for the exercise of their prowess and genius. They agreed to go beyond the borders of their accustomed field of operations.

After Otterville, a part of the gang went into St. Clair County, and the other members of the banditti proceeded to Clay County, to the vicinity of Kearney, where resided the mother of Frank and Jesse James, Mrs. Zerelda Samuels. That person was always true to the interests of her sons, and under no circumstances did she ever desert their cause or betray their designs. Mrs. Samuels was a very useful ally of Frank and Jesse, and when hard pressed in other quarters, they were always sure of a safe retreat and succour in the vicinity of the Samuels' house.

The successful robbery accomplished at Otterville, had created a profound sensation throughout the southwest, and the law-abiding citizens were vigilant and suspicious, and it was not a pleasant time to travel in any direction where the least possible suspicion in regard to the character of the traveller was once aroused. Therefore, the robbers of the train at Otterville sought their hiding places and remained quiet for a time.

But idleness under such circumstances became extremely irksome to the free riders, accustomed as they were to a life of activity and exciting adventure. The division of the band from St. Clair County, journeyed into Clay County, Missouri, and then began a series of conferences in regard to the next campaign which they contemplated inaugurating.

These consultations between the leaders of the banditti were held in a thick forest near the residence of Mrs. Samuels. The result of the deliberations was the development of a plan to pay a visit to Minnesota, and raid some bank there, the exact place of its situation to be determined when they should have arrived in that state.

Who originated the scheme is a question which, in all human probability, will forever remain unanswered. The credit of the project has been often given to Jesse James. Whether or not he originated it, we have good reason to know that he was one of the parties who went to Northfield, and in all probability, he was the leader of the band.

Be that as it may, a plan was concocted to pay a visit to Minnesota, and plunder as many of the banks in that state as possible before the beginning of winter, and then retire to winter quarters on the Texas and Mexican frontiers. The general plans were finally agreed upon, and about the middle of August, 1876, the bandit camp in the vicinity of the Samuels house was broken up, and the brigands, separating in couples, commenced their long ride through the country to the flourishing villages of Minnesota.

The party which left Clay County was composed of Frank and Jesse James; Coleman, Robert and James Younger; Clell Miller, Bill Chadwell and Charlie Pitts. It is related, on what appears excellent authority, that Cole Younger and Bill Chadwell preceded the other members of the gang, to fix upon a suitable rendezvous. Near Mankato, Bill Chadwell had "a friend," a man who had often before rendered him substantial service. Preconcerted "signs" of the route to be taken by the main body of the bandits had been left by the advance guard, Cole Younger and Bill Chadwell. The final rendezvous selected by these leaders was at Mankato, and the whole band then proceeded to Chadwell's friend's resting place, where their final councils were held.

A gentleman of the highest respectability, well known in Central Missouri, who is in a position to be informed, assures us that Cole Younger did not favour an attack on the bank at Northfield; indeed, that he was opposed to raiding any bank in Minnesota, but that he was overruled in his judgment by the other members of the gang. It is said that Cole favoured a movement into Canada, where the prospects for a large haul were believed to be very much better. But whatever might have been his wishes, the other members of the band did not accede to them, and, after due consideration, it was determined to strike a Minnesota bank. Cole Younger was too far committed to recede, and so he submitted to the will of the majority, and was among the law's victims after Northfield.

Bill Chadwell was for many years a border rough and horse-thief in Minnesota. He had committed depredations in many parts of that state, and was perfectly familiar with the geography and topography of the country. With a vast number of the dishonest and rough class in that state, he was on terms of intimate personal acquaintance. To him, as a guide, the other members of the brigand company looked with confidence to lead them successfully to a handsome deposit of spoils, and away from pursuers and pursuit. Chadwell's friends were relied upon to afford them succour in the hour of need, and Chadwell's skill inspired them with hopes of great gains, at a small sacrifice of time and little risk of danger.

All these things had been discussed, and the plans of the gang were well matured before the departure from Clay County. It was a long expedition, and the principal members of the company were unfamiliar with the country into which they journeyed. They based their hopes of success on the conditions which at that time existed in Minnesota. It was at that season of the year when the grain growers were disposing of their crops; when it was supposed grain buyers and shippers would have their heaviest deposits in bank, and when the farmers were "in funds," which the robbers doubted not would be placed in the country banks for safe-keeping. Moreover, they reasoned that inasmuch as the people of Minnesota were unacquainted with their bold methods, that, as usual, when they made an onset, the customary panic would ensue, and the risk taken would be small.

Thus, the preliminaries of the celebrated raid into Northfield were settled. Never before had this gang of *desperadoes* failed in accomplishing their object, and when the last council was held, and it was settled that Northfield should be the objective point of their great raid into Minnesota, "the signs" were propitious, and the superstitious element in the character of the outlaws rested satisfied.

The remainder of the band divided into couples. Jesse and Frank James, as usual, travelled the road in company. Bob Younger and Charlie Pitts went together, and James Younger and Clell Miller bore each other company by the way. These separate detachments travelled different roads, and kept a good lookout for favourable places for concealment in case of necessity, and they also noted the characteristics of the surface of the country over which they passed.

Previous to leaving Missouri, Jesse James wrote, or caused to be written, two letters for publication in the Kansas City *Times*, denying the charge of complicity in the Otterville robbery, and denouncing the statement of Hobbs Kerry as "a villainous pack of lies." These letters were printed, and lead to the belief that the Jameses were still in Missouri. The latest one of these letters was dated "Safe Retreat, August 18th, 1876," and appeared in the Kansas City *Times* August 23rd, 1876.

Divided as they were, their passage through the country excited no comment. They travelled as respectable persons might have travelled. In the evenings, they would put up at a respectable village inn, or country farm-house, and in the mornings they paid for their accommodations as any other reputable citizens might have done. They did not hurry, because they did not want to break down their horses. The distance was great, and they were many days on the road. It was about the 1st of September, 1876, when the whole band had arrived in the neighbourhood of Mankato. Their advance agents, having found a suitable place for a rendezvous at the house of Chadwell's friend, met their comrades, and, without exciting suspicion among the people, they directed the various detachments to the designated place of meeting.

The robbers were now in Minnesota, but as yet they had not determined which of more than half a dozen banks they would rob. First, the claims of some one of the three banks doing business in Mankato to the distinction were considered. But the proposition to rob any one of them met with little consideration in the council of the brigands. They reasoned that three banks in such a place would naturally cause the business and investment funds of the community to be divided into three parts, no one of which could be very large, and as they "played for high stakes" at a great risk, they concluded to let Mankato banks alone. Then they considered the claims of the bank at St. Peter to be plundered. But there was not enough business done in the place, and it was not surrounded by a community deemed wealthy, and the brigands concluded to pass St. Peter, believing that they would not get a large haul in case they should raid the place. Several other banks were considered, and the probabilities as to the amount of treasure likely to be obtained were all considered. Finally, indications pointed to the bank of Northfield as probably richer in the treasures contained in its vaults than any other in that region of Minnesota.

Northfield, the place selected by the desperadoes as the scene of their attempt at plundering, is a flourishing town on the line of the Milwaukee and St. Paul railroad, situated in the northeast corner of Rice county, Minnesota. The town is compactly built, and contains a population of about 2,000 souls. The country around Northfield is very productive, and there is considerable activity in commercial pursuits in the village. The bank building is situated in the very centre of the business portion of the town. At the time the raid was made a large sum of money had accumulated in the vault of the institution. But Northfield happened to be peopled by a hardy and courageous race of pioneers who were not made of the material to submit with a good grace to be plundered by strange outlaws from another state.

But the leaders of the brigands had selected Northfield, and it only remained to fix upon a time when the attempt should be made. That time was set for the afternoon of September 7th, 1876.

CHAPTER 38

The Attack at Northfield—Haywood's Death

Sometime before noon on the 7th of September, four well mounted and well-armed men approached Northfield from the north. They did not at once enter the town, but remained on that side of the bridge in the suburbs for the advance of the other division of the band, which came *via* Dundas, a small station on the line of the railway about four miles south of Northfield. The brigands from Dundas were Cole and James Younger, Bill Chadwell and Clell Miller. On the north side were Frank and Jesse James, Charlie Pitts and Robert Younger.

About 2 o'clock in the afternoon. Cole Younger and his party appeared, then the brigands rode into town and directly to the bank, the exact position of which had been before ascertained. Jesse and Frank James and Cole Younger dismounted and entered the bank. The brigands had entered the town at a full charge, shouting at the top of their voices and firing off their pistols as they rode. The inhabitants were taken by surprise, but were not at all panic-stricken. The movement on the bank was noted, and its object at once comprehended.

The three leading brigands who had entered the bank proceeded to business at once. They sprang over the counter and confronted the surprised cashier, Mr. J. L. Haywood, with a huge knife, which they placed at his throat, and ordered him to open the safe, threatening him with instant death in case he refused. The knife had already marked his throat, but the brave cashier refused to comply with their demands. Again, with fearful threats the command was repeated. But Haywood still persisted in his refusal, when one of them, now generally believed to have been Jesse James, placed the muzzle of his pistol to Haywood's right temple, and fired.

The cashier fell, and expired ere he had touched the floor. Besides the cashier, there were Mr. A. E. Bunker, assistant cashier, and Mr. Frank Wilcox, clerk. These were ordered to hold up their hands when the robbers first entered. Of course, under the circumstances, they could not do otherwise than to obey. After Haywood fell they turned to Mr. Bunker and ordered him to open the vault. That gentleman declared that he did not know the combination. Then they thrust a pistol into his face and made other threatening demonstrations.

Mr. Bunker, acting under an impulse to preserve his own life, fled out through the backdoor. As he ran, the robbers fired at him, the ball taking effect in his shoulder. They seem not to have paid any further attention to Mr. Wilcox, but occupied the remainder of the brief time allowed them in efforts to find the cashier's money drawer. The nickel drawer was found, and they scattered the contents of that over the floor.

Meanwhile, an exciting scene was transpiring in the street in front of the bank building. A Mr. Wheeler, a young gentleman who occupied a second-storey room in a building opposite, happened to possess a gun. Seizing this weapon, he took deliberate aim and fired. The ball took effect, and Charlie Pitts, a notorious Texas *desperado*, fell from his horse, shot through the heart. The shots fired by the brigands who had remained on the street did not have the desired effect in intimidating the citizens of Northfield. In a few moments, many citizens who had seized guns and pistols, and whatever other weapons came in their way, were rushing toward the bank. Mr. Wheeler having been so successful in his first shot, fired a second time, and Bill Chadwell fell, mortally wounded, from his horse. By this time others were firing from windows, and one of the horses was struck and fell dead. Another horse which had been ridden by Charlie Pitts ran through the street. Another one of the band was struck by a bullet, but managed to keep his place.

The situation was desperate. The leaders in the bank had not succeeded in getting anything, when the events happening in the street admonished them that their only salvation was in immediate flight. They rushed out of the bank, mounted their horses, and the six living bandits galloped away. Indeed, there was need that they should. Already a band of fifty citizens, well mounted and well-armed, were nearly ready to take the road in pursuit. At the head of this party rode Wheeler, who had already proved himself to be cool and daring.

The flight of the discomfited robbers was rapid. These free riders would never mount an inferior horse. But chances for escape were very few. The robbery, or rather, bold attempt at robbery, and especially the death of Mr. Haywood, a gentleman held in the very highest esteem by the community at Northfield, had created a state of feeling in the public mind which would not allow the people to rest satisfied until the murderers were either captured or killed. In less than twenty-four hours the whole region about was notified of the occurrence at Northfield, and not less than four hundred well-armed and well mounted men were in hot pursuit of the six surviving brigands.

The excitement occasioned by the events at Northfield was at fever heat. Efforts to capture the outlaws were further stimulated by the proclamation of Governor Pillsbury offering a reward of $1,000 for the apprehension of each of the robbers, or $6,000 for the capture of the survivors of the band.

The bandits fled in a southwestern direction, toward the little hamlet of Shieldsville, situated about 20 miles on an air line, southwest from the scene of the tragedy at Northfield. The route taken by the robbers made the distance more than twenty-five miles; yet they were at Shieldsville before dark. They passed straight through the place and made no concealment of their identity. Shieldsville is a small post village, containing a population of no more than 175 souls. As they passed through the village, they shouted to the citizens who were on the streets to get into their houses, and they made such demonstrations by firing off their pistols that the people were greatly alarmed. The pursuers meanwhile were gathering about them. Sheriff Davis and posse were behind them; Sheriff Estes and posse were before them, and there were officers and armed citizens to the right and to the left of them. Their situation became extremely critical after leaving Shieldsville.

But the indomitable courage of the bandits seemed for a time to promise them a final escape.

From Shieldsville the bandits travelled in a westerly direction toward Kilkenny, a post town and railway station in Le Sueur county. They were now avoiding the towns and travelled highways, and keeping in the forest, and travelling through the farms. All the crossing places on the streams were guarded by armed citizens. The guards at the ford on French Creek became alarmed at the approach of the bandits and fled, so that they met no resistance at the crossing place. They remained one night for rest in a large forest near Kilkenny. The next morning, they crossed the ford at Little Canyon. They pressed on toward the west. The route was beset with difficulties and dangers for them. They were anxious to reach the borderland, the frontier region, where men are few and wild.

There was no rest for them. It was at length necessary for them to abandon their horses. They had camped in the depths of a great forest. The officials had taken to the by-paths and scoured the woods in search of them. Leaving their horses and some of their heavier clothing, they trudged on foot, skulking among the thickets. Their progress was slow. One day they camped on a sort of a peninsula, about half a mile from a church. They were now thoroughly exhausted. Their diet had been green corn, potatoes and watermelons for several days, and they had been constantly on the move. Here a stray calf came along and they shot it in the head, but the calf did not fall, on the contrary, it ran away. A small pig passed by their camp, and one of them shot him in the head. But the pig refused to succumb, and ran away.

After leaving their isolated camp in the evening, foot-sore and worn out by reason of the anxiety and fatigue, they pushed forward in a more southerly direction, leaving Cleveland and the forest where they had abandoned their horses to the right. At midnight, they had reached Marysburg, a small post village in the southern part of Le Sueur county. Finding a convenient hiding place, they kindled a fire, and had a meal of roasted potatoes and corn.

The village clock struck six. They heard the bell and judged themselves to be about a mile from the town. They left the Marysburg camp somewhat refreshed, and with buoyant hope of an ultimate escape from impending peril. Thus far they had eluded their pursuers.

Place of the Last Conference before Northfield.

Their route from Marysburg lay south-westward through Blue Earth County, to Mankato. They made good headway during the day, and late in the evening they found a nice hiding place in a thicket in a cornfield, and lay very quiet without making a fire. Twice during the night, they were alarmed by persons passing near them. Their hiding place happened to be near a neighbourhood path which ran through the fields.

Six days after the affair at Northfield, when the worn robbers were struggling along through a great forest near Shaubut's, a few miles in a north-easterly direction from Mankato, they came suddenly upon a man named Dunning, who was one of a posse of citizens in pursuit of them. They at once captured this man, and a question arose as to the course to be taken with him. At once it was suggested by some one of the band to bind him fast to a tree and so leave him. Dunning pleaded hard for his life, and to be spared the terrible ordeal of such an uncertainty as that of being left bound in that great forest. It might be days before he would be discovered, and it might be that no human being would pass that way until he would be starved. Finally, from motives of humanity, as they claim, they administered to Dunning the most terrible oaths that he would not say one word about having seen them until they had ample time allowed to get out of the country altogether. Dunning gladly consented to take upon himself these solemn obligations, and they let him go.

The released citizen sought the haunts of men and made haste to communicate to others all the particulars of his adventure with the robbers in the woods; and then the pursuit was renewed with new ardour and zeal. At midnight, six days after Northfield, the weary bandits trudged through Mankato in a very different plight from that in which they had made their entry into the place but a little more than a week before. As they approached the town with which they had made themselves familiar as they went to Northfield, they were alarmed by the shrill whistle of the oil mill. They concluded that their approach had been noted, and the steam whistle was the signal agreed upon to call the citizens together in case the approach of the robbers was noted.

They therefore turned aside from the main streets, and sought the lanes and alleys back of the oil-mill. Here they hid awhile, but as there did not seem to be any movement among the citizens, they stealthily passed on, across the bridge. The guards had retired, or were not disposed to attack the six *desperadoes*. At any rate, they were not interrupted. After crossing, they raided a field of watermelons, selected four large ones, and under the deep shade of the trees, at the hour of one o'clock, they had a feast on the melons. They visited a house nearby and got one spring chicken, and would have secured more had time been allowed. But they heard a great shouting of people, and saw one man looking for tracks. They fled at once up a bank, and pushed forward through the woods bordering the Blue Earth River. During the day, they crossed that stream.

It was on the day after they passed Mankato that Frank and Jesse James, who appeared to have suffered less from the fatigue and exposure than the others, bid a last *adieu* to their comrades in the ill-starred Northfield enterprise. Only Cole Younger and his brothers, Jim and Bob, and Clell Miller, were left. The pursuers struck the trail of the Jameses, and these *desperadoes* now had a terrible time in eluding those who sought them. They were repeatedly fired upon, and were both wounded severely several times.

The four men left in the Blue Earth River forest struggled on toward the west. They had passed through the county of Blue Earth, and entered Watonwan County, full seventy-five miles on a straight line from Northfield, and a hundred and twenty-five miles by the route they had travelled. They had reached the swamps bordering the Watonwan River. They had been now exposed to untold hardships from the afternoon of the 7th of September to the 21st of the same month, a period of fourteen days. They had subsisted on green corn, potatoes and melons for the most part during that whole time. They had had but little sleep, and had been constantly harassed by their pursuers. For nine days and nights they had been compelled to walk through forests and thickets, and their clothes had been literally picked from their bodies by the thorns and brambles through which they had struggled. Their feet were in a most terrible condition. But their pursuers still followed them with a grim resolve that nothing could equal.

On the afternoon of the 21st, Sheriff McDonald, of Sioux City, having tracked the brigands to a swamp a few miles from Madelia, the county seat of Watonwan County, Minnesota, the final struggle commenced. The sheriff's forces had surrounded the swamp where the brigands lay concealed. The armed citizens then began to close in upon the surrounded men, keeping up a continuous fire as they advanced. The bandits were not the men to yield, even to a superior force, without making a desperate resistance.

One of the sheriff's men was severely and another was slightly wounded as they closed in upon the wearied but still determined men.

The continuous volleys poured into the thicket where the bandits had concealed themselves were not without effect. First, Clell Miller fell, moaned once, and then his lips became mute forever. A heavy rifle ball then crashed through Jim Younger's jaw, shattering the lower jawbone in a most frightful manner. Cole Younger received seven wounds, and Bob was shot in the right elbow. They fought desperately, but what could four men do? Sheriff McDonald commanded a hundred and fifty courageous men, whose lives had been spent on the frontiers.

Resistance could no longer be offered, when one of their number had fallen, and the other three were wounded, two of them nigh unto death. It was the last struggle of four as daring and dangerous men as ever rode over the Western prairies. When resistance had ceased, the sheriff's men gathered around them. They were prisoners; their last hour of freedom had expired. They were placed in spring-wagons and carried into Madelia. The people of the whole surrounding regions came flocking into the town to see the renowned outlaws, for they had confessed that they were the Younger Brothers, whose fame as daring freebooters had already been extended over the entire country.

In a few days, the wounded robbers—Cole, Jim and Bob Younger—were carried to Faribault, the county seat of Rice County. They were closely guarded, as well to prevent excited citizens taking the law into their own hands as to insure the safe custody of the bandits. The body of Clell Miller was conveyed to St. Paul to be embalmed.

While confined at Faribault, the Youngers received every attention, and rapidly recovered from the effects of their long exposure and the terrible wounds which they had received. During this time a strong guard was maintained about their prison.

Early in October, the Rice County Circuit Court met at Faribault, and Thomas Coleman, James and Robert Ewing Younger were arraigned at the bar to plead to an indictment for murder in the first degree, and for conspiring to commit murder and robbery. Advised by counsel that under the laws of the state the death penalty could not be inflicted in cases when the parties charged entered the plea of guilty, the three brothers plead guilty, and were sentenced to the penitentiary at Stillwater for the terms of their natural lives. A few days afterward they were removed to their life-time place of abode, and the stormy career of the Youngers closed. Since their incarceration, it is understood that Jim Younger has died. Cole and Bob, in their dreary isolation, still survive, without hope of breathing the air of freedom again.

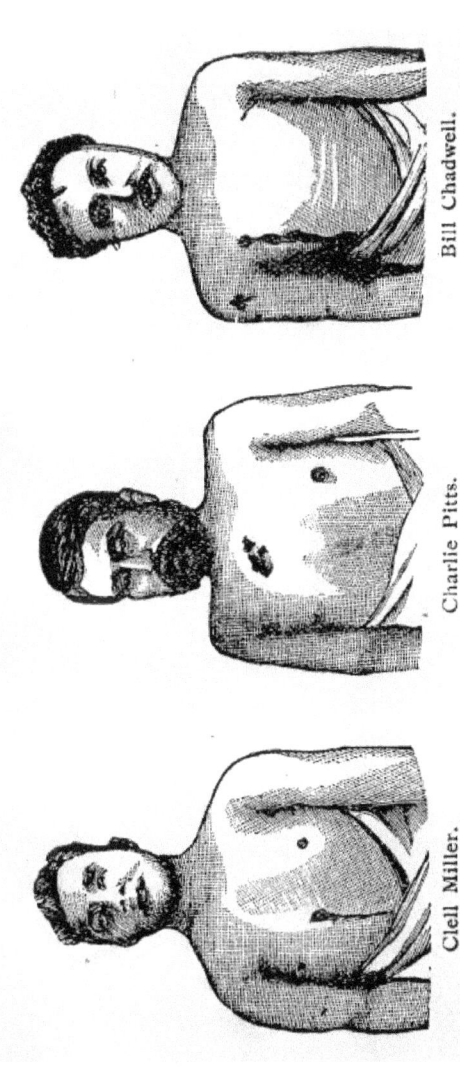

Clell Miller. Charlie Pitts. Bill Chadwell.

THE OUTLAWS KILLED AT NORTHFIELD.
(From Photographs of the Corpses, Before Embalming.)

CHAPTER 39

Escape of Frank and Jesse James

The most formidable band of robbers in this country had suffered terribly in consequence of the raid on Northfield. Charlie Pitts, Bill Chadwell and Clell Miller—the last-named a formidable lawbreaker, who was raised in Clay County—had lost their lives. Cole, Jim and Bob Younger had been captured. Jesse and Frank James were still free, but numerous officers of the law were on their trail.

When the Jameses left the Youngers in the Blue Earth River bottom, they were on foot. The Youngers and Miller had entrusted to them their watches and jewellery and most of their money, believing that there was a possibility for the Jameses to escape. The departure of Frank and Jesse created a diversion in favour of the Youngers and Miller. The bands of armed citizens followed the Jameses. For two days and nights the brothers travelled westward, their footsteps constantly dogged by wary citizens. The hardships through which they were passing were almost incredible. The men were sometimes almost completely surrounded by the citizens.

Three days after they had separated from their comrades, they came to a wilderness region, where the timber was heavy and the underbrush thick. Here they proposed to rest for a season. But they were tracked to their hiding place, and fired upon by a band of pursuers. Frank James received a wound in the hip. The brush was so thick that the pursuers, who were on horseback, could make no headway, and three of them dismounted to continue the chase on foot. The direction taken by the hunted men led to a swamp, but the season being dry, there was but little mud in the basin. The bushes were close together, and aquatic plants were high. The three men seemed resolved to close up with them. Several times the hunted bandits could have killed the citizens, but for the fact that their ammunition was giving out, and they desired to take care of what remained for the last emergency. It was getting late; the sun was low in the west, and the shadows were deepening in the forest. The three pursuers were determinedly following them. Once or twice the hunted men were tempted to turn and try the issues with their foes.

But they kept on. Just when daylight faded away, they emerged from the swamp, and found themselves in a travelled highway. They had lost their determined foes in the darkness of the sombre swamp behind them. They started down the road, which lay along the bank of a stream of considerable size. Wearied into a state of exhaustion, they hoped to find a snug place where they could rest and take some food. But their trials were not yet at an end. In the lonely depths of the forest, with the dark, still river on one side, and the timbered wilderness on the other, they heard the ominous sounds of horses' hoofs. They listened. There were horsemen behind and before them. In another moment, sounds came from the woods, which indicated that they were being surrounded.

The wearied freebooters quickly stepped into the deep shadow of a great tree which stood upon the bank of the stream, to await further developments. That the horsemen were gradually closing around them they were speedily convinced. Their situation was critical. What could be done? The stream below them was evidently deep and dangerous to ford. Their plans were quickly formed and consummated. They quietly dropped down the bank to the margin of the stream, which at that place flowed close by an abrupt bank. "They were there by that tree but a moment ago," they heard one man remark, as a party came up to the spot where the outlaws had stood but a moment before.

It was evident that their numbers must exceed twenty. Stealthily the hunted brothers moved down the stream along the margin of the water, and close up under the overhanging bank. They heard their pursuers discuss the situation. "They are still near at hand, no doubt," the brothers heard one remark. Then the movements indicated that they were preparing for a more careful examination of the situation where they were. Soon several men came riding down the road just over their heads. They had reached a place where the river runs under a shelving bank and the brothers could go no further without taking to the water. Four men came down the bank above, and came toward them.

The brothers were constrained to take to the stream. The water was about two feet deep. They clung close to the bank, and silently reached a place they deemed safe, in a cave-like excavation made by the water under the roots of a great tree. The hunters came to the place where the bank and the waters met, and, apparently satisfied, they turned and went back. The brothers heard the clash of horses' feet on a bridge below, and then they knew that the crossing below was guarded. After a time, all became still around them. They concluded to swim or wade the river from the point where they were, and, once on the opposite side, to strike through the country.

Silently as possible, without any splashing, they came from their place of concealment and waded out into the stream until they were compelled to swim. The night was quite dark, and they passed over without being discovered. Climbing the opposite bank, they found themselves in an open wood. With all the haste, which they could make, they proceeded westward. A mile away they came to a cornfield, and in the field, there was a thicket. Here they found a hiding-place, and, as wet as they were, they partook of a repast of green corn, and lying down on the grass, they slept soundly until the sun was up. Waiting some time in a sunny place until their clothing had partly dried, the brothers started on their weary way. All day they travelled without being molested.

In the evening, while travelling along a country road, they met a man leading two horses, one of which was saddled. They spoke to him, and from his manner and the answers he made them, they were convinced that he had not heard anything about the affair at Northfield. They asked him if he would like to sell the horses he was leading. He answered that it was his business to deal in horse-flesh. What would he take for the pair? The man named the price, and, after some bantering, a trade was effected, and even the saddle on which he rode was transferred, the horse-trader declaring that he did not own anything which he would not sell.

Jesse and Frank James were once more mounted. They stopped at a cabin in a lonely locality and asked for supper. A woman and two children were apparently the only inmates. They learned from her that her husband had been summoned to help catch a gang of horse-thieves, and had not been home for three days. Frank carefully concealed his wound, and the woman quickly prepared a good supper for them, and, after settling with her, they mounted and rode away.

The brothers rode all night, and as their horses were fresh and good travellers, they traversed many miles. They had already begun to congratulate themselves on their escape, when one day when they were in the neighbourhood of a town on the western border of Iowa, they were fiercely attacked by seven men, all well-armed, but, fortunately for the outlaw brothers, not very well mounted. A running fight ensued, and Frank received a desperate wound. But the good fortune which had so often attended them came to their aid, and in the darkness of the night they rode far away, and in the morning reached a house where the services of a physician were secured, who dressed Frank's wounds. The physician was afterward arrested, but no evidence of his having knowledge of the character of his patient was produced, and he was discharged.

The brothers had reached the borders of Nebraska. Jesse had a "friend" somewhere on the confines of that state, and they proceeded to his place by easy stages. Here they rested for some days while Frank's wounds were attended to by a physician. But the news of Northfield had reached there, and suspicions of their friend and his strange guests were aroused. It was deemed best to take an early departure. An ambulance was procured. One of the horses was disposed of, and the Boys by easy stages drove into Kansas. Their horse and ambulance was disposed of there. At a station, not a thousand miles west of Kansas City they took the cars, and were transported to Texas. At Waco, Frank was placed under the care of a physician, and nursed until restored to health again.

Thus was terminated one of the most remarkable escapes from capture ever recorded. None other than men of very superior genius could have succeeded. As it is, the exploit is one of marvellous adroitness, one which cannot fail to excite our admiration.

Frank James' Escape from Seven Pursuers.

CHAPTER 40

A Visit to Carmen

After Northfield, Missouri was deemed an unsuitable field for operations by the James Boys. Nor did it afford a safe place of retirement for persons who had engaged in such a desperate warfare against the established order of society. But they were accustomed to make long expeditions, and they were at home anywhere. The shelter of a rock sufficed for them in the wintry nights, and the branches of a tree, with their spreading leaves, furnished roof enough for them when the summer nights came. Far away, in that region of the great state of Texas known for many years as the Territory of Bexar, where a beautiful stream flows down from the rugged mountains toward the west, to unite with the Rio Pecos, Jesse and Frank had established a retreat which they called Rest Ranch.

It is many miles east of Fort Quitman, and a long way from San Estevan. To the west there are rugged hills and low mountains, covered with chaparral almost impenetrable to man or beast. Far away in a southern direction is the little frontier post called Fort Lancaster. There are no frequented trails near the place which they had selected. The Rio Grande road, from Fort Quitman to Fort Lancaster, runs southwest of the rugged region alluded to above, and the usual line of travel from Fort McKavitt to the military posts and settlements on the Upper Rio Grande, in New Mexico, was a long distance from their chosen retreat. Toward the northeast are the Salt Plains, and, further away still, the Staked Plains, the dread of all travellers in those regions.

In this retreat, they were free from the intrusion of prying neighbours, and the inquisitiveness of passing travellers. It was and is a lovely place. There are few traces of the presence of man in that wilderness land. The Pecos flows miles away from their place through a valley full of natural beauties. But the region is lonely—so lonely! There are only trails occasionally followed by a band of predatory Lipans, or traversed by marauding parties of Comanches and Kickapoos, on raids to the Mexican border through that vast region. It was in such a country the daring bandits found repose; and, when occasion suited, to ride untrammelled by fears.

> *When the wild turmoil of this wearisome life,*
> *With its scenes of oppression, corruption and strife;*
> *The proud man's scorn and the base man's fear,*
> *And the scoffer's laugh and the sufferer's tear;*
> *And malice and meanness, and falsehood and folly,*
> *Disposed them to musing and dark melancholy;*
> *When their bosoms were full, and their throughts were high,*
> *And their souls were sick with the outlaw's sigh—*
> *Oh, then there was freedom, and joy, and pride,*
> *Afar in the broad plains alone to ride!*

Such seasons of reflection concerning that which is, and that which might have been, come to all mankind, and it came to the outlawed brothers, because they are members of the great family. It was doubtless at some such time, when their spirits were subdued by their lonely communion with the grander mysteries of nature, that the James Boys plead for pardon of past offences, and promised future amendment and conformity to the laws established for the government of society. They have often manifested a desire to be at peace with the world. But such resting did not wait upon them.

Issuing from their retreat, they dared the danger of the border, plunged through the chaparral, ascended rugged mountain steeps, plunged down their western slopes to the sand plains which border the Rio Grande. Passing through the poor *pueblo* of San Estevan, noted as the haunt of cattle raiders and bandits; alarming the people at early morn by their imperious behaviour and skill as pistol-shooters, exhibited by bringing down a chicken for their breakfast at a distance of sixty paces, they rode away to the Grande River, crossed over to the Mexican side, and passed westward until the *adobe* walls of Mojmia rose before and around them.

The brothers had grown weary of secluded living. They had now started on an expedition destined to create a profound sensation all along the border. They passed on through Santa Rosa, and through the desert lands, and over the mountains to the westward of that place. These men never pause before obstacles which would appal others.

Neither the rugged mountain passes where the Mexican Guerrillas have their hiding places, nor the desolation and terrors of "the Dead Man's Journey" arrested their course.

Carmen is a village of considerable size and importance in the northern part of the State of Chihuahua in Mexico. Surrounded on three sides by rugged hills rising into mountains, it is situated on a line with an important pass through the Sierra Madres. Carmen is therefore a halting place for caravans of traders, and through its *plaza* passes treasure-*conductas* from the mines of Chihuahua. The bold riders from the north of the Rio Grande had an object in going to Carmen, which was made plain in due time.

Arrived at Carmen, Jesse and Frank, who had been joined by three other members of the band at Santa Rosa, among them Jack Bishop, put up at the leading *posado* of the place. They were a well-behaved company, and as they paid liberally for all they desired, the people regarded them as a valuable accession to the population. The Boys had a delicate way of demonstrating their capacity to shoot, by killing a fowl, or pig, or dog, by shooting it with a revolver from a great distance, taking care always to make the exhibition as public as possible. So it happened on this occasion. The guerrillas and other rough characters about Carmen had a very respectful manner toward such persons. The Mexican, whose pig had been shot, received four times its value and conceived thereafter a very ardent affection for the American gentlemen of the north.

It was in the late spring-time and the road through Carmen was travelled by many traders and miners, bound north through New Mexico, to the markets of this country.

The adventurers from Rest Ranch noted everything. There were little parties travelling together with considerable money, on their way to purchase supplies in the United States. But it was not for such small profits that they proposed to practice their profession. One day, six pack mules, each loaded with 150 pounds of silver, and each with a muleteer to control him, moved out of the city of Chihuahua. With these rode twelve men as a guard. They kept on until Carmen was reached, without anything unusual happening.

At this place, they halted for a day's rest. The outlaws went among the guards, sought out the persons to whose charge the treasures had been committed, and ascertained the direction of their future movements. Nay, further, they simulated fears of the lurking Indians and plundering guerrillas along the road before them. They claimed to be anxious to get into the United States, but had heard so many stories of the dangers of the road that it had deterred them from undertaking the journey.

They professed to be American gentlemen who had been looking over the mines of Chihuahua. Their manners were affable, and their story plausible. When they made overtures to the chief of the *conducta*, to be allowed to journey with the treasure party for mutual protection across the dangerous border, their desires were acceded to, and when the cavalcade moved slowly away from Carmen the next day, the unsuspecting merchants and treasure-bearers were accompanied by five men of the most desperate character. For the first three days of the march the Americans were watched with some degree of vigilance, and the Mexicans maintained a strict guard over the treasure-pouches.

But the deportment of the outlaws was such that they soon succeeded in allaying any suspicion which might have attached to them. Carmen was a long way from the border, and the bandits did not care to strike the blow which they had resolved upon when too far away from their retreat, and that, too, on unfamiliar ground. So, they journeyed on with their intended victims on the most amicable terms. A suitable opportunity to seize the treasure was now all that they wanted, for the Mexicans had grown somewhat careless in consequence of their confidence in the numbers of their party.

One day they halted by a crystal stream which flowed down from a gorge in the mountains, and where a spring of pure, cold water gushed from the rocky bank. It was noon time, and the weary travellers took the burdens from their beasts, and allowed them to graze in the fresh, tall grass in the valley. It was a lovely day, and the scenery about them was very charming. The muleteers and guards, all save two, who stood sentinel over the treasure-pouches, had thrown themselves on the verdant bank, and were lazily conversing about the beauty of the situation; the length of time yet required in which to complete the journey before them, and like topics of small interest to our readers.

There were in the company a Senor Molines, and another Mexican gentleman, both merchants of Chihuahua. The American *desperadoes* stood upon the bank under the shade of a tree, a little apart from the group of guards, who were in fact largely owners of the treasure they watched. The muleteers formed a little group not far away. The guns which the Mexicans carried had been stacked, or rather leaned against a tree. Mr. Molines and his friend sat smoking on a mossgrown rock by the bank of the stream. It was a picturesque scene, and the surroundings heightened the effect of the picture. The two guards on duty carried their guns carelessly on their shoulders. Suddenly, Jesse James called out,

"Let's go, Boys!"

There was a sharp report of pistols. The two armed guards sank quivering to the earth. The outlaws rushed to the tree where the guards had left their arms, and placed themselves with presented revolvers between the guardians of the treasure and their weapons, The two Mexican merchants were ordered to throw up their hands, and with the forcible argument of levelled dragoon pistols, presented as an alternative, they yielded, and one of the gang went and disarmed them. The muleteers were paralyzed with fear, and remained sprawled upon the grass carpet. The place has been well named *La Temido* (the place of fear.) It had been but a minute since the first act in the drama was presented, and in that time the whole tragic play had been completed. What a revolution in the circumstances of the actors had taken place? Two were dead, and sixteen survivors were prisoners, and at the mercy of five of the most desperate men who ever played the part of freebooters on this continent.

They took the horses of the merchants and guards, broke their guns, forced the muleteers to place the treasure pouches upon the best and fleetest of the horses; shot the mules and other horses not required, and threatened the frightened men who were in their power with death, and finally left them a long way from any human habitation, without horses and without food, and proceeded to the Rio Grande at an unfrequented part of its course, many miles above Fort Quitman, where they had provided a boat before they ventured on their expedition, ferried the captured treasure and swam their horses across, and in less than twenty-four hours after their surprise and capture of the treasures of the caravan, they had disappeared in the rugged region which lies between the Rio Grande and the Pecos, in the Territory of Bexar, Texas. They had so completely hidden their trail that all attempts to follow them were futile.

In a few days after this successful foray into Mexico, Jesse and Frank were at their ranch enjoying much-needed repose. How the members of the wealthy party, with which they travelled from Carmen, managed to get once more into the haunts of civilized men, we have received no information. The great heap of silver which they had taken was brought by the outlaws into their retreat in the mountains, and there divided among the five daring brigands.

CHAPTER 41

The Robbers and Their Friends

Wherefore, in the hour of need,
Shall a people house them?
Wherefore did our brothers bleed,
When great wrongs did rouse them?
Is this the sod, So blest by God,
That slaves swear by its clay, men?
Or are we still,
The men of will?
We ask you that today, men!

Why have the James Boys so many friends? Is it because there are so many people disposed to lawlessness? Are the friends of the Jameses, like themselves, all outlaws? If they are not, why do they yet sympathize with them? How can any honest man succour and shelter them? Can it be possible that anyone can be so impervious to testimony as to believe these men to be anything but outlaws? These are the questions asked by those who believe that the Boys ought to have been caught long ago, and lay a large part of the blame for their escape from arrest so long on the people of the states where their most notable deeds have been committed.

Some persons point to the results obtained in Minnesota, after Northfield, as an evidence that a large part of the population in Missouri, Arkansas, Texas and Kentucky, where their most successful raids have been made, must necessarily be in sympathy with them, if, indeed, they are not in direct collusion with the great outlaws. Such a charge is evidently made by persons who have not examined into the circumstances of the case, and the conditions which have favoured them in escaping apprehension by the officers of the law. It will be remembered that the James Boys have committed successful robberies in both Iowa and Kansas, and it will not be claimed by the most prejudiced mind that the people of Iowa and Kansas, resident in the neighbourhood where these exploits were committed, were more in sympathy with the marauders than were the people of Northfield and vicinity. And yet the Jameses escaped capture.

Without in any way assuming a defence of the people of the states named above, on account of their failure to capture the outlaws—for they need no service of the kind from us—we may be permitted in this place to state a few facts which may enable cavilers to form a more rational judgment in this matter.

That the Jameses have friends scattered through many states we readily admit. That all those who have a friendly feeling toward them are not in the lower classes of roughs, is undeniable; that some who move in respectable circles of society, and who are above reproach, so far as their individual actions are concerned, are yet disposed to apologise for them, is unfortunately true. But such "friends" as these have nothing to do with obstructing the execution of the law. The Jameses have numerous friends in Missouri, Kentucky, Arkansas, Texas, New Mexico and Colorado.

And under like conditions they would have equally as large a list of friends in Illinois, Iowa, Wisconsin, Minnesota, Dakota and Wyoming. Their active, helpful friends are to be found among that class which the law is ever pursuing but never subduing. They are called "thugs" in New York and all the other large cities; and on the border everywhere, the same elements in human nature which create "the thugs, pariahs and roughs," of the urbane populations, produce the desperadoes and road agents of the wilderness regions.

Now the fact is, the Jameses have ranged over the entire country, from the Ohio River to the shores of the Gulf; from the borders of Iowa to the Sierra Madres, and from the Blue Ridge to the Rocky Mountains. Their reputation as daring men and skilful leaders has made them known to all that class of people who are without the pale of society, as that term is applied—and there are members of that class in every community—who at once seek an alliance with such distinguished leaders of their class—the outlaws. The result is, that these people embrace every opportunity to serve such men as Frank and Jesse James. Why has not Pinkerton, with all his ability and resources as a catcher of law-breakers, caught these men?

The answer is simple enough. They know the country thoroughly;

they have, not one, but many places to which they can retreat, and when hard pressed or sorely wounded, they go to their retreats, where they are nursed and cared for until they choose to go away.

Again, there may be, and doubtless are, a few persons who have known the Boys from early childhood—knew their father before them—and afterward remembered the deeds performed by them in a cause which they regarded as right, who are loath to believe that the Boys are brigands and robbers. And then it is certain that some of their "friends" are persons who are free to admit that the Boys have degenerated into lawless marauders, but excuse them on the ground that they were driven to it by the terribly bad treatment which they received at the hands of those who were enemies of the Southern cause in the struggle of long ago.

It is barely possible that a limited number of people, whose whole mind and strength were devoted to the success of the South during the great conflict, yet look back with deep regret at the melancholy failure of their efforts, and have apotheosised every man who engaged on that side and fought for the cause which had become sacred in their eyes—a very few persons who belong to that class, representatives of which are to be found everywhere, who can neither forgive nor forget—who only remember that Frank and Jesse James were fighters in that struggle, and hence all subsequent bad conduct cannot exclude them from a place in their affections. This is in accordance with the laws of human nature. All men are not cosmopolitan in their views, and hence, when disasters fell upon a cause which was believed to be right and sacred, the little world in which these persons lived and moved and had their being, suffered a moral convulsion from which it has not yet recovered, and, in their minds, can never recover.

With the social conditions and mental state which enshrouded people like those described above, and rendered them insensible to the requirements of social order, we have nothing to do. Such people are found in all climes now; and such people have lived in all ages since the human family commenced the struggle for existence.

But the "friends" of the Jameses are for the most part persons who, like themselves, have rebelled against the established order of society. They are scattered all over the country, and among that class, from the Rio Grande to the Ohio, the Boys have personal acquaintances and active allies. Even beyond the lofty range of the Rocky Mountains they have confederates in spirit, if not in action. These children of an ill-starred destiny roam over a vast extent of country. And wherever they go, they are likely to find someone who, from some cause or other, open their houses to them and willingly afford them succour and shelter. Some of these men doubtless share with the renowned freebooters the spoils gained in their daring profession.

The "friends" of the Jameses—even those who are active allies and participators in their lawless deeds, are many of them respected in the communities where they belong. Among their neighbours, they are known as liberal-minded men of unquestionably good character. Some of them have families who are respected and honoured by their associates. Some of them, when at home, are regular in their attendance at church, and liberal in their donations for the support of the ministry.

Some affect to patronise the educational interests, while there are others who are promoters of improvements in horticulture, agriculture, and all other movements intended to benefit the communities of which they are members. Who would surmise that these staid and respected members of society are leagued with outlaws? Generally, their evil deeds are committed far away from their places of residence. They are not often mixed up in any affair nearby, and when they join the band for the purpose of committing depredations, they always give out that they are about to make a journey in a way directly contrary to that in which they intend to travel.

But the most valuable of the members of the band of friends of the Jameses are those who never go abroad to depredate. They are of infinite service to the Boys. In all their relations with their neighbours and the members of the society with which they are brought in contact, these allies of the brigands are scrupulously exact and strictly upright. The consequence is, no suspicion attaches to their character, and with them the outlaws are safe.

Not only do these "friends "not go abroad to plunder, but when their confederates who "do the work" commit a deed of outlawry in their vicinity, they first conceal the robbers, and then turn out as leaders of the hunters of the outlaws. They are sometimes loudest in their execration of the plunderers, and strongest in their expressions of hatred toward all lawless men. Being good citizens of honourable repute, no one suspects them, and their friends, the robbers, rest until the storm has swept by, and then quietly they ride away. Many of these men are well-to-do; have good farms, live in comfortable houses, and have many fine horses and fat cattle. Of course, these valuable allies have a liberal allowance of the brigands' spoils set apart for their use and behoof. It must be borne in mind that these men are residents of regions of comparatively recent settlement, where the antecedents of newly-arrived citizens are not strictly inquired into by those who only arrived yesterday themselves. So long, therefore, as the citizen deports himself as "a clever man," so long will his neighbours implicitly trust him.

Such is the character of the men which Jesse James' fertile brain has called into service; the character of the organisation, which all the devices of the shrewdest detectives, all the bravest executors of the law have failed in ten long years of effort, to disintegrate or destroy. The very fact that such an organisation does exist, and that Jesse James furnished the brains which summoned it into existence, and has maintained it for so long a time, stamps him as an extraordinary man—one who, under other circumstances, might have become a leader of men, and passed into history along with George Cadoudal, Paoli, and other like actors on the world's wide stage.

CHAPTER 42

Excursions into Mexico

The wild, adventurous career of the Boys has been wonderful. They loved the road, loved to ride at will over the land, and set at defiance the officers of the law.

Nor have they confined their excursions to the American side of the Rio Grande. Not unfrequently they ride far away over the Sierra Madres into the valley of the lakes; in Coahuila and San Luis Potosi, they are known of many. In some of these expeditions they pass through thrilling experiences and innumerable dangers. Those border rovers of Mexico who have crossed the path of the Boys once and have escaped with their lives, evince no disposition to renew hostilities with the "gringo devils," as they affectionately call the American outlaws.

In this chapter, we propose to relate some of "the hair breadth escapes" of the daring outlaws in the land of the Otomis. These tales of wild life will not fail to interest the reader.

One time—it was in the spring of 1877—Frank and Jesse James rode down to the bank of the "River of the North." Piedras Negras is a favourite crossing place, both for Mexican cattle thieves and American outlaws. To this point came Frank and Jesse James. The river was high and the crossing difficult. It was not the season for successful raiding, and the enterprising Mexican raiders had turned their attention to the business of revolutionizing their own country. In this pious undertaking, they had not met with that degree of success which justified them in rejoicing. The *lazaroni*, gathered at Piedras Negras, were particularly ill-humoured, and the lonely Texan who came in their way could expect nothing better than to be plundered.

Such was the situation of affairs when Frank and Jesse James arrived on the Texas side of the river in front of the wretched Mexican *pueblo*. The surly "greaser," who acted as the Charon at that point, was even more surly than usual. But the Boys had passed that way before, and the ferryman had a vivid recollection that one Estevan Sandoval, who had molested them on one occasion, was now no more in the land of the living. He complied with the usual tedious alacrity of his countrymen to set them across the stream.

There was an unusual number of ill-looking fellows about the place, a fact which did not escape the immediate attention of the Boys. There were regular brigands from the passes of the Sierra Madres; thieves from Matamoras, cut-throats from Saltillo; smugglers from all along the border, and rogues of all grades. The Boys knew there was "fun ahead."

It must be said to the credit of the Jameses that they neither seek nor run away from a fight. In this case the character of the Boys was sustained. They proposed to pass on without stopping. In this benevolent intention, they were not destined to succeed. Riding through the square, or *plaza*, as the Mexicans call it, they passed on toward the country of woods beyond. They had not got out of the straggling village, when a mob of half-drunken, howling Mexicans, mounted on horses, came after them, cursing and firing off their pistols as they came. It would have been well for some of them if they had never beheld the face of a gringo. Doubtless the leaders expected to see the Boys use their spurs liberally and make time out of town. In this they were disappointed. The American outlaws were not accustomed to flee before such "outfits."

Instead of galloping away, they deliberately halted, and the inevitable pistols were drawn and "the fun began." The Jameses do not have occasion to kill unless they desire to do so, as they can easily disable an enemy without taking his life. In less time than is required to state the incident, four of the foremost of the rabble were on the ground, with broken right arms. The remainder of the crowd turned and rode with all speed through the *plaza*. Actuated by some wild impulse which sometimes seems to possess them, the Jameses turned and rode back again to the square.

It came near proving a fatal ride to Frank. Some of the Mexicans had taken refuge in an *adobe* house on one side of the *plaza*, and seeing the daring American outlaws sitting on their horses in the very midst of the place, in an attitude of defiance of all "the brave men" of Piedras Negras, they mustered courage to open fire upon the Boys. A perfect shower of bullets was discharged, and one of them cut the brim of the hat worn by Frank James, narrowly missing the side of his head. Then the Boys felt that they were in for "a good deal of fun," and all scruple as to killing vanished. They shot to kill, and death was the doom of any greaser who came within their deadly range. Two were killed outright, and then the ill-natured mob that had sought to avenge the death of Estevan Sandoval, fled from the village in terror, leaving the brothers in undisputed possession of the place.

It was not their purpose to remain, and they rode on in a short time. That evening, when they were crossing a stream, swollen by the recent spring rains, a party of brigands in ambush on the opposite bank opened fire upon them, and Jesse received a slight wound in the left shoulder. The Boys charged the thicket which had afforded the robbers shelter, and the whole ten broke and fled, not however, before one of their number was made to atone for the hurt which Jesse had received.

This journey into San Luis Potosi, was one fraught with many perils, and only the fate which seems to protect them, enabled them to return into Texas. They met with a singular adventure on this trip.

They had reached Monclova, a large town in Coahuila. Here they found an acquaintance—an old comrade of the Guerrilla times. He had taken up his residence in Mexico, had married a handsome Mexican girl, and had settled down to a quiet life in a strange land. Of course, he was glad to see the Boys whom he had not met since they parted in Kentucky, when he was captured and sent to prison. His home was placed at their disposal, and his Mexican wife received them with that cordial hospitality which is a characteristic of her countrywomen. Here they proposed to remain a day or two and rest.

In accordance with the customs of the country, the Mexicanised American gave his old comrades a reception on the following afternoon, or rather evening after their arrival. A reception in Mexico means a ball or *fandango*. Many of the leading citizens of Monclova attended the reception, for the friend of the Jameses was esteemed a very worthy citizen and respectable gentleman.

Among the guests was a young lieutenant of the Mexican Army, and an American long resident in the country, who came from the vicinity of Matehuala. These two men scrutinised the faces of the Boys in a very peculiar manner, and a careful observer could have seen the flushes of anger which ever and *anon* overspread their countenances. Jesse had noticed their behaviour, and called the attention of his brother to the strangeness of their conduct. He was sure that he had seen the American before somewhere, at some time, just when and where he could not remember.

Frank was enjoying himself in the society of a fair *senorita*, and seemed to attach little importance to his brother's suggestions. But Jesse watched them closely, and became thoroughly convinced that he had met both men before, and he knew that the meeting had been that of enemies.

The lieutenant and his companion did not remain long, but took their departure. There was at that time encamped, in the environs of Monclova, a brigade of the Mexican Army, and the regiment to which the lieutenant belonged had barracks near the *plaza*. On leaving the ball-room, the two men went directly to the headquarters of the regiment, and found there the colonel and lieutenant-colonel. The young officer at once laid before them the knowledge which he possessed concerning the character of the men who were being entertained in Monclova that night. Both men had a score to settle with the Jameses. The account of the American dated back to 1865—that of the young officer only a little more than a year, at which time, unfortunately, in one of the border broils, frequent about that time between Mexicans and Texans, the Boys had killed a brother of the officer.

The superior officers looked with favour on the scheme to arrest the Boys. The more readily, too, did they agree to the plan of capture when informed that the American authorities were offering a reward of $50,000 for the apprehension of these men. It was a bonanza which the impecunious colonels hoped to gain.

Silently as possible a company of eighty men was mustered, and marched to the house, and immediately surrounded it. The merry makers were just in the midst of an evening of enjoyment. Indeed, "there was a sound of revelry by night," and the fair *senoritas* and chivalrous youths of Monclova were animated by high hopes and dreams of future bliss.

Suddenly there was an interruption. The doors were thrown open, and an officer, accompanied by a guard, strode into the room. The violinist dropped his bow; the dancers stood still; the faces of women blanched, and men quailed before this apparition of war and bloodshed.

The officer stepped briskly to the part of the room where the Jameses were standing, and addressing them in broken English, commanded them to surrender in the name and by the authority of the government of Mexico. Frank and Jesse looked at him with a disdainful, dangerous smile.

Would they surrender without his being under the painful necessity of using force, inquired the officer.

"Never!" The answer was firmly delivered.

The officer turned to the guards, and gave a signal of command for them to move up.

"Stop!" It was Jesse's voice of command. The officer waved the guards to halt.

"We have a proposition to submit. Will you hear it?"

"If it means surrender, yes," replied the officer.

"It is this:" pursued Jesse, not appearing to notice the purport of the officer's reply, "allow these ladies here to retire, and we will discuss the question with you."

"I shall be compelled to take you by force," said the officer.

"Let the ladies retire, I say!" exclaimed Jesse James, in a tone that betrayed his impatience.

The Boys were not surprised without arms. They never lay aside a pair of pistols. They are ever at their sides, and always ready for use. The officer parleyed. He did not desire to begin an affray in the midst of a company of ladies—his instincts as a gentleman revolted against subjecting them to alarm and danger. The house was surrounded; he had ample force to enforce the orders of his superiors; so he said,

"Let the ladies all retire."

The order was given at the door to the guards to allow the ladies to pass through. The bail-room was soon free from their presence. The men huddled in one corner, and finally were permitted to retire into another room.

"Now," said the officer, "lay down your pistols. I have an ample force to enforce these orders. The house is surrounded; you cannot get away."

The answer he received was a derisive peal of laughter. At the same moment, a pistol flashed before the eyes of the officer as he raised his sword to signal his guard. He saw it but for an instant, there was an explosion, and the officer fell dead to the floor. The guard, amazed, rushed forward to succour their fallen leader. They were thrown off their guard. One, two, three deafening reports, and three soldiers lay still, weltering in their gore. *Celerity of execution is safety,* was ever the motto of the Jameses.

The guards who had followed their officer into the house, fled when they saw their comrades fall. The Boys rushed out of the house.

The soldiers in the street met them with a volley of balls. But they were too much agitated to shoot well. The Boys escaped with two or three trifling scratches. They opened fire on the line of guards around the house. Seized with consternation, the soldiers fled from their deadly revolvers. The whole town was excited. The streets began to teem with surging throngs of men, women and children; the alarm drums were beat in the barracks; the soldiers hastily formed in line and marched to the scene of the disturbance. Never had Monclova been so shaken before.

It was too late. The cause of all the hubbub had reached their horses, hastily saddled them, mounted, and were then thundering far away through the dark streets. They did not travel the highways after daylight. They found a refuge in the mountains.

Fight with Mexicans at Monclova.

CHAPTER 43

Death to Border Brigands

The ranch of the James Boys furnished a temptation to the Mexican border brigands, which they were in no wise able to resist, even if they had possessed the least particle of that moral sense which enables men to withstand temptation. The Jameses were successful rancheros; they lived out on the confines of the white settlements in Texas. Their fat herds spread over the valleys and ranged over many hills. This wealth of cattle excited the cupidity of the Mexican border *banditti*. They envied the outlawed Boys their goodly possessions; and they were nerved to undertake to appropriate the herds, even if the lives of the owners should be taken in order to compass their wishes.

There was a robber chief of Nueva Leon, who had once been a faithful lieutenant of Cortinas, "the Robber Governor" of the State of Tamaulipas. This fellow, whose name was Juan Fernando Palacios, had achieved a local reputation about Piedras Negras, Eagle Pass, Mier, and other localities on the upper Rio Grande, as a daring freebooter and bloody minded murderer. He had gathered about him a band of men of like disposition with himself—principally fugitives from justice from the neighbouring states.

This gang of *desperadoes* numbered more than thirty men, and Palacios resolved to lead them over among the ranches of the Texans. There was much booty to be gained by a successful raid. It was at a season of the year when many herds were being pastured in the valley of the Pecos, and with thirty men and more he fondly hoped that he could come upon, and discomfit all the "cow-boys" in that region, and drive away the well-conditioned herds at his leisure.

It was in the autumn of 1877. The dry season had withered the grass on the hill slopes and the upland plains. But down in the valleys the grass was green, and the wild flowers bloomed in all the freshness of the spring time. Palacios and his brigands made careful preparations before they set out. There had been a season of quiet on the border. Several months had passed since the last raid was made. The Mexican brigand hoped to take the "cow-boys" unawares—surprise them—kill them, and drive away their herds. This was his hope.

Mexican brigands are good night travellers. Indeed, their most important movements are made in the night. During the day time, if possible, they take shelter in the chaparral, and remain quiet until the shades of night fall over valley and plain, and then under the starlight they ride—sometimes accomplishing long journeys in a thinly inhabited country without giving the least information of their presence, so secretly do they move.

It was a lovely evening in October. There was no moon, but the stars shone brightly from the cloudless sky. El Paso was unusually quiet that evening. There was not a *fandango* in progress in the place; the sound of the violin was not heard within its borders. The *senoritas* sang no vesper hymns. Palacios and his robber band had gone across the river into Texas, and not many young men remained in El Paso. All night, beneath the silent stars, the mongrel band of the bandit chief rode on toward "the settlements" of the hated, as well as dreaded Texans. Before dawn, they found shelter in a patch of chaparral in the valley of an affluent of the Rio Pecos. No one had seen them. Thirty miles and more they had ridden in the direction of the fat herds of the Texans.

The day passed away, and once more the curtain of night fell, and the Mexican raiders rode in its shadow. By dawn they had reached the vicinity of a well-stocked ranch. A convenient shelter was sought and found near a little stream. The raiders were many miles from El Paso now, and the valleys and the hill slopes, and the lower plains were dotted with great herds of cattle. But the *rancheros* had not yet discovered the presence of the enemy, and rested in fancied security.

Palacios and his band hovered near the herds all day. Men were sent out to ascertain the number of herdsmen attending the different droves. All this time the horses of the raiders were carefully concealed in a thicket by the bank of the stream. When the evening came on, Palacios was well informed of the locality of all the herds in his immediate neighbourhood. Dividing his men into two bands, over one of which he appointed a notorious murderer from Mier, named Jesus Almonte, and assumed command of the other in person. The time appointed for "the stampede" of the herds was ten o'clock at night.

An Alarmed Cattle-Boy.

At that hour, the western herdsmen are almost always sound asleep. Palacios was certain that his presence on the American side of the Rio Grande was not known. He had met no one, and his scouts had reported everything quiet among the herdsmen. Ten o'clock came. The Mexican robbers, well-armed and splendidly mounted, quietly left their covert. Almonte and his band proceeded two and a half or three miles up the stream where a large herd of cattle were corralled. Palacios went down the creek to "stampede" another herd of seven or eight hundred head. The process of "stampeding" is thoroughly understood by the Mexicans. The herdsmen were aroused by the approaching horsemen.

But it was too late. The Mexicans were among them, and Almonte's gang killed two of the "cow-boys" at the upper herd, and Palacios' crowd killed one at the lower herd. The "stampede" was complete. The herds were turned toward the Rio Grande, and driven rapidly away. All the remainder of that night, and all the next day, the robbers pressed forward toward their place of concealment and shelter beyond the Rio Grande. As yet, no pursuers had appeared, but Palacios knew well that they were not safe on this side the river. He knew that the avengers were on his track, and he cared not to see the face of a Texan at that time. Coming at night time to the river some distance below El Paso, he crossed over with all his booty, and speedily made himself comfortable among his sympathizing countrymen and countrywomen.

It chanced about that time that Frank and Jesse James rode down toward the Rio Grande to make observations, and enjoy life just beyond the borders of civilization. Being somewhat in the outlaw business themselves, they cared very little for "the borders of civilization," or for that matter, for the interior. While riding, they met one of the sorely disconsolate herdsmen, who told the story which we have related, with many embellishments; for instance, that a band had come out of the south country, killed all the herdsmen in the valley, driven off *all* the herds, and that *he* only was left alive to tell of their fate.

To this doleful tale, Frank and Jesse James gave good heed, for one of the missing herds had been their property.

The two brothers consulted together as to what could be done under the circumstances. They had been into Mexico on many occasions before, and, although the frightened herdsman had magnified the numbers of the raiders, so that they appeared a mighty host, Frank and Jesse James were not the men to submit tamely to downright robbery. The brothers resolved to pursue the raiders. And so, they rode on and on until they came to the Rio Grande.

It was in the early morning. The October sun had not yet appeared above the horizon, but all the eastern sky was refulgent with the coming glories of a lovely day. Frank and Jesse James had ridden far, but their horses were not jaded, and as for themselves, physical endurance is their normal characteristic. They were ready for any desperate adventure, such as they were then engaged in. Only for a moment did they pause when they emerged from the river. Their firearms were carefully examined, and then they urged their horses onward.

El Paso was silent. The inhabitants had not yet awakened from their slumbers. Palacios and his band, with their stolen herds, had passed on through the village in the direction of the mountains. Their trail through the sand was still fresh. The James Boys rode on. Three miles away they came to the camp. Deeming themselves safe, the Mexican raiders had taken no precautions to guard against surprise. The herds had been corralled, and the bandits, wearied by their long marches, slumbered heavily.

Cautiously approaching the Mexican camp, the two brothers, with that quick perception for which they are distinguished, saw at a glance the situation of the camp and the position of the sleeping robbers. The dreamers were suddenly aroused by the reports of the avengers' pistols. Jesse and Frank James were in their midst, and dealing death to the miscreants ere they could grasp their weapons. Some who dreamed were sent to their account before the phantasy had cleared from their brains. With a death-dealing pistol in each hand, they fired with incredible rapidity, and at each discharge an unfortunate wretch fell to rise no more. Terror-stricken, the robbers fled in every direction. Some were arrested in their flight by the unerring aim of the outlawed brothers; and some more fortunate escaped to the mountains with life only, everything being left behind in order that they might save it.

The corral was broken up. The Boys are skilful herdsmen, and soon the great tramping drove was turned toward the Rio Grande. Ten dead robbers, stark and still, among the cactus patches, testified to the prowess of the American *desperadoes*. They passed back through the village. Not a man was visible. They had heard of the fate of their robber friends. Terror-stricken, they had abandoned their homes and fled into the chaparral beyond the hills, which at this point approach the river. The Boys were hungry after their morning's engagement, and halting at the little *adobe posado*, they ordered breakfast, taking care that it was prepared under their personal supervision, in order that no treachery on the part of their unwilling entertainers should succeed.

The feat which they had accomplished was one of the most daring ever recorded in the annals of border strife. Then, the nonchalant way in which they ordered the trembling inhabitants to minister to their physical comfort, furnished another proof of the admirable nerve of these remarkable men. After refreshing themselves, the Boys, at their leisure, recrossed the Rio Grande with nearly the whole number of cattle which the bandits had driven away.

Desperadoes as they were, Palacios and Almonte were indisposed to surrender the rich prize which they had secured, as they thought,

After the "Greasers."

without any effort. The two chiefs had stopped in the village the night previous to the arrival of the Jameses, and were not in the camp at the time of the attack of the Boys. In El Paso, they lay hidden in a heap of hay, while Frank and Jesse regaled themselves with "the best the market afforded." The Mexicans were convinced that a large force of *Gringo Diablos* were at hand, and they feared for their lives. They waited for the appearance of the squadrons of rangers in vain.

Gradually it began to dawn upon their dull comprehension that the whole force of the *Gringos* numbered just two men. Palacios, Almonte, and a few of their followers rallied some hours after the Boys were on their march over the rolling plains of Texas. They were furious, and boasted of what great things they intended to accomplish. Sometime, toward noon, they cautiously approached the river, reconnoitred, and finally ventured to cross over. There was no enemy in sight, and the twenty-five brigands of the border became valiant, and set out on the trail of the Boys who were marching on with the recaptured herds.

Encumbered as they were, by a vast drove of cattle, their progress was slow. Toward evening the Mexican bandits came in sight. But they did not venture to attack. Hovering on the rear, and galloping along the flanks of the moving herd, the Mexicans made a thorough reconnaissance of the force of Americans. There were just two men, and no more. Emboldened by this knowledge, they approached with a view of "stampeding" the herd. Five well mounted men were sent to engage the Boys while the others advanced on the left flank of the herd. But they did not know the character of the men they sought to kill out there on the plains. Secured to the saddles which they bestrode, each carried a long range sixteen shot Winchester rifle.

The bandits came within range. If they ever prayed, the time for prayers had arrived. They were approaching, unwittingly it may be, the margin of the river of death; the black angel hovered over them, the sun of time was being surely extinguished. Detaching their deadly rifles from the fastenings, each singled out his man, took deliberate aim, touched the trigger, and instantaneously two Mexican robbers fell to the earth pierced through their hearts. Their comrades marked their fall, and knew the cause. They turned to flee. It was too late. Even as they turned two more of them fell, pierced through and through by the unerring bullets from the steadily aimed rifles of the American outlaws. The other one of the five fled, and succeeded in making his escape.

The Boys fully comprehended the designs of the Mexicans, and

Jesse suggested that he would ride to the summit of "the swell" to the left, to see what "those other devils are about."

Riding rapidly up the slope, his horse was soon reined up on the crest of the ridge. There he discovered on the slope below him a party of some fifteen armed men. Bringing his rifle to bear a Mexican saddle was emptied in an instant. The raiders replied; but their guns would not send a ball so far. They were not less than four hundred yards away. Jesse continued to empty saddles until four men were down. The Mexicans turned and fled, and Jesse gave them a parting salute, which brought down a horse. When he rejoined his brother he remarked sententiously, "Well, I've prepared a feast for the vultures over yonder."

"How many are down?" asked the other.

"Oh, only four men and one horse," he answered, with a grim sort of smile.

The dangerous time for them was the shadowy hours. They knew that all the brigands of that region would take their trail. They were a hundred miles from any certain succour. The Mexican raiders are not to be despised in a night affray. They expected attack, and it is one of the peculiarities of the Boys, that they never sleep when there is danger surrounding them. The severe losses which they had sustained only rendered the pursuers more wary; but they still hovered around. The Boys expected an attack that night. The sun was sinking low in the west, and the brothers were earnestly consulting as to the best means of guarding against the consequences of a night attack.

"See," said Frank, "away there on that ridge whose top the sun is gilding! Are those moving objects men on horseback, or a herd of buffalo? What do you think?"

The brothers halted. Since their removal to Texas they never ride abroad without carrying with them a field glass each. They now raised their glasses and looked long and earnestly at the dark objects moving between them and the horizon.

"They are mounted men," said Jesse.

"Texans, Mexicans, Lipans or Commanches? Which do you say?" asked Frank.

Jesse looked again. The mounted men were nearly two miles away—a long distance to determine the character of men, or designate their nationality. Long and carefully did he scrutinize the movements of the horsemen.

"Soldiers—Federal soldiers—by Jehovah!" he exclaimed. "Well, I've seen the time that I would not like to see such a company, but

I'm confounded glad they've come around this evening. I'll get a nap tonight, anyway."

It was agreed that Jesse should ride forward and inform the officer in command of the presence of Palacios' band of raiders. He spurred his horse forward over the high rolling swells of prairie toward the horsemen, who were also advancing. The Mexicans saw this movement, and saw the horsemen. They at once surmised that a detachment of McKenzie's command was out looking for them, and turning about, they rode hastily back the way they came.

The Boys were left in peace. The detachment of cavalry swept onward in pursuit of the fleeing raiders, and the herd, fatigued by long driving, were indisposed to scatter. The return to the pastures from whence they had been driven was leisurely made. The Boys returned safely to their abode, and Jesse was welcomed by one who worships him as the world's noblest hero.

Fight with Mexican Cattle Thieves.

CHAPTER 44

A Golden Harvest Reaped by Outlaws

Wide is our home, boys,
Freely we roam, boys,
Merrily, merrily, o'er the brown lea;
Brief though our life, boys,
With peril rife, boys,
Oh! it has wildness, and rapture, and glee.

In the mellow days of September, 1877, a party of seven men came to the neighbourhood of Ogallala, Nebraska, and went into camp there. They were "stockmen," they said, and only wished to rest awhile before entering upon the long, wearisome march across the plains to Texas, which lay before them. They had brought droves of cattle from the pasture-prairies of the "Lone Star" state to supply the markets of Chicago and other cities to the east, and it was their intention, according to their statements, to return to Texas to be in readiness for "the spring drive."

There was in this party Jim Berry, of Portland, Callaway county, Missouri, an old-time guerrilla in the days of Anderson; Jack Davis, formerly of the vicinity of Fort Smith, Arkansas, a man of sinister reputation; Billy Heffridge, a Pennsylvanian of no good repute; Jim Collins, a brother of Brad, the well-known Texan *desperado*, who was killed in an encounter with a sheriff who attempted his arrest, and Sam Bass, the somewhat distinguished outlaw, whose name figures so prominently in the criminal annals of the period between 1865 and 1878. There were two others, the identity of one of whom has never been discovered. Of these, Berry, Collins, Davis, and one other, had sometimes ridden with Frank and Jesse James, and exchanged the civilities of the craft with them. Who the seventh man of the party of "campers at Ogallala" was, the detectives have never been able to discover.

The "stockmen," as they styled themselves, remained in camp near Ogallala for a number of days, and were frequent visitors to the village. Jim Berry had been in business at Plattsmouth, Nebraska, and had made some acquaintances along the road. Among the business men residing at Ogallala, which is the county seat of Keith county, and a station of some importance on the line of the Union Pacific railway, was Mr. M. F. Leach, a gentleman of great mental acuteness, and an excellent judge of men.

One day some of the "cattlemen" came to Leach's store in Ogallala, among them Jim Berry, and purchased a number of red bandana handkerchiefs. Of course, nothing was thought of the circumstance at the time, but subsequently the red bandanas afforded "a clue" to the identity of the robbers of a train on the Union Pacific railroad.

Big Springs is a station on the railroad, about twenty-three miles west of Ogallala, nearly on the line between Keith and Cheyenne counties, Nebraska. At this place, there is an excellent supply of water, which constitutes its greatest claim to importance, for on other accounts Big Springs possesses little to interest the traveller. One evening—it was the 17th of September—the people of Brule and Ogallala were thrown into a great ferment of excitement on the arrival of the train from the West, bringing, as the conductor and passengers did, a full account of the great robbery of the express car, and all the passengers, at Big Springs station, which event had occurred just after nightfall that same evening. It was a great sensation at the time, and interest in it has not yet ceased to operate on the public mind. A brief account of the robbery, and pursuit and death of several of the robbers, will not be regarded out of place in this volume, inasmuch as some of the robbers had an acquaintance with the principal characters who are the subjects of this work.

The train from the Pacific slope arrived at Big Springs on the evening of September 17th, 1877, a little after nightfall. No sooner had the locomotive come to a standstill at the little station, than a band of seven men, all of whom wore red bandana handkerchiefs on their heads, which fell over and concealed their faces, sprang upon the train with drawn revolvers. Four of the men guarded the engineer, and entered the express car. Wells, Fargo & Co.'s safe contained $62,000 in gold. This was opened, and the contents taken out and deposited in a sack which one of the robbers carried. Another one kept guard over the train's crew, and two men, well-armed with heavy revolvers, went through the train to take the purses, watches and jewellery of the passengers.

One of the fellows carried a sack, and whenever the other handed him a watch, a pocketbook or some jewellery, he thrust it into the receptacle which he carried along. There were many passengers, and they were on a long journey. Many fine watches, much valuable jewellery, and innumerable pocketbooks were collected in the sack, in a miscellaneous heap. When the golden treasures of the express safe, and the valuables of the passengers were all secured, the brigands released the train and rode away over the plains. The train then proceeded eastward, by Brule and to Ogallala. The particulars of the robbery were detailed, and the inhabitants of those places were aroused by the intelligence. It was late and nothing could be done that night.

The next morning the "stockmen" were in camp as usual, and Mr. Leach and some others of the inhabitants of Ogallala were preparing to hunt the robbers.

Mr. M. F. Leach had performed some amateur detective work, and had exhibited so much acuteness that he was regarded as one of the ablest catchers of law-breakers in the West. He was at once secured to work up the great train robbery. To him is due the larger share of the credit for tracking down the Big Springs bandits. And the men Leach had to deal with were keen, adroit, and endowed with extraordinary effrontery. We cannot enter into detail concerning his remarkable pursuit of Sam Bass and his companions, from Ogallala. A full narrative would fill a volume. To show the character of the men with whom he had to deal, we will relate an anecdote of a meeting he had with Jim Berry, one of the gang, the morning after the robbery. As before stated, the "stockmen," who were no other than the brigands, had returned to their camp at Ogallala, and were there as if nothing had happened, the morning after the robbery. Leach was preparing to go after the robbers. He encountered Jim Berry, who addressed him in a familiar manner:

"Well, are you going out after those fellows?"

"Yes," said Leach, "that's what I am going to do."

"I wonder what they would give me to go along? I might be of service to them."

"Well, I can say," said Leach, "that you would certainly receive a liberal compensation for any service you may be able to render."

The two men talked together some time, but Berry did not go on the hunt for the train robbers. Mr. Leach proceeded out the road to Sidney, in Cheyenne County, not forgetting on his way to stop off at Big Springs to find, if possible, some clue to the robbers' course after leaving that place. He found part of a red bandana handkerchief, which he secured, and went on to Sidney in a special train which had been provided for his use. A careful examination of the situation in that place was barren of results, and Mr. Leach returned to Ogallala. The "stockmen" had remained in camp two days after the robbery, and then they had marched away—whither—no one knew.

Leach had brought with him the piece of red bandana from Big Springs. He was sure the goods had come from his store in Ogallala. While looking about the deserted camp of the "stockmen," Leach discovered the other piece of the bandana which he had brought from Big Springs. The ragged edges of the two pieces fitted exactly. The inevitable inference was that the "stockmen" were the robbers. The direction taken by them was not known, but Leach soon discovered their trail. Then commenced one of the most remarkable pursuits ever known. Leach ascertained that the robbers would probably cross the Kansas Pacific railroad at Buffalo Station, Gove county, Kansas. He was ever on their track, and on many occasions, he escaped with his life in a marvellous manner.

Once he saw them count the spoils of the robbery, and divide the money, watches and jewellery among themselves. Then he sent a ranchman a long distance, a hundred miles or more, with a dispatch to the *commandant* at Fort Hayes to have a guard of soldiers at Buffalo. The bandits divided into couples, and pursued their course. At Buffalo, some of the robbers and the soldiers had a conflict, and Billy Heffridge and Jim Collins were killed. Sam Bass, Jack Davis and two others escaped. Jim Berry made toward Missouri. It was ascertained that he would probably return to Callaway county, and detectives were at once hurried into that county and quietly waited around Fulton and Portland for the appearance of "the game."

One day Jim Berry made his appearance at Mexico, in Audrain County, Missouri. It was known that he had been in the Black Hills, and when he went to the bank in Mexico with a large amount of gold coin, principally twenty dollar pieces, to exchange it for currency, the circumstance seems to have aroused no suspicion at the time. Berry then "went on a big bender." While in Mexico he had ordered a suit of clothes from a tailor there. In a few days, information was received by Sheriff Glascock that Jim Berry was known to have been engaged in the Big Springs robbery.

Concerning this nothing was said at the time, but the sheriff made all necessary preparations, and patiently abided his time to make an attempt to capture Jim Berry. One day, an old comrade of Berry made his appearance in Mexico, bearing an order on the tailor to "deliver to the bearer" the new suit of clothes which had been ordered by Berry. This fact was at once communicated to Sheriff Glascock by the tailor. The friend of Berry was seized, and persuaded in a manner frequently employed by officers of the law, to reveal the whereabouts of his friend.

The friend of Berry was a man named Bose Kazy, Sheriff Glascock and John Carter were in company when Kazy was seized. The sheriff then called to his aid John Coons, Robert Steele, and a young man named Moore. They then set out, compelling Kazy to act as a guide. It was on Saturday night, October 14, 1877, when the party rode quietly away from Mexico, on their way to Callaway County, to find the lurking-place of Jim Berry, "the best man in Callaway." It was a long ride. Daylight had not dawned on the landscape Sunday morning when the officers arrived within a half-mile of Kazy's house. They did not go to the house to alarm those slumbering there. The officers took Kazy into the woods and bound him to a tree, leaving Robert Steele to guard him. They then secreted themselves in thickets to await results. As the men in the posse were assigned to their respective stations, the sheriff gave the following command:

"Boys, if you see him, halt him; if he shows fight, shoot him; if he runs, shoot him in the legs. Catch him, at all hazards."

Half an hour after giving this order. Sheriff Glascock heard the neigh of a horse about half a mile away, as he judged. The sheriff and Moore then crept cautiously about three hundred yards down the course of a branch. They came to a fence, and crossed over it. They discovered the tracks of a horse, freshly made. They were in a thicket at this time, and listening intently. In a few moments, they heard the snort of a horse, apparently not more than fifty yards away. The sheriff then crawled through the thicket about twenty yards toward the spot from whence the sound had proceeded. He was on his knees, and, cautiously peering through the autumn-tinted leaves of the tangled thicket, he saw the back of a horse, about forty yards away.

Laying aside his hat, Sheriff Glascock crept twenty yards nearer. He then rose to his feet and saw Jim Berry unhitching the horse, which had been tied to a tree. Berry started to lead the horse in a direction nearly toward Glascock. The sheriff cocked both barrels of the breech-loading gun which he carried, ran about twenty yards and within twenty feet of Berry, and commanded him to halt. Berry, taken by surprise, started on a run. The sheriff then fired. The charge of buckshot passed over the head of the trainrobber, but in an instant, he fired again, and this time seven buckshot took effect in Berry's left leg, below the knee, and he fell to the ground. Glascock sprang forward. Berry was endeavouring to draw a pistol, as he lay writhing on the ground.

It was too late; the sheriff was upon him, and, seizing the pistol, he wrested it from the grasp of Berry. Finding himself overpowered, the wounded man, in his helplessness, besought the sheriff to shoot him, as he did not want to live any longer. The officer told him that he did not want to kill him, but that he wanted him to have justice. By this time, Moore arrived on the scene. Berry was wounded and defenceless in the hands of the officers of the law.

Sheriff Glascock then summoned the other members of the posse to the scene of the conflict. When they had arrived, Berry was searched. In a belt worn on his person they found five $500 packages of money, and in his pocket-book was found $304; in all, $2,804 were secured. Berry also had a gold watch and chain, a dress-coat, three overcoats and a comforter. He had slept there in the thicket the night before. Afterward, Berry was removed to Kazy's house, and a messenger was sent to Williamsburg for a surgeon.

After taking breakfast at Kazy's, Sheriff Glascock and John Carter proceeded to Berry's house to search for the balance of the money. Arriving there, they asked Mrs. Berry concerning the whereabouts of her husband. She did not know; had not seen him for several days, and she thought he had left the country. The sheriff then showed her Berry's watch and chain. On seeing it, one of the little children exclaimed:

"Oh! I thought that was papa's!"

Poor child! Perhaps it was too young to fully comprehend the tragic meaning of those tokens.

To Mrs. Berry the whole story of the tragedy in the thicket that Sunday morning was repeated. In response, she said,

"I never thought he would be taken alive. He has said a great many times that he would never be taken alive."

Then ensued a scene deeply affecting. The robber had those at home who loved him. The wife and mother began to weep bitterly, and the wailings of her little boy and five little girls, made a scene calculated to touch the deep chords of emotion in the breasts of the stern men, who in the performance of lawful duty had been compelled to inflict all this misery on the family of the robber.

They searched the house, but they found no hoards of money. Then Glascock and Carter returned to Kazy's, a conveyance was procured, and the officer and his posse with their wounded prisoner set out for Mexico, where they arrived late in the evening. Berry was placed in a room in the Ringo House, and received the attention of Dr. Russell, of Mexico. Berry's wounds were painful, and he did not rally from their effects. On Monday, gangrene supervened, and a little before 1 o'clock Tuesday, October 16th, 1877, Jim Berry, one of the robbers of the train at Big Springs, quietly passed over the dark river, and the records of his stormy career were closed forever.

Sam Bass escaped from Buffalo station, and finally, after many thrilling adventures, reached his haunts in Texas. A little more than one year afterward he met his fate in a manner equally as tragic as the event which closed the career of Jim Berry.

Of the seven men who plundered the train and its passengers at Big Springs, Billy Heffridge, Jim Collins, Jim Berry, Sam Bass, and one other, have met violent deaths. The robber who went by the name of Jack Davis has disappeared. The seventh man—the only one whose name was never ascertained by the detectives—succeeded in getting away. Who he was, from whence he came, and whither he went, are, until this day, unanswered questions.

Much speculation in regard to the identity of the seventh man, whom we shall call the Unknown, has been indulged in, and the question has been asked. Was it Jesse James? or was it Jack Bishop, Dave Pool, John Jarrette or Jim Cummings? We have no means of answering such interrogatories. Whoever the Unknown is or was, he has probably not a single comrade of the occasion alive, and is therefore in little danger of being betrayed.

There are people who believe that Jesse James was with the Big Springs bandits. Upon what particular grounds such belief is based, we have been unable to ascertain. He may or may not have been present. Our readers may well be left free to draw their own inferences. But certain it is, a mystery, which perhaps may forever remain such, surrounds the personality of one of the daring raiders who accomplished one of the greatest robberies which has yet taken place on any American railroad.

Chapter 45

A Visit to Frank James' Home

In Southern climes where ardent gleams the sun,
Gilding each rivulet, and tree, and flower,
With crimson radiance—and gaily flings
On all around of light a golden shower—
Where lavish nature mingles in the breeze.
Refreshing odours with her spicy hand;
The rare Nepenthes wave their flexile form,
The floral wonder of that fragrant land.

During the autumn of the year 1878, a young gentleman of the highest respectability, a citizen of the State of Georgia, being on a tour through Texas, expressed to his friends a desire to make the personal acquaintance of the celebrated outlaws, Frank and Jesse James. His friends endeavoured to dissuade him from making the attempt to see them at their own retreat. They represented to him that such an undertaking would be fraught with no little personal danger. The Boys have been hounded and hunted over so large a territory, through so many years, that they have become extremely cautious, and very suspicious of all strangers.

But the young Georgian was courageous and determined. There was a tinge of romance in his composition, and the career of the Boys, to his mind, was the most romantic in all history. He felt that he would venture farther to see them than to behold the face of any living man. The advice of his friends fell unheeded upon his ear. He resolved to seek their retreat at whatever hazard. He had learned to admire their cool bravery, indomitable energy, and shrewd ability to evade the snares laid for them by the officers of the law.

The Jameses, outlaws as they are, do not want for friends. They have devoted admirers and staunch friends even in the ranks of respectable circles—persons who would suffer death rather than betray them. Such a friend was a Texas relative of the young Georgian. Finding that his kinsman was resolved upon a visit—that he would in all probability be able to discover the retreat of the outlaws, and, believing that he might possibly meet with a misfortune by venturing to penetrate to their place, the Texan gave his relative a letter addressed to a certain name—which is not that of James—described the route to be taken, and gave a minute description of the personnel of the renowned *desperadoes*, and with many admonitions and cautions, after having solemnly pledged his kinsman to reveal nothing concerning the exact whereabouts of their home, the Texan bid his Georgia kinsman God-speed, and they parted.

Many days he rode over the plains, and crossed many a limpid stream, and pushed his way through many a tangled wold before he approached the retreat of the outlaws. He found it, however, but in what county or division of the state, he declines to say.

In a letter written to the author, subsequent to that visit, he gave a most interesting account of his reception and sojourn with the outlawed brothers on their own ranch. We have obtained his permission to use that portion of the letter relating to the Jameses, which we herewith present to our readers:

> It was a lovely afternoon. The grass was brown and sere. A few late autumn flowers relieved the otherwise monotonous landscape. The country through which I was passing was high, undulating prairie. Here and there, from the tops of the long swells in the surface, the course of streams far away to the right and the left, were well defined by dark lines of trees from which the foliage had not yet been cast. The journey had become lonely and irksome. I had lost interest in the landscape. The faded grass and the golden-hued flowers no longer possessed charms for me. The limpid brooks and darting minnows in their clear waters even failed to awaken the slightest interest. The truth is, I was worn out by the excessive fatigue of the long journey.
>
> I had just crossed a small stream, skirted by some wind-twisted trees, and was ascending a long slope. Looking toward the crest of the ridge, I saw two horsemen, splendidly mounted, riding rapidly directly toward me. They wore low-crowned, broad-brimmed felt hats, looped up at the side. I could see at

a glance that they were heavily armed. A repeating-rifle was swung behind the shoulder of each, and a holster was attached at the saddle-bow. When the horsemen had approached within seventy-five yards of me, they suddenly halted, and each drew a heavy pistol, and simultaneously presented them at me, calling out at the same time for me to raise my hands. I confess that I felt a little shaky about that time.

I readily complied with their command, and held up both hands as high over my head as possible. The horrible thought occurred to me that I was to be shot, and left out there to make a feast for voracious vultures and ferocious wolves. A cold shudder thrilled through my veins. I had dropped the reins, and my horse stopped still. It was a dreadful moment. There were the two men, grim in features and steady of hand, with their horrible, yawning repeaters pointed at my heart. I felt sure they were murderous highwaymen. Strange that I never once thought of the renowned outlaws! I know not how long I looked at those dreadful pistols; it seemed half an age. I was aroused by the voice of one of the men calling out,

'Why don't you come on?'

I did go on. Once I let my hands droop slightly, as I advanced up the slope.

'Up with your hands, I say!' exclaimed one of them.

You may readily suppose that I threw up my hands without further admonition.

When I had arrived within fifteen paces of the spot where the men were sitting on their horses, the thought that these were no other than the men whom I was seeking, flashed through my brain.

'What are you doing here?' asked the larger one of the two.

I must have stammered a little, and appeared awkward and frightened as I made answer that I had a great desire to meet Mr. —— and his brother—naming the person to whom the letter was addressed—and I have a message for Mr. —— here with me now.

One of them—it was Frank—turned to me sharply, and asked me what I knew about Mr. ——. I told him that I had never met the gentleman, but that I had a great desire to do so. He then asked me when I was last in St. Louis. I replied that I had not been in St. Louis for a period of more than five years. 'What

are you doing here?' he asked.
'Looking about the country,' I replied.
'You like it, do you?' he inquired.
'Very well,' I said.
'You go to Chicago, do you?'
'Never was there in my life,' I answered.
'Do you know Allan Pinkerton?'
'I don't,' I said.
'What state do you hail from?'
'Georgia.'
'A very good state,' he soliloquized. 'From whom did you say you had a message for Mr. ——?'
'From Col. ——, of ——,' I answered.
'You know where you can find ——?'
'I do not.'
'Give me the message; I'll see that he gets it.'
'Are you Mr. ——?'
'No matter,' he answered. 'I'll see that he gets the communication.'
'But I've come all the way here to see him myself. I do not want to go back without seeing him,' I remarked.
'What do you want to see him for?'
'Well,' I stammered, 'I have heard a great deal about him and his brother, and I just wanted to visit them at home.'
'You know who he is then?'
'"Certainly, he is Jesse James and —.'
'An outlaw!' he interrupted me. 'Mind how you act, young man.'
The tones of his voice were dry and harsh, and the pistol which had been allowed to droop was once more raised, and pointed at my breast.
You may be sure I was thoroughly alarmed, and it required some effort to speak distinctly. At last, I managed to say in a tolerably low tone, 'I wish you would read this letter which I have brought.' The pistol was lowered and he reached out his hand to take the letter from the breast-pocket of my coat.
Meanwhile, Frank kept me under cover of a pistol. Jesse secured the letter, and commenced to read it. I watched his features closely. A change came over his countenance. The cold, stern look relaxed, and his face put on a sunny smile as he read on.

When he had finished, he turned to Frank and said, 'I guess this is all right.' Then he turned to me and said,

'So, you are a kinsman of Colonel ——?'

'I am,' I replied.

He continued, 'He is a good friend of ours, and I reckon you're all right. You wanted to see the James Boys. You see before you what is left of them. I guess you had better give us your pistols to keep for you until you are ready to leave again, for you know we are the only armed men allowed around our place. This is a very odd world anyhow. We do not trust anyone.'

"'I have but one, and here it is,' I said, presenting it to him, while I held the muzzle. He took the pistol and thrust it into a side-pocket, and turning full toward me, he said with a smile on his face, and a merry twinkle in his bright blue eyes:

'So you wanted to see the *notorious* outlaws?'

'Yes.'

'Well, did you expect we wore horns, and had split feet, and spouted fire and brimstone, eh? But you see you are mistaken. There are a hundred, yes, a thousand, worse men along the borders here than the James Boys. But they have not been lied about as we have been; they have not been hunted all over the states as we have been; they have not been so grossly misrepresented and abused, and we must bear not only our sins, but the sins of many others. It is a pretty hard fate, young man.'

The hard, unpitying expression came upon his features once

The Home of Frank James, in Texas.

more, but it was only for a moment, and the cloud passed away, and his countenance was illuminated by a smile that was genial and pleasant, and whoever could have gazed into the face of Jesse James at that moment, would not have concluded that he was a *desperado* and an outlaw.

'I suppose,' said Frank, 'that you will accept an outlaw's invitation to his humble retreat?'

'Most gladly,' I said.

They turned their horses' heads, and Jesse taking a position on one side and Frank on the other, we rode on to the crest of the ridge. 'There is where we camp,' said Frank, as he pointed away to the northwest. Camp! Indeed, it seemed more like the residence of a well-to-do planter in Georgia. The situation which they had selected was beautiful as any I had yet seen in the West. Before us a broad, green valley lay spread out in the sunlight, bounded by a line of high hills toward the northeast, and widening toward the southwest. A noble grove of timber skirted the margin of the stream, which appeared to be of considerable size, and meandered through the valley. Beyond the stream and the grove, situated on a gentle slope in the midst of gardens and cultivated fields, and vigorous young trees, rose a pleasant house of two storeys in elevation, with a garden in front. Some distance away were the barns, stables and other outbuildings.

'A lovely home!' I exclaimed. Frank smiled at my evident delight, and remarked that he found it very comfortable, after the exposure and hardships through which he had passed.

So, we rode on down the slope into the grove, and across a beautiful broad pebble-bottom stream, and up the slope to the front of the mansion, talking, by the way, of many things in the past, and expressing views and opinions concerning the future. The James Boys are far from being loquacious. They seem to maintain a perpetual guard over their words. Sometimes this reserve is momentarily cast aside, and the brothers will converse with considerable freedom. But the fits of relaxation do not last long. They speedily relapse into their accustomed reticent state, and then they answer questions only in monosyllables.

It was not long before I discovered that I was at the home of Frank James, and that Jesse and his family were only visitors. My peculiar reception was due to the fact that a person supposed to be a detective, had been making inquiries concerning the Boys at San Antonio, some weeks before my arrival.

Arriving at the yard gate, we dismounted, and I was invited into the house. At the door, we were met by a neatly dressed and handsome lady, whose deep blue eyes and regular features produced a favourable impression at once, to whom I was introduced. It was Mrs. Frank James. She received me with much dignity, yet with a genial cordiality which assured me that I was a welcome visitor. Her manner toward her husband was trusting and affectionate. 'We welcome you,' said Frank, 'as a relative of one of our best friends. We hope you will prove as manly as he. Annie, this is Mr. ———, a near relative of Colonel ———, who was so kind to you when you arrived at ———, on your way out here.'

'I am very, very glad to meet you. We all feel extremely grateful to Col. ———, for his kindness toward us, and we are only too glad to serve any of his friends,' she said.

Such was the welcome which I received at the home of Frank James. I felt myself quite at ease very soon, and the four days and nights which I spent under their hospitable roof gave no occasion for me to think hard of the outlaws. Indeed, I could not bring myself to think of them in that light. Mrs. James is a lady who is suited by education and disposition to grace any circle. And where is this model home? you ask. Well, it is in Texas—just what part of Texas I must leave you to find out. I know that I ever met with better treatment in any home, anywhere.

CHAPTER 46

Epistles of Jesse James

Jesse James is not an educated man in the scholastic sense of that term. In this respect, he differs widely from his brother Frank, who has a fair knowledge of the Latin and Greek languages, and is said to be able to converse fluently in the Spanish and German tongues. Frank was a college student when the war was commenced, and Jesse a school boy in a country place.

He had made some progress, had learned to "read, write and cipher," and was wrestling with "the knotty intricacies" of English Grammar and Geography, when his career in school was stopped short by the political events occurring about him.

It cannot be expected that Jesse's literary performances should exhibit the classic finish of an Addison or an Irving, and yet barring his faulty orthography, his style is direct and pointed, and under other circumstances he might have become a very good newspaper reporter. Although Jesse is deficient in the command of language to express his views in accordance with the canons of literary criticism, yet his letters, if not elegant specimens of composition, are at least vigorous and clear. It is a matter of regret that so few specimens of his epistolary ability are available.

We have succeeded in obtaining copies of a few of his letters, but unfortunately none which reveal the domestic relations and characteristics of the man. Such of Jesse's letters as we have been able to secure, which have any interest for the public, we present in this chapter.

The following note was addressed from Jesse to "a friend" in Missouri, and came into the hands of a gentleman who, for reasons which the author is bound to respect, desires his name to be withheld. The orthography alone is revised. The year, it will be observed, is not given.

Commanche, Texas, June 10th.

Dear Jim:

I hear they are making a great fuss about old Dan Askew, and say the James Boys done the killing. It's one of old Pink's lies, circulated by his sneaks. I can prove that I was in Texas, at Dallas, on the 12th of May, when the killing was done. Several persons of the highest respectability know that I could not have been in Clay County, Missouri, at that time. I might name a number who could swear to this, whose words would be taken anywhere. It's my opinion Askew was killed by Jack Ladd and some of Pinkerton's men. But no meanness is ever done now but the James Boys must bear the blame for it. This is like the balance of the lies they tell about me and my brother. I wish you would correct the lies the Kansas City papers have printed about the shooting of old Askew, and oblige,

Yours faithfully,

Jesse.

The date of the murder of Askew, given in the above letter, is wrong. That event occurred on the night of *April* 12th, and not *May*, as the writer of the above note assumes.

The following is a characteristic note. It contains several allusions unintelligible to the uninitiated. It was written to an old comrade, who long ago abandoned a "wildlife," and is living as a respectable citizen.

Ft. Worth, March 10th, 1877.

Dear ———— ————:

The beeves will soon be ready. As soon as the roads dry up, and the streams run down, we will *drive*. We expect to take a good bunch of *cattle* in. You may look out. There will be plenty of bellowing after the drive. Remember, it is business. The range is good, I learn, between Sidney and Deadwood. We may go to pasture somewhere in that region. You will hear of it. Tell Sam to come to Honey Grove, Texas, before the 'drive season' comes. There's money in the stock. As ever,

Jesse J.

The following letter was obtained in Colorado, by a gentleman who claims to be well acquainted with the handwriting of Jesse James, and claims that it was dropped by Jack Bishop. As to its authenticity, we leave the reader to judge. It is in style much such a letter as Jesse

James might have written.

Rest Ranch, Texas, January 23rd.

Dear Jack:

We had a little fun on the other side of the line lately. A lot of Greasers came over and broke up several ranches. Some of us were down that way, and "the cow-boys" wanted us to help them and we done it. Some of our cattle had been taken, and I don't owe the yellow legs anything good anyhow. Well, we left some half a dozen or more for carrion-bird meat. We brought the cattle back. I was confounded glad we met some cavalry out after raiders. There was a big lot of them motley scamps, and we would have had a pretty rough time, I expect. But the sneaks got back as fast as they could. You would have enjoyed the racket.

As ever yours,

J.W.J.

The last letter, to an individual, which we here present, is vouched for as being in the handwriting of Jesse James, by Marshal James Liggett. It was written to George W. Shepherd about two weeks after the Glendale train robbery. In this, as in the other notes given above, we have revised the orthography, without correcting the grammatical errors. The letter is without date, and runs as follows:

Friend George:

I can't wait for you here. I want you to meet me on Rogues Island, and we will talk about that business we spoke of. I would wait for you, but the Boys wants to leave here. Don't fail to come, and if we don't buy them cattle, I will come back with you. Come to the place where we met going south that time, and stay in that neighbourhood until I find you.

Your friend,

J.

On many occasions Jesse, has written, or caused to be written, exculpatory letters for publication in the public journals. We present a few of these as specimens of Jesse's epistolary style, and because of the interesting character of their allusions to his own conduct. It will be observed that the dates of outrages on banks and railways, are wrong in several instances, as given in these letters. For instance:

The following communication appeared in the Nashville (Tenn.)

Banner, of July 10th, 1875:

Ray Town, Mo., July 5th, 1875.

Gentlemen:

As my attention has been called, recently, to the notice of several sensational pieces copied from the Nashville *Union and American*, stating that the Jameses and Youngers are in Kentucky, I ask space in your valuable paper to say a few words in my defence. I would treat these reports with silent contempt, but I have many friends in Kentucky and Nashville that I wish to know that these reports are false and without foundation. I have never been out of Missouri since the Amnesty Bill was introduced into the Missouri Legislature, last March, asking for pardon for the James and Younger Boys.

I am in constant communication with Governor Hardin, Sheriff Groom, of Clay County, Mo., and several other honourable county and state officials, and there are hundreds of persons in Missouri who will swear that I have not been in Kentucky. There are desperadoes roving round in Kentucky, and it is probably very important for the officials of Kentucky to be vigilant. If a robbery is committed in Kentucky today, detective Bligh, of Louisville, would telegraph all over the United States that the James and Younger Boys did it, just as he did when the Columbia, Kentucky, bank was robbed, April 29th, 1872. Old Bly, the Sherman bummer, who is keeping up all the sensational reports in Kentucky, and if the truth was known, I am satisfied some of the informers are concerned in many robberies charged to the James and Younger Boys for ten years.

The radical papers in Missouri and other states have charged nearly every daring robbery in America to the James and Younger Boys. It is enough for the northern papers to persecute us without the papers of the south; the land we fought for for four years, to save from Northern tyranny, to be persecuted by papers claiming to be Democratic, is against reason. The people of the south have only heard one side of the report. I will give a true history of the lives of the James and Younger Boys to the *Banner* in the future; or rather a sketch of our lives. We have not only been persecuted, but on the night of the 25th of January, 1875, at the midnight hour, nine Chicago assassins and Sherman bummers, led by Billy Pinkerton, Jr., crept up to my mother's house and hurled a missile of war (a 32-pound shell) in a room among innocent women and children, murdering my eight year old brother and tearing my mother's right arm off, and wounding several others of the family, and then firing the house in seven places.

The radical papers here in Missouri have repeatedly charged the Russellville, Kentucky, bank robbery to the James and Younger Boys, while it is well known, that on the day of the robbery, March 20th, 1869, I was at the Chaplin Hotel in Chaplin, Nelson County, Kentucky, which I can prove by Mr. Tom Marshall, the proprietor, and fifty others; and on that day my brother Frank was at work on the Laponsu Ranch in San Luis Obispo county, California, for J. D P. Thompson, which can be proven by the sheriff of San Luis Obispo County, and many others. Frank was in Kentucky the winter previous to the robbery, but he left Alexander Sayer's, in Nelson County, January 25th, 1868, and sailed from New York City, January the 16th, which the books of the United States mail line of steamers will show. Probably I have written too much, and probably not enough, but I hope to write much more to the *Banner* in the future, I will close by sending my kindest regards to old Dr. Eve, and many thanks to him for kindness to me when I was wounded and under his care.

Yours respectfully,

Jesse James.

The following communications appeared in the Kansas City Times during the excitement succeeding the great train robbery at Rocky Cut, near Otterville, Missouri. The first one appeared in the *Times* in its edition of August 14th, 1876, and the second one came out on the morning of the 23rd of the same month.

JESSE JAMES' FIRST LETTER.

Oak Grove, Kan., August 14, 1876.
You have published Hobbs Kerry's confession, which makes it appear that the Jameses and the Youngers were the Rocky Cut robbers. If there was only one side to be told, it would probably be believed by a good many people that Kerry has told the truth. But his so-called confession is a well-built pack of lies from beginning to end. I never heard of Hobbs Kerry, Charles Pitts and William Chadwell until Kerry's arrest. I can prove my

innocence by eight good, well-known men of Jackson county, and show conclusively that I was not at the train robbery. But at present I will only give the names of two of those gentlemen to whom I will refer for proof.

Early on the morning after the train robbery east of Sedalia, I saw the Hon. D. Gregg, of Jackson County, and talked with him for thirty or forty minutes. I also saw and talked to Thomas Pitcher, of Jackson County, the morning after the robbery. Those two men's oaths cannot be impeached, so I refer the grand jury of Cooper County, Mo., and Gov. Hardin to those men before they act so rashly on the oath of a liar, thief and robber.

Kerry knows that the Jameses and Youngers can't be taken alive, and that is why he has put it on us. I have referred to Messrs. Pitcher and Gregg because they are prominent men, and they know I am innocent, and their word can't be disputed. I will write a long article to you for the *Times*, and send it to you in a few days, showing fully how Hobbs Kerry has lied. Hoping the *Times* will give me a chance for a fair hearing and to vindicate myself through its columns, I will close,

    Respectfully,

                                       J. James.

Second Letter.

                        Safe Retreat, Aug. 18, 1876.

I have written a great many articles vindicating myself of the false charges that have been brought against me. Detectives have been trying for years to get positive proof against me for some criminal offense, so that they could get a large reward offered for me, dead or alive; and the same by Frank James and the Younger Boys, but they have been foiled on every turn, and they are fully convinced that we will never be taken alive, and now they have fell on the deep-laid scheme to get Hobbs Kerry to tell a pack of base lies. But, thank God, I am yet a free man, and have got the power to defend myself against the charge brought against me by Kerry, a notorious liar and poltroon. I will give a full statement and prove his confession false.

Lie No. 1. He said a plot was laid by the Jameses and Youngers to rob the Granby bank. I am reliably informed that there never was a bank in Granby.

Lie No. 2. He said he met with Cole Younger and me at Mr. Tyler's. If there is a man in Jackson county by that name, I am sure that I am not acquainted with him.

Lie No. 3. He said Frank James was at Mr. Butler's, in Cass County. I and Frank don't know any man in Cass county by that name. I can prove my innocence by eight good citizens of Jackson county, Mo., but I do not propose to give all their names at present. If I did, those cut-throat detectives would find out where I am.

My opinion is that Bacon Montgomery, the scoundrel who murdered Capt. A. J. Clements, December 13, 1866, is the instigator of all this Missouri Pacific affair. I believe he planned the robbery and got his share of the money, and when he went out to look for the robbers he led the pursuers off the robbers' trail. If the truth was half told about Montgomery, it would make the world believe that Montgomery has no equal, only the Bender family and the midnight assassins who murdered my poor, helpless and innocent eight-year old brother, and shot my mother's arm off; and I am of opinion he had a hand in that dirty, cowardly work.

The detectives are a brave lot of boys—charge houses, break down doors and make the grey hairs stand up on the heads of unarmed victims. Why don't President Grant have the soldiers called in and send the detectives out on special trains after the hostile Indians? A. M. Pinkerton's force, with hand-grenades, and they will kill all the women and children, and as soon as the women and children are killed it will stop the breed, and the warriors will die out in a few years. I believe the railroad robbers will yet be sifted down on someone at St. Louis or Sedalia putting up the job and then trying to have it put on innocent men, as Kerry has done.

Hoping the *Times* will publish just as I have written, I will close.

Jesse James.

CHAPTER 47

Glendale

The eastern part of Jackson county, the western part of Lafayette, and down southward through Cass county, constitute the very centre of the field of operation chosen by the old Guerrilla leaders—Quantrell, Todd, Anderson, Younger, Pool, Clements, and the Jameses—during the war. The Sni hills and the timber-crowned undulations bordering the Big Blue, afforded them excellent hiding places when sorely pressed, and from their fastnesses in the hills they could easily make forays into the very suburbs of the garrisoned towns of Kansas City, Independence, Lexington, Pleasant Hill and Harrisonville. They knew every pathway over the hills, and every crossing place along the streams.

Around and among these forests were the farms and dwellings of their friends, and warm sympathizers in their cause. Time has wrought some changes in the country since those days; but the forest-crowned hills and the deep, tangled thickets, and the sparkling streams still are there. The face of Nature has changed but little among the hills of the Sni, or along the banks of the Blue. It was meet that the bandits, who are believed to be the same men who once were guerrillas, should come back to the scenes of their earlier adventures, to consummate their latest and most daring robbery.

October 7th, 1879, was a beautiful, sunny, warm day. The woods had not yet assumed the sober brown hues of autumn, but nature was lovely in the rich ripeness of the summer's close. The great tide of human life flowed on in its accustomed channels. Some were engaged in the pursuit of pleasure; some were in search of gain; others were toiling for bread; some were happy in having accomplished their designs; others were wretched in realising the bitterness of disappointment; some were glad in the knowledge that they had contributed to the happiness of their fellow-mortals; others were miserable because they beheld the gladness of their neighbours, and knew of the triumphs of their rivals; some planned good deeds; others plotted dark crimes. These all go to constitute the atoms of the mighty tide of human life; and their plans, purposes and deeds all contribute to the production of the surges and swirls of the stream as it flows through time to the gulf of eternity.

There were always plotters. Since the world began men have schemed, and until the end of time there will be the good and the bad in humanity, sometimes one and sometimes the other quality predominating. And so, while the autumn sunshine was golden, and the wood-cricket's chirp was mournful, the schemers were prodding their brain in the devising of a scheme to commit a grievous crime.

Glendale is a lonely wayside station in the western part of Lafayette county, Missouri, on the line of the Chicago & Alton railway, Kansas City branch. There is a water-tank, a little station-house, and a few houses in a narrow vale, wedged in between rugged hills, which are covered with lofty trees and tangled thickets, a fit place for the rendezvous of a *banditti*.

Glendale is about twenty miles from Kansas City, and on the line of the road between Independence and Blue Springs, in the very midst of a region where many of the darkest crimes and deeds of blood which marked the guerrilla warfare of the border were committed both by the Federal militia and the Confederate Guerrillas. The country about Glendale is one of the wildest regions in Western Missouri, and the hills and dark ravines afford excellent opportunities for the concealment of both men and horses. A better situation for a successful foray by brigands does not exist on the line of the road between Chicago and Kansas City.

The night express train, bound from Kansas City to Chicago and St. Louis, left the Union Depot in the first-named city on the evening of the 7th, at six o'clock, and consequently was due at Glendale at about seven o'clock—a short time after daylight had faded from the west.

Now, as we have before intimated, Glendale is a place with a nice name, but few inhabitants. Though perhaps it is not destined to go down to history with the historic interest attached to Arbela, Malplaquet, Shiloh, Kennesaw or Waterloo, yet so early in its history Glendale has become famous. The incident which contributed so much to this result occurred on the evening of the 7th of October, 1879. In addition to the station-house, the business of Glendale is represented by a post-office and a general store, kept by the postmaster. The evening in question was very pleasant outside of houses, and when the curtains of night were drawn, and the store was lighted, the postmaster and four others, who constituted the male population of the place, except the station agent, Mr. McIntire, had gathered in front of the little store to discuss the neighbourhood's affairs. They were quietly interchanging views. Suddenly a stranger joined the circle, and, walking quickly to where the proprietor was sitting, he tapped him on the shoulder and said:

"I want you."

"What do you want?" asked the other.

The new arrival did not deign to answer the question, but quietly stepped away, and said:

"Here, Boys."

In a minute—nay, a moment—half a dozen rough-looking men, muffled and masked, stood by his side, armed with huge pistols and wicked-looking knives. Their pistols they held cocked in their hands. Then the leader, in a harsh, grating voice, said:

"Now, take care, make tracks out of this!"

The terrified citizens started to obey. As they were going, the leader said:

"To the depot, do you hear!"

In great consternation, the little company of citizens filed away to the depot. In the depot was the operator and agent, Mr. McIntire, and Mr. W. E. Bridges, assistant auditor of the Chicago & Alton railway company, already under duress. When the citizens were all assembled in the room, the leader said:

"Now, sit down, act clever and keep still, or you will not have heads left on you."

Of course, obedience to such an order was just then regarded by all the parties as a great virtue, and they therefore obeyed.

The masked men, who had now assembled to the number of twelve, according to one account—fourteen by another witness—tore away the telegraphic instrument and went out and cut the wires. The instrument was smashed.

"Now," said the leader, whose only mask was a long dark beard, "I want you to lower that green light!"

"But," said the agent, "the train will stop if I do."

"That's the alum! precisely what we want it to do, my buck, and the sooner you obey orders the better. I will give you a minute to lower the light," said the bearded leader, at the same time thrusting a cocked pistol to the face of the agent.

The operator could see the long, bright barrel of the pistol and the dark, cavernous interior of the tube had a forbidding appearance. He looked up into the face of the long-bearded man. He saw a cold, fixed look, and every indication, so far as features could reveal intentions, that the robber chieftain meant just what he said, and he lowered the light. Of course, the position of the light was an order to the conductor to stop at Glendale and receive fresh instructions, according to the code of signals in use among railway men.

But to be perfectly sure of the expected plunder, and in order to destroy even the possibility of the train passing without making a stop, the robbers heaped a pile of cross-ties, fence rails and other lumber across the track. Having completed their preparations, the robbers quietly awaited the coming of the train.

It was a little after seven o'clock. The prisoners in the station-house were wondering about what would happen next, and especially were they concerned and anxious respecting what should happen to them. Then the distant rumbling of the train as heard; louder and louder it fell upon the ears of the listeners. The engineer saw the signal displayed which commanded him to stop. He sounded the whistle and ordered the brakes on. The train stood still on the track, with the engine at the tank.

The conductor, with lantern in hand, sprang upon the platform ere the wheels had ceased to revolve, and was about to proceed to the little station-house to receive his orders. But he had made little progress in that direction, when a man rushed up to him with a cocked revolver, which he held out as if about to fire. This man was speedily joined by another, who was also armed in like manner. Both the men wore masks. Mr. Greeman, the conductor, was of course powerless to resist such odds, and with mingled feelings of alarm and disgust was compelled to await the pleasure of the strange men whom he now knew to be robbers. Two men rushed up to the cab of the locomotive and made prisoners of the engineer and fireman by the presentation of pistols, and the stern declaration that instant death would certainly follow a failure to obey, or an attempt at resistance. One of the robbers, addressing the engineer, called out:

"Hand me that coal hammer of yours!"

"What do you want of it?" asked the other.

"Hand it here very quick, or you'll never have use for another," was the emphatic command of the robber, accompanied by a very significant movement of the pistol arm.

Thus appealed to, the engineer obeyed. The large hammer used by stokers to break coal was handed to the masked *desperado*.

Then a group of the masked men, with the long-bearded man at their head, gathered at the door of the express car. One of the men with the coal-hammer then commenced beating in the door of the car. The messenger, who was in charge of a large sum of money—more than $35,000 in currency, and much other valuable property—was inside, but had refused to open the door. The messenger, Mr. William Grimes, could hear the blows of the ponderous hammer, and knew that his place would soon be open to the marauders. The door was already yielding—it was falling to splinters, and a minute later the car was broken into by the masked and armed robbers. Grimes, in the meanwhile, had formed a hasty plan to escape with the money. While the robbers were beating in the door, he opened the safe, took therefrom a large amount of money, hastily deposited it in a satchel, re-locked the door of the safe, and was in the act of attempting to escape by the other door.

He was too late. The robbers sprang into the car before he was ready to leave it. In any event, escape was rendered impossible by the fact that the other door of the car was guarded. He could only have escaped a part of the band to fall into the hands of their comrades.

When the robbers rushed into the car, after having broken the door open, one of them cried out to the messenger:

"Here, you! Give me that key!"

"I will not. You may take it," answered the messenger.

The words had no more than escaped his lips, when one of the gang in the car dealt him a terrible blow with the butt of a heavy revolver, which felled him to the floor. They took the key, opened the safe, and rifled it of all its contents which were of value to them. They then took the packages from the messenger's satchel, and the great railway and express robbery at Glendale was an accomplished fact.

During the time occupied by a part of the robber band about the express car, a patrol was distributed along the sides of the train, and these were discharging fire-arms at intervals, for the purpose, as is supposed, of intimidating the passengers.

The whole time occupied in completing this great robbery probably did not exceed ten minutes. The whole amount of booty secured was probably fully forty thousand dollars. The passengers were greatly alarmed during these proceedings. Valuables were hastily concealed under seats, about the persons of the owners, and wherever else a place not likely to be examined by the robbers could be found. After concluding the work which brought them to Glendale, the brigands, amid the reports of pistol shots, set up a shout which echoed among the hills for a long distance around, sought their horses, mounted, and rode away through the gloom. They had locked the citizens in the little station-house. These waited until everything seemed still about the place, for the train had moved on, and then they broke down the door and walked out of their temporary prison-house.

CHAPTER 48

Hunting Clues

After the affair at Glendale, the marshal of Kansas City, Major James Liggett, a cool-tempered, clear-headed man, took charge of the case and directed all movements intended to result in the discovery of the robbers. It was soon ascertained beyond a doubt that Jesse James had been in Kansas City only a few days before the robbery. Then the inquiry proceeded as to who else had probably been participants. It came to the knowledge of the marshal that Jim Cummings, Ed. Miller, and a hard character named Blackamore, had been moving about the country in a suspicious way. Little by little, fragmentary scraps of information were secured, and a generalisation of all the facts led to the general conclusion that the train robbery at Glendale had been effected under the direction of the James Boys; that certainly Jesse, and probably Frank, had participated in it, and that Jim Cummings, Ed. Miller and Blackamore were probable accomplices.

The next important point to gain, was information concerning the route travelled by the bandits in their retreat from the scene of their lawless depredation. This was not so easy a task as the uninitiated might conclude. The character of much of the country in western Missouri, with the thorough knowledge of the region possessed by the principals in the outrage, forbade an easy discovery of the route which they had taken. But the marshal had called about him men as well acquainted with the country as any of Quantrell's old raiders could be, and the little information gathered by each one, finally brought together, led to the inference that they had gone in a southerly direction toward the Indian Territory. The inference afterward became a certainty. Their "trail" was discovered.

Men were at once placed at various points on their probable line of retreat; men were dispatched on their trail to hunt them to their places of concealment. There were men in western Missouri who had ridden with the old Guerrilla band, bold, daring men, who laid aside the weapons of destruction when the war closed; men who had never learned the meaning of the word fear, who yet became weary of turmoil and strife, and settled down in life as quiet citizens, who long ago ceased to sympathize with their old comrades in their acts of outlawry, and who, notwithstanding their peaceable demeanour, were subjected to annoying suspicions at every recurrence of the visitations of their former associates; who felt when the train was robbed at Glendale that it was time to take a positive stand on the side of the law and to co-operate with the officers in every endeavour to put an end to such depredations for all time by capturing the depredators.

These persons became active allies of Marshal Liggett in his efforts against the bandits, and materially contributed to the discovery of the robbers and the line which they had chosen on their retreat. So, the active campaign began. There is reason to believe that after the robbery was consummated, at least a part of the band went into Clay County, and remained in seclusion there for some days. Then they started south. It was pending these events that Marshal Liggett made an arrangement with George W. Shepherd, formerly a guerrilla captain, under whom Jesse James served near the close of the war, to take part in the campaign, then about to be prosecuted against the bandits. As subsequent events have brought Shepherd prominently before the public, and the mystery which attaches to some of the proceedings will continue to excite the interest of the public until it is cleared up, it is deemed best to present a brief history of the career of George W. Shepherd in this connection.

CHAPTER 49

George W. Shepherd

The name of George W. Shepherd, which attained prominence during the old Guerrilla times, when he was one of Quantrell's most trusted lieutenants, had passed out of the public mind, in a measure, until the events following the Glendale train robbery once more brought it prominently before the country.

At the time of the affair at Glendale, Shepherd was following a peaceful avocation in Kansas City. It was known to the marshal of that place, and other officers of the law, that the relations subsisting between the James Boys and Shepherd had been rather unfriendly for several years, and overtures were made looking to his engaging in the pursuit of the outlaws. Shepherd's reputation for desperate courage was not inferior to that of any other man in the days when he led a band of Quantrell's men, and when Marshal Liggett, of Kansas City, had obtained his consent to engage in the desperate undertaking, everyone expected some sensational denouement. A history of the Jameses, after the events which occurred since Glendale, would be incomplete without some notice of George W. Shepherd, the man who is credited with engaging in a terrible conflict with Jesse W. James and his followers, near Joplin, Missouri, resulting in the alleged death of the outlaw, and in Shepherd's receiving a severe wound in the left leg.

George W. Shepherd is a son of the late James Shepherd, a respectable farmer of Jackson county, Missouri. He was born near Independence, January 17th, 1842, on a farm now belonging to the Staten heirs. There were two brothers older than George, namely, John and James M., and one brother his junior, whose name was William. J. M. Shepherd is now a respectable farmer in Jackson county. During his boyhood, George resided with his parents on the farm, and when of sufficient age he attended the neighbourhood school for a few months every summer and winter until he was able "to read, write and cipher," as he expressed it. In early youth, he manifested an adventurous and somewhat wayward disposition.

In 1857 he left home and proceeded to Utah, where he joined the army, at that time operating against the Mormons under the command of General Albert Sydney Johnston. The Shepherd family, which originally came from Virginia, were a race of pioneers, and the disposition of the subject of this notice to seek exciting adventure on the borderland of civilization was legitimately inherited.

After a varied experience, and absence of two years, George returned to Missouri in the autumn of 1859, and resumed farming operations with his brothers. He continued in this employment on a farm about one mile and a half distant from Independence, until the commencement of warlike preparations in 1861. Seized by the prevailing military fever, and his surroundings being all Southern, George W. Shepherd was among the first to cast his lot with the Confederate recruits. He enlisted in company A, Captain Duncan's, of Rosser's regiment. This command participated in the great battles fought at Wilson's Creek and Pea Ridge, and engaged in many other skirmishes in Missouri and Arkansas, in all of which he took a part. When the Confederate army, under the command of General Sterling Price, was ordered to the east of the Mississippi, young Shepherd returned to Jackson county, and soon afterward joined Quantrell's command of guerrillas.

The war record of Shepherd would fill a volume if written out in full. For this we have not the space. We can only summarise the chief events in this part of his career. We first hear of George Shepherd in a desperate charge made by Quantrell's men on the garrison at Independence, in February, 1862. On that occasion, he and a comrade, William Gregg, swept down one of the streets of Independence, causing the greatest consternation, an inflicting no little damage on the soldiers of Col. Burris' command. From that day forward Shepherd took rank among the most daring of Quantrell's men.

When Quantrell's small command of twenty men was surrounded at night by a large Federal force, while asleep in the Tate house, near Santa Fe, Jackson County, Missouri, in March 1862, Shepherd was with the guerrillas there, and was selected to guard one of the doors of the house. The conflict which ensued was terrible. After some minutes' fighting, and when the house had been fired, the Federals desired a parley with a view of inducing the guerrillas to surrender. Shepherd commanded the men who defended the lower rooms of the house. He asked for twenty minutes' time.

It could not be granted. For ten minutes. No. For five minutes, then. No, if the guerrillas did not yield within one minute, not a man of them should escape, was the ultimatum of the Federal officer. "Then count sixty," exclaimed Shepherd, "and take the consequences." The fight was renewed. That house had become a pandemonium. In it were such men as Cole Younger, Stephen Shores, John Jarrette, James Little, Hoy, Haller, and others. The Federal commander permitted Major Tate and his family to leave the house. Then the fighting was resumed more fiercely than before. The building was on fire. It was manifest that the guerrillas would be forced to evacuate their fortress. It was resolved to break through the Federal line. Quantrell led the desperate charge, followed by George Shepherd, Jarrette, Younger, Toler, Little, Hoy and others. Seventeen men made the attempt, and succeeded in making their escape. Three had surrendered before the attempt was made.

Once, in the spring of 1862, George Shepherd, Cole Younger and Oliver Shepherd were surrounded at the house of John Shepherd, in Jackson county. Their peril was imminent. The Federal force numbered ten to their one. Cole Younger was about to lead a desperate sortie, when Martin Shepherd, Scott, Little and John Coger came up and attacked the Federals in the rear. The diversion enabled the Shepherds and Younger to escape from the house.

Soon after the incident noted above, George Shepherd and Cole Younger were detailed to go into Jackson County for the purpose of collecting ammunition. They had collected a large amount of the ma-

Burning the Tate House at Santa Fe.

terials of war which were most needed in Quantrell's command. One day they went to find a wagon to convey the ammunition to camp. They were at a house behind which was an orchard, and this had been sown in rye which was now tall and luxuriant. While at this house seventy-five Federal troopers surrounded the place, and demanded their surrender. They refused, and made a rush to the rye-grown orchard ground, where they had hitched their horses.

Beyond the orchard was a skirt of timber, now clothed in luxuriant green. They gained the orchard in safety, although followed by a storm of bullets. Mounting, they made a dash for the forest. But they were not destined to reach it unscathed. Three buckshot had penetrated the body of Cole Younger, and George Shepherd was hit hard and badly wounded. He, however, continued his flight until he reached a shelter where he could, receive surgical attention.

It was about harvest time, 1862, that Major Peabody undertook to capture Quantrell's band by a vigorous movement with superior forces. The two joined issue at Swearingen's place, a few miles from Pleasant Hill, Cass County. A series of desperate encounters followed. The guerrillas were forced to seek shelter in the woods. In the fights which ensued, George Shepherd lost his horse. The guerrillas suffered fearfully, both in the neighbourhood of Swearingen's barn, and later in a depression near Fred. Farmer's house. A number of Quantrell's followers were seriously wounded. George Shepherd had great difficulty in escaping from this sanguinary engagement. He was again wounded, though not severely.

Col, Upton Hayes, Col. Gideon Thompson and Col. John T. Hughes, co-operating, resolved upon attacking Independence, then garrisoned by a Federal force of about five hundred men, under command of Col. J. T. Buell, now of St. Louis. The Confederate forces numbered about seven hundred. Quantrell was requested to aid the enterprise, and joined his forces with the regular Confederate troops in an attack on Independence. George Shepherd was there, and fought with desperate valour. After the battle was over, when Quantrell was asked to name the men of his command who had most distinguished themselves for daring courage, George Shepherd was designated as one among half a dozen others.

In the early days of the autumn of 1862, George Todd, commanding about fifty men, prepared an ambuscade, with rifle pits, on the road leading from Kansas City to Harrisonville. The place was admirably selected, and the utmost caution and vigilance was observed in guarding it, but it came near being a slaughter-pen for the guerrillas. One evening he succeeded in destroying a wagon train, and scattering the escort which accompanied it. But sometime afterward, Gregg, Scott, Haller and Shepherd, with a number of followers, re-occupied the rifle pits. George Shepherd was sent out on the road toward Harrisonville, south of the ambuscade. It was, perhaps, past ten o'clock at night. The rifle pits were still, and the droning hum of insects was the only sound to break the silence. Shepherd was motionless at his post down the road. Suddenly he was made conscious of the presence of an enemy, by a tall form which rose up at his right stirrup—a form which had apparently come from the shadows around him. But it was no apparition conjured up by a disordered brain.

The levelling of a gun barrel at his breast, and the sharp utterance of the single word, "Surrender!" convinced George Shepherd that the form was very real. A glance satisfied him that crouching forms were all about him, and all were armed. He threw himself forward, shot the dismounted trooper in the breast as he whirled his horse around, and received a scattering volley as he dashed away to arouse his comrades in the rifle pits. The Federal forces were under command of Major Hubbard, a gallant officer of the Sixth Missouri Cavalry. He had received full information about Todd's rifle pits, had dismounted his command, and but for Shepherd's extraordinary nerve and presence of mind, he would have made a complete surprise of the guerrilla garrison. As it was, a terrible conflict ensued, and a number of Federals were killed and eight of the guerrillas were wounded, among them Shepherd, who received a slight flesh wound.

In August, 1863, Quantrell began to rally around his standard all the small, detached bands in Western Missouri for his expedition against Lawrence, Kansas. At this time, Shepherd was one of his confidential advisers. In that grim council of war, summoned by the guerrilla chieftain to consider the feasibility of engaging in such an enterprise, George Shepherd sat among the stern, relentless warriors of the border.

When Fletcher Taylor returned from Lawrence, whither he had gone to obtain information concerning the military situation there, and made his report at Quantrell's headquarters to the assembled leaders, the Chief spoke:

"You have heard the report. Before you decide, you should know it all. The march to Lawrence is a long one; in every little village, there are soldiers. We leave soldiers behind us; we march between garrisons of soldiers; we attack a town guarded by soldiers; we must retreat through swarms of armed men; and when we would rest after such an exhaustive march, we must do so with soldiers all about us, and do the best we can. Come, speak out, somebody! What is it. Shepherd?"

Thus appealed to, the answer came deliberately and firmly from George Shepherd:

"Lawrence! I know the place of old. They make no difference there between negroes and white people. It is a Boston colony, and it should be cleared out."

And the others gave similar replies, and so the expedition, which was destined to be fraught with consequences so baleful, was resolved upon. George Shepherd went with the rest of the command, and in the terrors and tragedies of that dreadful day, he had his share.

The winter of 1863-4, Shepherd spent in Quantrell's camp, in the vicinity of Sherman, Texas, leading a comparatively inactive life; but the following summer he was engaged in innumerable skirmishes. At Pink Hill, in Johnson County, at Pleasant Hill, at Keytesville, and many other places the fighting was severe. Then came the mustering to aid General Price. In that summer campaign the guerrillas took a conspicuous part. Toward the middle of September, Bill Anderson was carrying destruction to many neighbourhoods in North Missouri. Todd and Anderson combined, had a force of a little more than two hundred men. In this troop rode George Shepherd. He was present at Centralia. The particulars of that dreadful day's work are given in another place in this volume, and need not now be recited. It may be accepted as a fact that George Shepherd performed his part in that carnival of Death.

Price and Shelby were compelled to retire from Missouri. In a desperate encounter with the Federal advance, in pursuit of the retiring Confederate Army, Todd, who was protecting the rear, was killed. George Shepherd succeeded him in the command, and after lingering awhile in Missouri, he led the remainder of the once formidable band of guerrillas, save about twenty men, who went with Quantrell into Kentucky—to Texas.

The forces under Shepherd had fighting all the way. The Indians beset their pathway and struck at them viciously as they marched. Among those who went to Texas with this force was Jesse James. In the following spring the guerrillas, or at least a part of them, returned. The cause of the Confederacy had suffered. Lee surrendered. Johnston followed. The catastrophe came; the Confederacy was no more. Then the guerrillas of Missouri were permitted to go in and surrender, and all save eight men of the band which Shepherd had led back from Texas surrendered. His career as a guerrilla had ended, and Shepherd went to Kentucky soon after the close of the war.

Geo. W. Shepherd.

CHAPTER 50

Pursuit of the Glendale Robbers

During the days succeeding the robbery, the marshal had learned sufficient to satisfy him that the robbers had gone into retreat in Clay County; and becoming aware of the fact that Shepherd was working in Kansas City, the officer sought him out and engaged him as a detective to assist him in the pursuit. Shepherd consented, and it was arranged that he should, in some way, place himself in communication with the gang. The unfriendly relations existing between Shepherd and the Jameses presented a serious difficulty. The plan adopted to overcome this was shrewdly devised.

A story was told, and industriously circulated, that it was a matter of little doubt that George W. Shepherd was engaged in the robbery, and that in consequence he had tied to parts unknown. This was not all; Marshal Liggett had printed on a slip of paper, already printed on one side, an item to the effect that Shepherd was believed to be implicated in the robbery, it was reported to have been clipped from one of the Kansas City papers.

What follows in relation to this enterprise is based upon the statements of Shepherd. He relates that he went to Clay County, visited the residence of Mrs. Samuels; saw that lady; told her a story about his persecution by the detectives about the Glendale business; showed her the pseudo newspaper clipping, and expressed a desire to become a member of the gang; that he was blindfolded; led a long way, and when relieved of his eye bandages, he found himself in the midst of the gang confronted by Jesse James; that his reception was anything but pleasant, but that finally he was able to convince them that he, like themselves, was hunted; that he became cognisant of all their plans, and then sought and obtained permission to go into Kansas City after having taken a terrible oath to reveal nothing and act true in every respect with the band.

He came into Kansas City, related all that he had seen and heard to the marshal; was furnished a fleet horse, pistols and blankets, and returned to the gang. Liggett was informed by Shepherd that they would leave Clay County at a certain time; that they would cross near Sibley at a certain other time, and would be at a certain place at a certain hour, where he could see them if he so desired. Marshal Liggett, acting upon this information, proceeded to the point designated, and at the hour named he had the satisfaction of seeing a party of armed men cross at the previously announced place, and among them recognised his chosen detective. Shepherd. The robbers passed on southward. Rogue's Island is in the River Marais des Cygnes, not far from Fort Scott. Here the band camped one night. Their plan was to rob the bank of Street & McArthur at Short Creek, Kansas. This was to be effected on Sunday evening, Nov. 2nd, at 3 o'clock.

When Shepherd arrived in the camp on Shoal Creek, about nine miles southeast of Short Creek, he exhibited his pseudo news item to Jesse James, and in other ways succeeded in convincing him that he was also an outlaw, and Shepherd was thenceforward treated as "a man and a brother." He states that the party consisted of Jesse James, Jim Cummings, Ed. Miller, and Sam Kaufman. It has been ascertained that the person who was supposed to be Sam Kaufman was one Blackamore. The plan to rob the bank was known to the authorities, and contrary to the pre-arranged measures for the capture of the outlaws, the guard of armed men who were to have been in waiting at the hour appointed for the raid, went on duty early in the morning. Jesse James that morning went from the Shoal Creek camp to Short Creek, and was in the town when the guardsmen assumed their places, and he noted everything.

Of course, this mistake on the part of those engaged in the efforts to capture them, caused a change in the plans of the gang. Shepherd, well-armed and mounted, rode to the camp in the afternoon, after having been informed by Jesse James of the situation at Short Creek in the morning when they met. He found the brigands much alarmed, preparing to break camp. Mike and Tom Cleary, two of Shepherd's assistants, were to form an ambuscade, but this part of the arrangement failed because of the sudden movement of the band. Shepherd was to proceed to camp, provoke a quarrel with Jesse, shoot him and flee, when of course the other members of the gang would follow.

But the camp was broken up too soon. The ambushers could not reach their place in time. Shepherd relates that they were riding scattered out in the woods; that he was riding near, and a little in the rear of Jesse James; that he suddenly drew a pistol, called out, "Damn you, Jesse James! thirteen years ago, you killed my cousin, Frank Shepherd." At the first word Jesse wheeled his horse and sought his pistol. He was too late. Shepherd fired, the ball taking effect just behind the left ear, and Jesse James fell heavily to the ground. After firing. Shepherd says no one moved for a few seconds, when he, suddenly realising his position, wheeled his horse around, and driving his spurs deep into the animal's flanks, dashed away.

At the same time, Cummings rode furiously toward him, while Miller went to the assistance of the fallen chief. The pursuit of Cummings was persistent and rapid. Blackamore soon fell behind in the chase, but Cummings gained on Shepherd until at last it became necessary for the latter to make a stand and fight it out there. As he wheeled his horse to carry out this resolution, a ball from Cummings' pistol took effect in the calf of Shepherd's left leg. The firing which had been maintained during a chase of three miles, now became quick and furious, and the result for a time was doubtful. At last, Shepherd says, a ball took effect in Cummings' side, and he turned his horse and rode back through the woods by the way they came. Shepherd rode into Short Creek to have his wound attended to.

The foregoing is Shepherd's account of his pursuit of the Glendale robbers and contest with Jesse James. But developments since do not sustain the statements in many important particulars. The relation appears to be correct up to the time of the shooting, but it is now clear that he did not wound Jesse James.

The truth is, that Jesse James was at all times suspicious of Shepherd's motives, and from the time he joined them he was watched with a ceaseless vigilance. The outlaws had little confidence in his protestations, and his movements were carefully observed. They went into camp on Shoal Creek, Shepherd being with them. According to their custom they arranged to remove to another camping place about three miles away the next day. It was Saturday night, and Shepherd obtained the consent of his ostensible confederates to go into Short Creek. One of the brigands, assuming a disguise, followed him for the purpose of watching his movements.

This man discovered that Shepherd was laying a train for the capture of the band. During Sunday morning, it appears Shepherd met Jesse James, who informed him that "the game was up" in Short Creek, and that they had been given away. Shepherd agreed in this view of the situation, and the two separated. Later in the day Shepherd went to the camp, where he had left them. It was deserted, but he found their trail, and followed it to where the new camp was established.

The fact that it was not the place which had been selected in Shepherd's presence ought to have warned him that his situation was one of extreme peril. But it appears that he did not consider this evidence that he was distrusted, and approached the camp. The moment he appeared Jim Cummings opened fire upon him, and mounting his horse gave chase. Both men were well mounted, but Cummings' horse was the superior one of the two. Shepherd, placing the reins of the bridle in his teeth, and drawing two revolvers, the fight commenced. He received a bullet wound in the calf of his left leg, and in turn shot Cummings in the right side, which fractured the sixth rib and wounded the intercostal artery. Some fragments of clothing, driven into the wound, arrested the flow of blood from the artery, else the probabilities are that the wound would have proved fatal. As it was, the surgeon, who has furnished the above facts, removed the foreign matter, took out some fragments of bone, put a ligature on the artery, and in a short time the wounded bandit went on his way.

It is asserted as a fact, that Jesse James was neither wounded nor killed, but rode away a picture of health and vitality. The peril of Shepherd was imminent. Had he not wounded Cummings, that *desperado* would soon have come up with him, when the death of one or both of them would have been inevitable.

The whole relation but confirms what has been reiterated in the pages of this volume, that the resources and shrewdness of Jesse James are truly wonderful; that in all respects he and his brother are men of extraordinary capacity, and that in courage, skill, adroitness, and vitality, they are men strangely endowed. What they may yet accomplish is hidden in the unrevealed future, which to our questioning returns no answer.

CHAPTER 51

Allen Parmer

Allen Parmer is a Missourian. His boyhood days were passed principally in Jackson county. When the late war broke over the country, Allen Parmer was a youth, little fitted to enter the ranks with fighting men. Yet he became a member of Quantrell's band. He first came into prominence among his comrades in August, 1863, at the capture and sack of Lawrence, Kansas. That day Parmer was a member of the squad led by Bill Anderson, who murdered without compunction and destroyed without feeling. He escaped with the rest of the band. He was at Independence; at Lone Jack; at Camden; at Weston; in their lairs among the Sni Hills, and along the waters of the Blues.

He was one of the six men who remained with Todd at Judge Gray's house, near Bone Hill, Jackson County, when Captain John Chestnut arrived in that neighbourhood, in September, 1864, bearing a communication from General Price to the guerrillas, which at once caused a rally of the old partisans. He was selected by Lieut. Geo. W. Shepherd as one of the picked men ordered on a dangerous expedition to the north side of the Missouri. The guerrilla campaign there was short, but bloody. The; terrible massacre and rout at Centralia was the crowning event, and Parmer performed a conspicuous part in that conflict. All through the operations of the guerrillas he was one of the most daring in the band. He was one of the executioners of Bradley Bond, a militiaman of Clay County. He and Frank James captured the man, and afterward he was shot.

When Missouri no longer offered a field for operations, and Quantrell entered upon his last campaign in Kentucky, Allen Parmer was one of the old guerrillas who followed him. The Federal garrison was compelled to surrender at Hustonville, Lincoln County, Kentucky. Thenceforward Quantrell was known in his true character. In a fight in Jessamine county, George Roberson and a member of Quantrell's command, was captured, taken to Louisville, and confined in prison, but subsequently escaped. Afterward he was captured again, taken to Lexington, transferred to Louisville once more, and there arraigned before a court-martial, tried, convicted and sentenced to be hanged on a charge of murdering the Federal major at Hustonville, who fell by the hand of Parmer. Roberson was afterward publicly executed at Louisville.

Parmer took part in all the dreadful frays of Quantrell's little band in Kentucky.

When peace once more brooded over the land, he returned to Missouri, and commenced a commission business in St. Louis, with J. W. Shawhan for a partner, under the style of Shawhan & Co. This was in 1866. It does not appear that the firm was very successful. Parmer is said to have lost several thousand dollars in this venture. Later, the business was closed out. Payne Jones, and some others, among them Jim White, a friend of Parmer, were implicated in a bank robbery at Richmond, Mo. Mayor Shaw was killed at that time. Suspicion attached to Parmer as being one of the robbers, and he was arrested, but, on examination, discharged. Then he led a sort of roving life, for some years, sometimes in Missouri, then in Texas, sometimes in Colorado, then in the Indian Territory. Finally, he came to regard Texas as his home.

In 1870 he returned to Jackson County, where his boyhood had been passed. For a long time, his relations with the James family had been friendly, and when he came to woo Miss Susan James, the sister of Frank and Jesse, she did not deny his suit, and they were married, and removed to Arkansas the same year. He remained in that state during the autumn and winter, and in the spring of 1871 he removed with his family to Texas. For a time, his wife taught a school at Sherman. Subsequently, Parmer established a ranch near Henriette, Clay County, Texas, about 120 miles west of Sherman. Clay County lies on the Red river, directly south of the Kiowa Indian reservation. Here he had all the freedom he desired, and for some years he tended his herds and was prosperous. He frequently made trips to Kansas City, St. Louis and Chicago with droves of cattle.

When the train robbery at Glendale took place, the authorities sought for clues to the robbers in every direction. Mr. Grimes, the express messenger who was knocked down by one of the robbers who wore no mask, was able to give a vivid and minute description of the features of his assailant, and that description suited the personnel of Parmer. Deputy Marshal Whig Keshlear was dispatched to Texas by Marshal Liggett to effect Parmer's arrest. He proceeded to Sherman, where he met and conferred with Mr. Everhart, sheriff of Grayson county. That officer readily consented to assist in the arrest of Parmer, and proceeded at once to his ranch, near Henriette. The officers effected the arrest without difficulty on the 2nd day of November, 1879, under a requisition from Governor Phelps, of Missouri.

Parmer was taken by the officers to Sherman. He was followed by a number of his friends from Clay County. There the prisoner attempted to regain his liberty by a writ of *habeas corpus*. But the judge before whom the writ was returned ruled out testimony, and remanded the prisoner to the custody of the officers from Missouri, in obedience to the requisition of the governor of that state. Parmer took exceptions and appealed. Marshal Liggett, however, had sworn out a warrant for his arrest before a United States Commissioner, charging him with interrupting the United States mail. But this was unnecessary, for, on hearing the case, the state authorities of Texas discharged the writ, and remanded the prisoner again to the custody of the Missouri officers, who at once set out for Kansas City, where they arrived with their prisoner Sunday morning, November 23rd, and Parmer was promptly incarcerated in the Jackson County jail. He emphatically denied all complicity in the Glendale affair, or any knowledge of the parties who accomplished the robbery, and after four weeks' imprisonment he was discharged by the Grand jury, the authorities failing; to connect him, in any way, with the Glendale affair.

ALLEN PARMER.

CHAPTER 52

Jesse James Still a Free Rover

It required no ordinary sagacity to escape the environments which his daring deeds had created for him, after the robbery at Glendale. Had Jesse James been other than a man of extraordinary capacity in great emergencies, his career would have been brought to an inglorious close before the clock of Time would have indicated the commencement of the New Year, 1880. But the destiny which seems to guide him once more manifested itself, and Jesse James, the bandit, rode through difficulties and dangers, and away to repose and freedom on the far-off plains of Texas.

There were many persons who believed that the reported death of Jesse James was true; that the account of the bloody duel between George W. Shepherd and Jim Cummings, was confirmatory of the statement of the former, that he had shot Jesse James. It is probable after that fateful Sunday in the deep recesses of a Southwest Missouri forest, and the terrible peril to which he was there subjected, that Shepherd really believed he had shot Jesse. But, be that as it may, there were many people who resolutely insisted upon it. that Jesse James rode away unscathed. Time has disclosed the fact that they were correct. Several circumstances combine to show that Jesse went away from the vicinity of Short Creek, after the Cummings-Shepherd conflict, in the enjoyment of perfect health.

A few days after Christmas, the newspapers of Kansas City announced the arrival in that city of Mrs. Jesse James, from what point they did not say, perhaps because they did not know. Mrs. James visited relatives and friends in Kansas City for several days, and her conduct was not at all like that of a recently bereaved widow. After spending some days pleasantly in the city, she proceeded with Mrs. Dr. Samuels to the residence of that lady near Kearney, Clay County, which fact was duly gazetted in the society notes of the St. Louis and Kansas City journals.

Mrs. Samuels herself, though professing to believe the reports concerning the death of her son, yet did not act as though the conviction had taken a very firm hold upon her mind. Mrs. Jesse James remained some days at the residence of her mother-in-law, and then suddenly she concluded to visit her relatives and friends in Logan and Nelson Counties, Kentucky. These movements of the supposed widow of the late dreaded leader of the Glendale robbers does not appear to have attracted any great amount of attention from the officers of the law. Indeed, it appears Marshal Liggett had not yet abandoned the opinion entertained by him, that George W. Shepherd had shot and seriously if not fatally wounded the noted outlaw.

One day, after the middle of January, 1880, a young man of respectability, residing in Kansas City, who had been entrusted with a certain message to deliver at Russellville, Ky., called upon another young gentleman of his acquaintance, and invited him to accompany the first-mentioned young man to Kentucky. It was a mistake on the part of the message bearer, for the young man was no admirer of the methods of the chief of the Glendale band, and, after revolving the proposition in his mind, he came to the conclusion to acquaint Major Liggett with the facts in his possession.

This he did. The marshal urged him to accept the invitation, and proceed to Kentucky with his friend. It is intimated that he supplied the necessary funds to enable the young gentleman to make the journey. The two men started. There lives in Kansas City a gentleman who has known the James Boys, and who is not their enemy, even now, (1880). This gentleman received an intimation of what was going on, and learned definitely the aims of the marshal. In half an hour, a message—it matters not what words were employed, they were significant—was sent to Louisville, to a friend. That friend received it, understood it, and a message was at once sent to a person in Russellville. Meanwhile, the conscientious young man and his friend journeyed in the ordinary course of travel toward Russellville. Arrived there, the message-bearer cut his companion of the journey, and the latter could learn nothing to report to the marshal of Kansas City. The person to whom the message came understood precisely what it meant, and the person whom Pinkerton and his employees have often sought, once more found a quiet retreat, where he cannot be readily discovered.

There are several stories afloat with regard to the course taken by

Jesse James after the Cummings-Shepherd conflict. The following is understood to be a correct narrative. Sunday night the party of robbers separated, each man taking a route of his own selection. Cummings was first cared for and left in a secure place. Jesse James made a detour toward the east, arid then turned northward. He remained in St. Clair County two days, and came into Jackson county while the attention of everyone was directed to the marshal's posse pushing down through the Indian Territory to Texas. In Jackson County, he remained for some days, and when it suited his convenience he proceeded to Texas by a route of his own selection, without molestation. Afterward he desired to enjoy a little civilized life and went to Kentucky, where he was joined by Mrs. James. But when the marshal's agent arrived in the region he was not there.

Thus, the great outlaw roves at will over the country, and all the skill of men clothed with authority to entrap him has for so long a time proved unequal to the task. But it is said by those who are in a position to know, that he longs to retire from the business of an outlaw, make peace with society and prove by an exemplary life in the future that his nature is not wholly bad.

CHAPTER 53

Changing a Five-Dollar Bill

The story that George Shepherd killed Jesse James at Short Creek has, in the preceding chapters, already been shown to be fictitious. It was generally accepted at first and continued to be credited; but those who know the Boys best, and who are most familiar with their remarkable resources in trying situations, their wariness, their almost superhuman instinct in detecting the aims of those by whom they are approached, never half believed that Jesse had fallen into the trap laid for him by the Jackson County Marshal. During the year and a half immediately following the Short Creek affair, some of Jesse's acquaintances had the strongest sort of proof that he was still in the land of the living, for he was seen by them, now in Kentucky, again in Texas, and yet again in Leadville and the mining camps of the far Southwest.

What other scenes he and Frank visited during this interval of leisure would be hard to tell, for the Boys are fond of travel and have many disguises. There would be nothing incredible in the story that, under the guise of wealthy ranch-owners, they had taken the waters at Saratoga and the White Sulphur with some of the bank directors whose vaults they had emptied; or that, in the character of Colorado miners with valuable claims to sell, they had sat with their legs under the mahogany of Wall street magnates, tipping champagne glasses with rich and robber-hating stock-holders upon whose trains they had levied tribute. If credulous people would believe that Jesse had been caught napping and shot in the back, so much the better for him; it lessened the vigilance of pursuers and gave the Boys time for a little innocent diversion.

Two incidents, which occurred during the month of July 1881, quickly dispelled any doubts yet lingering in the public mind, as to whether Jesse James was above ground or not.

The village of Riverton is situated in the extreme Southwestern corner of Iowa; and, previous to the date of the event here narrated, Messrs. Davis & Sexton did a right comfortable little banking business there. It was on the 10th of July that two well-to-do cattle traders appeared in the neighbourhood of Riverton and called at the farm of Messrs. Burks & Parsley to examine some thoroughbred horses with a view to purchasing. During the night two of the best horses in the stable disappeared, and next morning the well-to-do cattle traders rode into Riverton finely mounted. They visited the bank, inspected the village and carefully surveyed the roads leading therefrom. Having performed this duty, they went out to the house of farmer McKissick, not far from town, where they got dinner and had their horses well fed and groomed—a precaution which no good horseman neglects when there is a long, hard ride before him.

The mercury stood very high in the Riverton thermometers on the afternoon of Monday, July 11th; business was dull, and cashier Sexton was sitting alone in the bank when these remarkable cattle-traders rode up. They hitched their horses in the rear of the building and, entering by the front door, one of them politely requested the cashier to give him silver in change for a five-dollar bill. With equal courtesy, the cashier turned to comply with the request. Hearing a peculiar sound, he again turned to the man who had presented the bill, and found himself looking straight into the barrel of a long dragoon pistol.

At the same instant, his ear very distinctly caught the harsh command, "Throw up your hands." Though greatly surprised and somewhat shocked, Mr. Sexton did not hesitate about obeying. He elevated both hands as high as he could reach, maintaining his grasp upon the unchanged note; and while one of the strangers kept him covered with the long pistol, the other went behind the counter to get the change himself. The latter individual was naturally in a hurry to set out on his afternoon ride, and did not stop to count the money with any care, but swept into his pouch all the cash he found lying loose upon the table or in the safe. He gathered up all that there was. For when the visitors had taken their leave, the cashier found that he had never a cent to bless himself withal, except that five dollar note, one nickel piece and two copper coins of insignificant value.

Having pocketed their change, the two men requested Mr. Sexton to accompany them to the back door, still holding up his hands; which he did. Reaching the door, they hastily bade him good afternoon, sprang to the ground, bounded into their saddles and with a parting salute from their pistols, rode rapidly away toward the timber in the direction of the Kansas-Missouri line. By the time that his visitors left Mr. Sexton had become very tired of holding up his hands; and, having the fear of the big horse-pistol no longer before his eyes, he promptly slammed the back door, locked it and rushed through the front door into the street brandishing the remaining assets of the bank in the air and calling the people to witness that a couple of evil men had gotten away with a great deal more change than they were lawfully entitled to.

There was a cry, "to arms! to arms!!" and mounting in hot haste by the citizens of Riverton; but Thomas Thompson was the only man who got a shot at the departing bank examiners, and that shot missed its aim. And though the road they had taken was soon swarming with well-armed horsemen in eager pursuit, the pursuers never saw anything of the fugitives except their tracks.

The "cattle traders" got away with $5000 of the bank's money, leaving their five-dollar bill as a memento—clear profit $4,995.

CHAPTER 54

Winstonville

In Daviess County, Missouri, fifty-three miles from Kansas City, dwell the three hundred and odd villagers who have clustered around the railroad station of Winstonville. A few miles further up the railroad is Gallatin, the county seat, memorable as the scene of the famous bank robbery and murder of Cashier Sheets in December, 1869, for which indictments against Frank and Jesse James have long been on file among the dust-covered archives of the Daviess Circuit Court. Twelve miles to the southwest is Cameron.

About a mile east and north of Winstonville the railroad crosses Big Dog Creek, a tributary of Grand River, which in turn empties into Crooked River, and the latter into the Missouri, after traversing Ray County. For a distance of a hundred miles in length by twenty in breadth the valleys of Grand and Crooked Rivers are a continuous stretch of swamps and bayous, nearly every acre of which is covered with timber and underbrush, furnishing as good a cover as Spanish chaparral.

"That's the prettiest country to hide in you ever seed," said an old stock-man who had wintered his cattle in the Grand River bottoms for twenty years. "Thar are lots of them hiding thar, too, and you bet we keep our eyes peeled when we're thar or tharabouts."

But the country right around Winstonville is broad prairie, dotted in harvest time with waving fields of yellow grain, giving evidence of plenty and prosperity, while churches and school-houses at every cross-roads, bespeak the piety and intelligence of the people.

The Chicago, Rock Island & Pacific train which left Kansas City at 6: 30 o'clock on the evening of July 15th, 1881, had proceeded on its way as far as Cameron when it was boarded by four passengers of somewhat rugged aspect but not otherwise specially noticeable. Winstonville was reached a little after nine o'clock, and there three

253

more passengers were taken up, besides John McCulloch and two or three other stonemasons, employed by the railroad company, building bridge piers at the creek. The stonemasons intended, as was their custom, to jump from the train as it moved slow for them at the bridge.

When the train pulled out from Winstonville it carried seven men bent on mischief. Three of them rode in the smoking car; two stood on the rear platform of the baggage car, which was coupled immediately in front of the smoking car, while the two remaining members of the party took their stand on the front platform of the baggage car in good shooting range of the fireman and engineer. The plans of the robbers had been skilfully arranged to secure the contents of the express messenger's safe while the train was running the mile from Winstonville to the creek, and to jump off with their booty when the locomotive slackened speed at the bridge. The two men on the front platform of the baggage car had orders to keep the train in motion, while their confederates bagged the plunder. Fleet horses in the care of trusty confederates awaited the party at a convenient point in the woods.

The locomotive had hardly steamed a hundred yards from the Winstonville depot when Conductor Westfall entered the smoking car and began taking up tickets. The task was quickly completed and the conductor had nearly reached the back door of the car when a burly man in a long linen duster and big black beard, rose in his seat and called after him, "Hold up your hands!" At the same instant, a shot struck him in the shoulder; and, as he turned, a second shot, sped with more deadly aim, entered near the spine and pierced the body of the ill-fated conductor through and through. He staggered out upon the platform and fell off into the ditch. There followed a moment of indescribable confusion during which other shots flew about the car; one more death-stricken man reeled out into the darkness, and one other human form from which life had fled, was found near the stiffening corpse of the dead conductor. It was that of the stonemason, McCulloch; a bullet crashing into the brain had brought his earthly career to a sudden and tragical close.

Amid the consternation attending this bloody and unexpected attack, someone retained presence of mind enough to pull the bell-rope signalling to stop the train. Engineer Wolcott promptly obeyed the signal; but the driving-wheels of the locomotive had scarcely ceased to revolve when his eye caught the dusky outlines of two men, with ready revolvers, sitting on the box of the tender. With rough oaths, they commanded him to go on. The commands were accompanied by several pistol-shots, and the engineer obeyed these latter signals with even greater alacrity than he had shown in stopping the train at the signal of the bell. He threw the throttle-valve wide open, and as the train jumped forward with racehorse speed, all the lights about the locomotive were quickly extinguished, while the engineer and fireman retired to the cow-catcher, leaving those rude fellows in full possession of the cab.

The murderous work in the smoking car was quickly over, and the scene of action as quickly changed to the baggage car, where Messenger Charles Murray, in charge of the U.S. Express Company's safe sat looking over his papers, while Baggageman Frank Stamper occupied a chair near the open door. Four big revolvers were thrust into the faces of the two astonished men, and when the express messenger hesitated a moment about delivering up the key of the moneybox he was promptly knocked down.

Without any further ado the safe was rifled of its contents which were said at the time to amount to $15,000 in cash, though the express officers afterwards, and perhaps for prudential reasons, insisted that the sum total of their cash freight that night was far smaller than this. Having secured their plunder, the freebooters stopped the train about a mile from Winstonville, cut the straps by which their horses were tied to the trees and, quickly mounting, disappeared. None of the passengers on the train had been molested, and the sleeping coach was not even entered.

The robbers rode away in the darkness, and then the sad duty of caring for the dead devolved upon the friends and families of the victims. The remains of the stonemason, McCulloch, were taken to his home at Wilton Junction for interment. The body of Conductor Westfall was borne to Plattsburgh, in Clinton County, where he had provided a comfortable home for his wife and three young children, two boys and a girl. There, on the 17th of July he was buried in the presence of a large concourse of people from Plattsburg and neighbouring towns. The murdered conductor met his fate in the very prime of life and before completing his thirty-ninth year. The portrait, showing a man at the very pinnacle of strength and vigour, has been engraved expressly for this work from a photograph taken not many months before his death. Both the photograph and the facts of his biography here presented, were furnished by his family and friends in Plattsburg.

William H. Westfall was born on the 8th of January, 1843, in

McLean County, Illinois, where his earlier years were passed upon a farm. Later, he was employed as clerk in several neighbourhood stores; and in 1867 he was proprietor of a small confectionery at Kidder, in Caldwell County, Missouri. In September of that year he married Miss Eliza Sweeney, whose home was in Daviess county near Gallatin, and at once engaged as brakeman on the Hannibal & St. Joe railroad. After two years' service in that capacity he was promoted to the position of conductor, which he retained until 1878, when he was employed for a few months as conductor on the Central Branch of the Union Pacific. It was in March 1879 that he entered the service of the Chicago, Rock Island & Pacific road, where he remained until the time of his death. He was a member of the Conductors' Union and also of the Ancient Order of United Workingmen, so that his family was not left destitute.

Not the least weighty of the circumstances adduced to connect Jesse James with the Winstonville robbery is the alleged fact that Conductor Westfall piloted Pinkerton's detectives to the Samuels homestead on the night when the murderous bomb was thrown which shattered Mrs. Samuels' arm and mangled to death her eight-year-old son. But it has been denied that Westfall had any connection with that diabolical night's work, while, on the other hand, the killing of the stonemason and the shooting at the engineer and fireman might be taken to indicate that the conductor fell a victim to the safety or recklessness, rather than to the vengeance of his slayers. And yet, it is a curious coincidence that the long, black beard of the bandit who slew Westfall was also worn by the leader of the band at Glendale nearly two years before.

WM. H. WESTFALL.

Chapter 55

After Winstonville

When they galloped away from the scene of their bold exploit that July night, the Winstonville train robbers did not find it necessary to seek shelter in the thickets of the Grand and Crooked River bottoms. The chances of reaching that refuge, if the enterprise should go wrong or unexpected difficulties should arise on the retreat, doubtless entered into their calculations while planning the outrage. The retreat from Northfield, in which Clell Miller, Charlie Pitts and Bill Chadwell were killed and the Younger Brothers were captured more dead than alive, had doubtless taught Jesse James the value of having a safe cover close at hand in case of accident.

But everything went prosperously with the outlaws on this occasion and, after dividing their plunder at the first convenient place in the woods, the band separated into squads and spent the night under friendly roofs, where their entertainers either dared not or cared not to ask impertinent questions. It would, indeed, have been an easy task for Jesse James to have rolled himself into bed at his old home in Clay county before day-break the next morning, since the ride thither, less than sixty miles, could easily have been accomplished by him in four or five hours.

On Saturday evening, considerably less than twenty-four hours after the robbery, the principal members of the gang passed through Sni-a-bar township in Jackson County, making for Texas and the Indian Territory, over one of their old trails *via* Joplin or Osceola, through a thick belt of timber all the way, as they did after the Glendale robbery when George Shepherd joined them and was lucky to get away with a shot in the leg. By Monday morning the outlaws had ample time to reach their rendezvous around the headwaters of the Sandy River in Indian Territory, and they must have considered it a huge joke when they heard that the Sheriff of Jackson county had set out to head them off on Monday morning, sixty hours after the robbery.

"How far could Jesse James and his gang ride in sixty hours?" was asked of Sam Coffman, an old rough-rider who was always able to prove an alibi when accused of taking a hand in any of the dashing outlaw's exploits.

"Well," he replied after a careful calculation, "they might get in five hundred miles, but they could put in four hundred miles easily. I have done that myself when I was in a hurry. You see, those fellows plan their robberies a long time ahead, and have everything fixed. They have relays of horses every fifty miles or so, and all good stock, fast and gamey. They could have made the Panhandle country of Texas in sixty hours or thereabouts."

"Then the posse struck a pretty cold trail where Jesse crossed Jackson County."

"Cold! I should say they did. If they crossed the trail it was two days old, but I don't believe Jesse and his gang ever crossed Jackson County. I believe they are right around home. They don't commit robberies within a hundred miles of home for the purpose of running away from friends and relatives. They just go to some good hole and pull the hole in after them until the excitement dies away, when they pull up and take a little vacation on the money they made."

Another famous character who had the credit of being a friend and ally of the outlaws was Billy Hudsperth, a well-to-do farmer of Sni-a-bar township near Kansas City, a region whose inaccessible ravines and woods have long made it a favourite hiding place for outlaws. The old man was accidentally found in a communicative mood by a Kansas City journalist a few days after the Winstonville affair, and the explanation he gives of his relations with Jesse and the band will doubtless apply to many other farmers of the border country.

"I'm accused of being Jesse James' friend and confidant and all that sort of thing," said farmer Hudsperth, "but people don't understand it. Now, for instance, I was out in the field one Sunday morning doing some work, getting ready to go to church. I had a fine thoroughbred horse hitched to the fence, saddled and bridled, when who should ride up but Jesse James. Of course I says, 'Good morning Jesse.'

"'Good morning,' says he, jess so.

"'Then says he, 'That's a good horse you have. How much will you take for him?'

"I didn't want to sell the horse, but I knowed he'd take him anyway, so I says $200.

"'Says he: 'I'll give you $300. I've only got $100 with me, and I'll give you the other $200 when I meet you the next time.'

"I was blamed glad to get the $100, so I says 'All right' and he went away. In about two weeks he came riding along and hands me the $200. It's none of my business where he got it, and you bet your life I don't ask.

"Next week, maybe, he comes along with Jim Cummings and the gang, and says he wants to stop all night. Do you suppose I am going to say,'You can't stay here; you're train robbers, and you can't come in?' Not much I don't. I say: 'Come in Jesse; come in Jim, Dick, Ed; how's your mother and the folks? Make yourself at home'; and my barns and stock and family are safe. I pay my taxes, and help pay the county marshal, and I'll be damned if I turn out and do his work for him after paying him. He hasn't any barns, or stock or family to risk."

It is hardly necessary to state than on the day after the Winstonville robbery the Sheriff of Daviess County, with a large posse at his heels, went beating about the bushes in a vain search, or that all sorts of possible and impossible theories were set afloat as to who the robbers might be. Frank or Jesse James, Dick Little, Jim Cummings and Ed. Miller were named with some positiveness as four of the band, and the Coffman boys were mentioned-as probably being the other three; but these latter, on being interviewed at their home on the border of Clinton County, showed themselves ready to prove by trustworthy witnesses that they could not have been within thirty-five miles of Winstonville on the night of the robbery.

The railroad and express corporations doing business in Missouri were especially indignant, and declared that something must be done to stop such depredations upon their property. In the absence of any authority from the Legislature to offer rewards for the capture of the outlaws, Governor Crittenden met representatives of the railroad and express companies at the Southern Hotel, in St. Louis, to see what could be done about it. Several consultations were held and it was finally agreed that these corporations should make up a purse of $50,000.

Accordingly, on the 28th day of July the governor issued his proclamation offering a reward of $5,000 for the arrest and conviction of each person participating in either the Glendale or Winstonville affairs, except Frank and Jesse James, for whom larger sums were offered. For the delivery of each or either of these noted leaders to the Sheriff of Daviess comity a reward of $5,000 was promised, with an additional $5,000 apiece for their conviction of having had a hand in the wickedness done at Gallatin, at Glendale or at Winstonville. Formidable as the governor's proclamation appeared the rewards offered soon ceased to be looked upon as important. The sums named therein were to take the place of all previous rewards offered by any person or corporation, all of which had been previously withdrawn.

Since the mortifying and tragical experience of Pinkerton's men, when the prizes set upon the capture of the James Boys aggregated $75,000, the pursuit of these redoubtable bandits has not been considered the most profitable undertaking that an enterprising man could engage in. And after the narrow escape from their lair of George Shepherd, one of the coolest and boldest of the old guerrilla band, not one man in ten thousand feels the least inclination to stake his own life against the chances of making a capture. The probabilities are that if either of the Jameses is ever taken alive it will be after a most desperate conflict in which at least five of the assailants will be killed for every prisoner captured.

CHAPTER 56

Jesse's Last Exploit

Sam Coffman was right when he expressed the opinion, recorded in the preceding chapter, that Jesse James and his companions did not fatigue themselves by hard riding, after killing Westfall and plundering the express messenger's safe at Winstonville.

For several years, Jesse, had been living in Nashville, Tenn., but, after the capture of Bill Ryan, the bandit decided to leave that place. In March, 1881, Mrs. James went with her two children to visit relatives in Kentucky. In June, Jesse moved his family to Kansas City where they rented a neat frame house on Woodland Avenue, between Thirteenth and Fourteenth streets. It was in this house which they occupied for about three months, close to the scene of the dashing exploit which transferred the cash box of the Fair from the gate keeper to the gang, that the Winstonville robbery was planned.

In Nashville, Jesse lived under the name of C. Harvard; in Kansas City, he assumed the formidable title of T. J. Jackson, a name which might have excited some remark, if its real owner had not been better known to fame as "Stonewall" Jackson. Mr. Jackson appeared to be of a restless disposition, fond of moving. On the 13th of September, which happened to be just six days after the Blue Cut affair, Mr. Jackson rented a house on East Ninth Street, in the first block East of Woodland Avenue; after living there for one month, the family moved to 1017 Troost Avenue, where they remained till the 3rd of November, and then moved to St. Joseph.

Kansas City was about the last place the officers would think of hunting for Jesse, after one of his dashing exploits. Jesse's absence from home, at the time of the Winstonville affair, was accounted for by telling the neighbours that he had gone to some springs for his health; when he returned, greatly improved in health and considerably richer in pocket, he amused himself reading the daily papers and laughing in his sleeve at the smart detectives. Perhaps they were not any too anxious to find him; and even if they had been eager to rush upon certain death, Jesse concealed his identity too carefully for them to discover it.

Notorious as the man had become, and keen as was the curiosity of the public concerning him, the personal appearance of Jesse James was known to but few people, and of those few, not many were inhabitants of cities. With some rare exceptions, his familiars were outcasts and outlaws, who, like himself, avoided the public gaze and made themselves known only to men of their own mode of life. The piercing eye and retiring habits of Mr. Jackson were spoken of by some of his gossipy neighbours, but their surmises went no further than that the keen-eyed, well-dressed stranger, who seemed to have a comfortable living without working, was a gambler. His rent was paid regularly in advance.

For all that the family used cash was paid, so that there was no occasion for clerks or collectors to intrude upon the privacy of the household with bills. Mr. Jackson did not appear to be a sociable person, and when visitors dropped in, as visitors will, his crabbed manners caused them to feel that their room would be more acceptable than their company. Very different was Mrs. Jackson. She rarely or never visited, but the little that was seen of her left the impression that she was an exceedingly kind and neighbourly woman.

While Mr. Jackson and his family continued to live quietly in Kansas City, the sensation caused by the Winstonville exploit gradually faded from the public mind. Nobody seemed disposed to risk their lives in an attempt to earn the large rewards offered for the capture of the train robbers. Interest in the bandits was, however, suddenly revived by an event which occurred less than two months after the Winstonville affair.

On the night of September 7th, 1881, a passenger train of the Chicago and Alton road was pulling along at a comfortable speed through Blue Cut, not far from Glendale, when the waving of a red lantern warned the engineer, Mr. Foote, to tarry a while by the wayside. The engine was brought to a standstill a few feet from a cart-load of stones, which had been carefully piled across the track. The cause of the detention was promptly explained by two men who came down the bank with cocked revolvers in hand, and ordered the engineer and fireman to get the coal hammer and come down out of the cab.

It was an old story in that neighbourhood, and they obeyed without questioning. The admonition of the bandits to do as they were bidden, and all would be right with them, but that if they disobeyed, they would be shot, was wholly superfluous. They knew that without telling. Other members of the gang surrounded the train and began banging off guns and pistols, to encourage the passengers and trainmen to behave themselves as fitted the occasion.

All the robbers wore white masks except one, who wore a red handkerchief and said that he was Jesse James. Presently Mr. H. A. Fox, messenger for the U. S. Express Company, heard a pounding upon the door of his car. He opened the door and there stood two masked men, escorting the engineer with the coal-hammer. Mr. Fox knew at once what was wanted, but he waited for orders. He and the baggageman were ordered to get out of the car; the robbers then entered and messenger Fox went and sat down by the side of the track to await further developments.

Pretty soon he was told to come back into the car and open the safe, a proceeding which the robbers thought was easier than knocking it open with the coal-hammer. When the safe was opened only $500 or $600 was found inside, and the bold bandits began swearing at the smallness of the amount. Words being wholly inadequate to do justice to the occasion, they gave forcible expression to their disappointment by knocking Mr. Fox a double somersault with the butt of a pistol. They also made him surrender his own purse and watch. The watch he afterwards recovered from a pawn shop in Louisville, Ky., where "mine uncle" said Woot Hite had sold it. Having made a water-haul in the express car, the robbers decided to relieve the passengers of their spare cash and other valuables. Putting the trainmen under guard, three of the freebooters systematically went through the train, and demanded the passengers' contributions. Most of the passengers responded liberally, and, of course, promptly.

The man who called himself Jesse James seemed to take quite a liking for engineer Foote, and tried to induce him to leave the railroad and take to the highway, but the offer was politely declined. He also introduced Mr. Engineer to "my friend Dick Little," and the two men shook hands. Jesse then shook hands with Mr. Engineer, told him goodbye, and the train went on its way at a lively speed—to make up for lost time. Dick Little (whose real name is James A. Liddil) afterwards said in his "confession," that only six men were engaged in the Blue Cut robbery, *viz*: Frank James, Jesse James, Jim Cummings, Woot Hite, Clarence Hite, and Dick himself, but the trainmen all swore that there were from nine to a dozen. It has also been stated that Charley Ford, one of the men who afterwards killed Jesse James, took a hand in the robbery and pocketed a part of the plunder.

The Blue Cut robbery stirred up the officials to renewed activity, and a raid was made into the Cracker Neck region, where they arrested Creed Chapman, John Bugler and a well-digger named John Land. The prisoners were confined in the jail at Independence, and prodigious efforts were made to secure a confession. Finally, one was obtained from the well-digger. Land. Several other arrests were made on this man's statement, but he finally confessed that his "confession" was a string of lies from beginning to end, and all the prisoners were released.

Chapter 57

Gathering Clouds

In the days of peace and plenty, before the war, Mr. George Hite, a thrifty farmer of Logan County, Kentucky, married a sister of the Rev. Robert James, by whom he had three sons, George Hite, Jr., Wootson and Clarence. They were, of course, first cousins of Frank and Jesse James. George Hite, Jr., became a cripple owing to some spinal disease, and is, or was at the date of the events here narrated, a successful merchant doing business in a large country store near Adairsville, in Logan County.

George Hite, Sr., owned a fine farm about twelve miles from Russellville; until the bulk of his fortune was lost in a tobacco speculation, he was rich, and when Frank and Jesse found themselves in trouble at the close of the war, they were welcome visitors under his roof. Their visits continued, though in the course of time they became anything but welcome. The companions they brought with them often disturbed the peace of the household, and certainly added nothing to the old man's tranquillity of mind. His first wife having died, the old man married the buxom and dashing widow Peck, much against the wishes of the sons, with whom she was never on good terms.

It appears that after this marriage, Woot decided to go in regularly with Jesse James, and took part in the Glendale, Winstonville and Blue Cut robberies. Clarence Hite escorted Mrs. Jesse James to Kansas City from Kentucky, in June, 1881, and assisted in the Winstonville affair six weeks later, and was also at Blue Cut. Dick Little has since "confessed" that it was Woot and Clarence Hite who murdered Westfall, but slippery Dick's statements cannot be accepted as gospel truth.

After the Blue Cut robbery, Woot and Clarence Hite returned to their Kentucky home. The young stepmother had a special aversion for Woot, though neighbourhood gossip said that she entertained a tender regard for the gallant Jesse James. Woot had also incurred the hatred of Dick Little, with whom he had once had a shooting match in old man Hite's barnyard, in which neither combatant was hurt, and neither covered himself with glory. The hatred of this man and of this woman cost Woot Hite his life, and the murder of Woot Hite incidentally hastened the fate of Jesse James. When Woot returned to Kentucky, Mrs. Hite gave information to the authorities which caused him to be arrested for an alleged homicide committed in Logan County some time before. He made his escape, fled to Missouri, and sought refuge at the home of the Fords in Ray County.

There he was murdered about the first of December by Dick Little and Bob Ford. His body, with a bullet hole in the temple and clad only in under garments, was found buried in an old spring a few hundred yards from the house, and an inquest was held, Mrs. Bolton, sister of the Fords, being the only witness examined. This inquest was on April 5th, 1882. She testified that Woot Hite was killed in a desperate fight which took place in the breakfast room, his opponents being Bob Ford and Dick Little. But the fact that the body was almost naked when found, led many to believe that he was murdered while asleep in bed.

The Ford boys, who play so important a part in our story, were born in Fauquier County, Virginia. In 1871 their father, J. T. Ford, moved to Missouri and settled on a farm in Clay County, a few miles above Fredericksburg, Ray county. In 1877 the family moved to a farm near Richmond, Ray county, and then the farmers of the neighbourhood observed that their horses suddenly contracted the habit of "mysteriously" disappearing. It was also observed that the Ford boys occasionally made mysterious trips from home, and returned after several days pretty flush of money. Bob, Charley and Cap. Ford were all suspected of belonging to the train robbing band, though their neighbours never got much enlightenment on this interesting subject.

In the summer of 1879 the widow Bolton rented the old Harbeson place near Richmond, and she, Charley and Bob pretended to go to farming for themselves; but the latch of their door always hung on the outside for any member of the gang. According to Charley Ford's statement, it was here that he first met Jesse James, who visited the house in August, 1879, with Ed. Miller, and was introduced as Mr. Jackson, "a sporting man who gambled and drank a little," and "so did I" added Charley. From this incident, it will be seen that Jesse James acted a diplomatic part, and endeavoured to be "all things to all men."

On his first visit to the Harbeson place, he gambled and drank just enough to make a favourable impression on the Fords. They were already identified with lawlessness in that region, and Jesse was on the lookout for fresh recruits. Jesse made several other visits to the place at considerable intervals, and considered the Fords trusty members of the gang; he paid his last visit there shortly before the Blue Cut robbery.

For months before the death of Woot Hite, Bob Ford had been playing a double game. As early as the summer of 1881, he was in communication with the police at Kansas City, but he was careful not to tell them too much. His cupidity was excited by the large rewards offered for the train robbers, and after the murder of Woot Hite, it was easier for him to make terms with the officers of the law than with Jesse James. In the following January, he told Chief of Police Speers, of Kansas City, about the Woot Hite murder, and piloted a raid against the Harbeson place, where Dick Little was laid up with an ugly wound in the leg. The officers came near catching Dick, but he crawled out of the house with a pistol in each hand, and hid in the brush until the posse had left.

Dick, himself, was not anxious to meet Jesse James, and shortly after this incident, he surrendered to Sheriff Timberlake, of Clay county, on promise of full pardon and a cash reward for his services in entrapping the rest of the gang. Negotiations in behalf of him and Bob Ford, were conducted by the widow Bolton, the "veiled lady," who held several mysterious interviews with Gov. Crittenden at Jefferson City. Soon after "coming in," Dick went with a party of deputies to Kentucky, where they succeeded in capturing Clarence Hite, who was brought to Missouri about the first of February, and sentenced to twenty-five years in the penitentiary.

CHARLEY FORD.

BOB FORD, the slayer of Jesse James.

CHAPTER 58

Death of Jesse James

While Jesse James and his family were keeping house in Kansas City, the only resident who knew of their presence there was John Mimms, a brother of Mrs. James. Even her sister, Mrs. McBride, was not admitted to their confidence. In September Mrs. Frank James visited Kansas City, with her children, registered at the St. James Hotel under an assumed name, and met her husband at Jesse's house on Troost avenue, remaining in the city several days. One of the papers published an account of her sojourn at the hotel, but so improbable did the story seem that it was derided as a "newspaper sensation." The fact of the visit was, however, afterwards confirmed by Jesse's widow among her reminiscences of her husband's last residence in Kansas City.

Jesse used frequently to run over on the train to visit his mother at Kearney, and though careful to avoid the notice of inquisitive persons he sometimes ran considerable risk of detection. On one occasion, just after leaving Kansas City, the conductor taking up tickets noticed that a certain passenger had lost a finger-joint and on going through the train a second time he asked the passenger if he were not Jesse James, saying that Jesse was minus a finger. The passenger expressed much surprise and some indignation at such a question, and the conductor, perhaps, thought it prudent to keep his suspicions to himself.

In October, just before moving to St. Joseph, Jesse paid a farewell visit to the Samuels' place, and there he met Charley Ford, who said that he was fleeing from the officers, and asked to be protected. This appeal to the outlaw's generosity was not made in vain. He replied that the Fords had frequently protected him, and that he would befriend them; that he was going to St. Joseph shortly, and there Charley Ford should be sheltered and live safely under his roof. The plot to murder

FRANK JAMES, at the Age of Sixteen.   JESSE JAMES, at the Age of Fourteen.

Jesse James had already been formed between Charley and Bob Ford; and the story just mentioned was concocted simply that one of the assassins might be a spy upon his movements, while the other perfected the remaining details.

Jesse saw no imminent danger in remaining at Kansas City, but he knew the officials were on the alert, and he feared that some of them might accidentally stumble upon him. Accordingly, on the 3rd of November, his household effects were placed upon a wagon and with his family, accompanied by Charley Ford, he set out for St. Joseph. They arrived there on the 9th, and rented a house at the corner of Lafayette and Twenty-First Streets, Jesse taking a receipt for the first month's rent in the name of Thomas Howard—it was the last of his many disguises.

On the day before Christmas they moved to a neat frame cottage of seven rooms on Lafayette street, near Thirteenth. The house was painted white, with green shutters; there was a pretty yard around it, and a stable for two or three horses. It had been built some two years before by a solid citizen of St. Joe, an alderman, and stood on the brow of a lofty eminence, commanding a view of the city and surrounding country in three directions.

On the west, the plateau stretched away to a belt of timber, whither escape would be easy if danger threatened. A block or two away was the World Hotel, and the neighbourhood, though not the most fashionable, was occupied by many of the best and wealthiest citizens of St. Joseph. A less audacious man in Jesse's situation would have feared to intrude into such a neighbourhood, but audacity was part of Jesse's nature; besides, it was the last place that prowling detectives were likely to hunt for him.

Jesse generally kept himself pretty close withindoors during the day time, only going out in the evening to buy the Kansas City papers and to look about the town. But while he avoided exposing himself too freely to observation, he did not, by any means, make himself a close prisoner whilst the sun was shining. He turned out to see the sights on holidays, such as St. Patrick's Day, and his neighbours not infrequently met him on the street at all hours in various parts of the city. The family were under less restraint than at Kansas City, and some acquaintances were formed who will always remember "the Howards" pleasantly.

Speaking of the children—Jesse Edwards, an uncommonly bright lad of seven years, named for his father and Major John Edwards, of the Sedalia, Mo., Democrat, and a lovely little girl of three,—a St. Joseph lady who frequently visited the house is even reported to have said: "No children could be brought up better than they were. Mrs. Howard used to take them to Sunday school regularly. She would read to them from their Sunday school papers and teach them to pray, and I know that they were good children. I fairly adored them."

Mrs. James is said to have been a frequent attendant at the Presbyterian church, close by. The general impression of the neighbours concerning Mr. Howard was that he was a retired business man; he seemed familiar with the ways of the world; dressed plainly, but neatly; was cleanly about his person and always looked presentable.'

"I am sure," said the wife of the family physician who was fre-

The House where Jesse James was killed.

JESSE EDWARDS JAMES, only son of Jesse James.

MARY JAMES, only daughter of Jesse James.

quently called in to attend Mrs. Howard, "that, if he had been given an opportunity, he would have been an ornament to society."

While Jesse was living in this way, with the good will of his unsuspecting neighbours, fatal mischief was brewing. Charley Ford, under the name of Charles Johnson, a relative of the family, was eating his bread and patiently biding his time to act with foes from without. Dick Little's treachery and the capture of Clarence Hite, of course, were known to Jesse as soon as they became public—perhaps sooner. But the fate of Woot Hite he never knew, and the fidelity of the Fords he never doubted until he heard the click of their pistols the instant before he was hurled into eternity. In January Bob Ford proposed to Police Commissioner Craig, of Kansas City, to get rid of Jesse James, and earn the large reward offered for his capture.

Craig hardly knew what to think of the proposition, but Gov. Crittenden was sent for, and on the 13th of January, 1882, Bob had a secret interview with him at the St. James Hotel. Gov. Crittenden paid a second visit to Kansas City, ostensibly to take part in the ball of a militia company on Washington's birthday, and on the night of Feb. 22nd, he had a second interview with Bob Ford at which the final arrangements were agreed upon.

Bob's first plan was to go back to Ray County and raise a party to watch the Harbeson place, so that if Jesse came around they could surprise and kill him. But the weather became bad, and this plan was soon abandoned for an easier one, involving baser treachery. Towards

JESSE JAMES AT LONG BRANCH.

the end of the second week in March, Jesse set out with Charley Ford on a reconnoitring tour in northern Kansas and southern Nebraska, having previously addressed the following letter to Mr. Calhoun, a land agent at Lincoln:

> Mr. J. D. Calhoun, Lincoln, Neb.—Dear Sir: I have noticed that you have 160 acres for sale in Franklin County, Neb. Please write to me at once and let me know the lowest cash price that will buy your land. Give me a full description of the land, etc. I want to purchase a farm of that size, provided I can find one to suit. I will not buy a farm unless the soil is No. 1.
>
> I will start on a trip in about 8 days to northern Kan. & southern Nebrask., and if the description of your land suits me I will look at it and if it suits me I will buy it. From the advertisement in Lincol Journal I suppose your land can be made a good farm for stock and grain.
>
>   Please answer at once.
>   Respectful
>
>   Tho. Howard
>   No 1318 Lafayette St.,
>   St. Joseh
>
> March 2nd, 82.   Mo

The letter was answered by an epistle giving a glowing account of the land, and of the social, religious and educational advantages accessible thereto; but it seems that Jesse paid much more attention to a careful inspection of the banks in the villages along the line of his tour than to the character of the soil on that particular farm in Franklin County. Jesse declared himself best pleased with the bank at Forest City, and wanted to rob it forthwith, but Charley Ford begged off on the ground that he was sick.

Before returning to St Joseph, they went down among their old haunts, where Charley visited his brother Bob, "and told him what he wanted." They agreed to go together and to kill Jesse James at the first opportunity—when his pistols were off and his back was turned. Jesse received Bob as a recruit for the next bank robbery. The three men then proceeded to the Samuels homestead, where John Samuels, half-brother of the outlaw, was lying dangerously wounded, having received a bullet through the breast in a brawl at a neighbourhood dance. Two days were spent at the Samuels' house, and the two assassins, with their unsuspecting victim, then set out for St. Joseph on horseback, Bob Ford riding an animal that was stolen from a neighbouring barn for his special benefit. It was the bandit's last ride. The party arrived at Jesse's house on Sunday night, March 26, and then began the death watch which was never relaxed till Bob Ford fired the fatal bullet eight days later.

Monday, April 3rd, 1882, dawned warm and bright at St. Joseph. Mrs. James was unwell, and Jesse spent the early morning assisting her about the household duties. After breakfast Jesse and Charley went out to feed and curry the horses; between eight and nine o'clock they returned to the house and entered the front room, which was occupied by Jesse as a sleeping apartment. With an ivory handled pistol presented him by the man whom he was about to slay, Bob Ford was there patiently waiting for the golden moment to arrive when he should find Jesse James unarmed and with his back turned.

The opportunity came sooner than was expected. Jesse was heated by the labours of the morning, and with an exclamation of discomfort, pulled off his coat and tossed it upon the bed. Then, lest passersby might get a glimpse of the formidable weapons which he always kept belted around him, he unbuckled the belt, and that also was tossed upon the bed. At last Jesse James stood unarmed before the two men, but face to face with him, they still dared not draw a weapon; with even half a chance for the life which years of crime had placed

DIAGRAM ILLUSTRATING THE DEATH OF JESSE JAMES.

F. D.—Front Door.
B. R.—Bed Rooms.
1.—Jesse James standing upon a chair to dust a picture.
2.—Charley Ford, with revolver ready.
3.—Bob Ford, with revolver raised close to the back of Jesse's head.

beyond the *aegis* of the law, his wonderful nerve and quickness might still be too much for them. But see! He takes a dusting brush, steps upon a chair to sweep the cobwebs from a picture, and turns his face to the wall.

Instantly two deadly revolvers are drawn, one of them is thrust close to the bandit captain's head, and a quick pressure upon the trigger of Bob Ford's pistol sends a slug through his brain. Suddenly as it was done, the first movement did not escape the acute ear of Jesse. He turned his head a little at the click of their revolvers, but it was too late. The nerveless body swayed a little, and fell to the floor, whence it was raised a minute later by the faithful wife, who came hastily from an adjoining room. There was a faint semblance of life as the wife lifted her husband's head upon her lap, and an effort as if the dying man would have said something, the lips moved slightly, but no word came; they were silent forever.

Still the poor woman kept trying to wash away the blood which trickled from a gash over the left eye, but, she pathetically said, "It seemed to come faster than I could wash it away." The ball had lodged inside the skull, but the brutal slayers tarried a moment before running from the room, to strike the face with the butt of a pistol or some sharp instrument, and hence the wound over the left eye.

The news that Jesse James was killed flew quickly over the country, but at first was received incredulously. The assassins themselves were the first to tell it. They hastened from the scene of the murder to the nearest telegraph office, whence Bob Ford sent triumphant messages to Police Commissioner Craig, Sheriff Timberlake and Gov. Crittenden, saying:

"I have got my man."

They then sought the St. Joseph officials who took them into custody, detaining them rather longer, it must be said, than they had expected. Mrs. James also sent messages to her brother, John Mimms, and to Mrs. Samuels, asking them to come to her immediately. The body of the outlaw was taken to an undertaker's establishment, whither thousands of people flocked to gaze upon the placid features of the extraordinary man who in life had borne a name of terror.

At three o'clock in the afternoon, an inquest was begun at the Court House, the widow of the dead outlaw being the first witness. She who now for the first time publicly acknowledged that she was the wife of Jesse James, was an attractive looking matron of thirty-five summers, much of whose youthful beauty still survived the hardships, the sorrows and anxieties of an eight years' union with her wayward but ever affectionate husband. She was clad in a neatly fitting dress of black silk, and answered the questions concerning her married life with a simplicity and candour that were almost touching. She was married to Jesse James, she said, on the 24th of April, 1874. They first went to Texas, where they resided for about six months—on the ranch described in the earlier pages of this volume; then returned to Kansas City for a year; moved to Nashville, where they remained until March, 1881; then to Kansas City again, and lastly to St. Joseph, where the strange, eventful drama of the outlaw's life was brought to a tragical close.

Curious as it seems, the greater part of those eight years was passed by Jesse James in the bosom of his family, living much as other people live, for the most part frugally and economically. A wayward, unyielding nature, tempered to still greater hardness in the revengeful feuds of the border war, had made him an outlaw, put the brand of Cain upon him and shut him out from peaceful pursuits. It is a mistake to suppose that he earned his money easily, and spent it recklessly. For every dollar that he got, in whatever way, he incurred a terrible risk of violent death, of disabling wounds, and, worst of all, of capture. He seemed to be perfectly aware of all this, and went into those perilous enterprises of his only when necessity compelled. The sagacity and energy displayed, in planning his robberies, would have yielded a tenfold richer reward if they had been exerted in legitimate avocations, to which, during his later years at least, it is said he was anxious to settle down.

But what of the Fords? They were indicted for murder in the first degree, and on the 17th of April, plead guilty to the charge. The judge then sentenced them to be hanged on the 19th of May, but they were immediately pardoned by the governor. Bob Ford was at once re-arrested for his part in the murder of Woot Hite. In view of their many other offenses, and with the spectre of vengeance stalking at their heels, the future does not seem bright for them.

Mrs. Jesse James.
Formerly Miss Zee Mimms.

Chapter 59

Jesse's Last Resting Place

On the morning after the final tragedy, Mrs. Samuels, accompanied by her daughter, arrived in St. Joseph, and was at once driven to the late home of her son. The meeting between the mother and her widowed daughter-in-law was a sad one, and stout hearted men turned away unable to witness their emotion without shedding tears. As soon as the wife, between tears and sobs, had told her sad story, the three women re-entered the carriage and were driven to the undertakers to gaze upon the lifeless clay reposing there. When Mrs. Samuels entered the room she almost swooned, and with difficulty rallied and supported herself. Her grief over the inanimate form of her idolised son was uncontrollable, and her tears flowed fast.

At length, the party again entered their carriage and were driven to the Court House, where the coroner's inquest was still in session. Mrs. Samuels testified that the body at the undertakers was that of Jesse James, and bitterly denounced many of the falsehoods circulated concerning him. As she was leaving the court room, her eye rested for a moment on Dick Little, who was standing near the door; then she turned upon him with the fierceness of a tigress: "Traitor, traitor, traitor!" she exclaimed excitedly, "God will send vengeance on you for this. I would rather be in my poor boy's place than in yours."

Dick cowered like a whipped dog before the stormy rage of the bereaved mother, and turned pale and red by turns. "I did not hurt him," he stammered. "I thought you knew who killed him."

Half a volume would not suffice to narrate in full all the scenes and incidents enacted in St. Joseph during the days immediately succeeding the tragedy—the wrangling of officials, stories of armed comrades of the dead man riding about the city, other stories that Frank James was on the scene ready to wreak a terrible vengeance, etc. On Wednes-

FRANK AND JESSE JAMES.

day, April 5th, the mortal remains of Jesse James, in a handsome casket, were given over to the bereaved family, and a special train bore them to Kearney. On the train were Mrs. Samuels, Mrs. James and the children, Marshal Enos Craig, of St. Joseph, Sheriff Timberlake, of Clay County, and numerous friends and relatives of the deceased.

Never before in its history did the little village of Kearney contain such a throng as that which came on Thursday to witness the funeral of the famous outlaw. The country roads were deep in mud, but almost before the sun was up, singly, in couples and by groups, men began arriving on horseback. As the day advanced the throng increased, and among them were many women, some of whom carried children in their arms. The public schools were dismissed, and business of all kinds was suspended. Railroads trains were even stopped, to give the passengers an opportunity to look upon the face of the man whose exploits had, in times past, lent the zest of danger to western travel.

At two o'clock the hearse bearing the coffin led the way to the Baptist church, where Jesse had professed religion upon his return from the war, and where the funeral services were now to be performed.

The exercises were begun by singing the hymn "What a friend we have in Jesus." Prayer was then offered by Rev. R. H. Jones, of Lathrop, after which there was an impressive discourse by the pastor. Rev. J. M. P. Martin, and another hymn concluded the services. At half past four the procession was reformed and passed back to the principal street where the hearse, followed by carriages bearing the mourners and near friends, turned northward towards the Samuels residence.

Back from the main road, some four miles from Kearney, so hidden by a gentle eminence on its southern side that it cannot be seen by the chance passer-by, stands the early home of Jesse James. A grass-grown yard of perhaps an acre surrounds the house; and under the summer shade of a great tree in the southwest corner of the yard a deep-dug grave awaited its occupant. When the funeral procession arrived from Kearney, some three hundred people from the neighbourhood were ready to receive it; but none save relatives were admitted to the house when the casket was taken in for the purpose of permitting the dying John Samuels to look upon the face of his half-brother.

Those who ought to know say that John Samuels was not the only brother of the dead Jesse, who looked upon his face on that occasion. Frank James was in the house, having arrived on Tuesday night, and in this way alone could he view the body with comparative safety. But if Sheriff Timberlake and other officers present entertained such a suspicion, they made no attempt to take advantage of it. The crowd was

THE SAMUELS HOMESTEAD.
At C is shown the grave of Jesse James.

armed, from man to boy, and no arrest of one brother could have been made in that yard over the grave of the other. There were wild scenes of passionate grief on the part of the mother and widow during the final services at the grave, and Sheriff Timberlake quailed when Mrs. Samuels turned furiously upon him with the words:

"The blood money murderers! When you spend the money, Mr. Timberlake, remember where it came from."

A hymn at the grave, remarks by the Rev. Mr. Jones, suggesting that God and not man must judge the dead, a prayer by the Rev. Mr. Martin, a few softly thrown shovelfuls of earth, a reluctant dropping away of the throng until only scores remained, then little knots, and then a group of leave-taking relatives—these were made and seen and all was done. The great outlaw had gone from the sight of men to his allotted space of earth. After his soul, his body fled; memory alone remained to mark his name among the living—memory and a mound.

Mrs. Samuels, mother of Jesse and Frank James, is a woman of wonderful powers, great self-control and indomitable energy. Her children have inherited these traits of their mother, taking from the weaker nature of their mild-mannered father little but his name. To these qualities Mrs. Samuels adds a vindictive, unrelenting spirit which could not forget and would never forgive an affront or injury.

In person, Mrs. Samuels is commanding, but the effect of her height is somewhat lost by the breadth of her shoulders and an inclination to flesh, which is checked just this side of corpulence. She has been well educated and talks with a force and fluency which impress everyone with whom she comes in contact.

The writer has frequently met her, and just after the body of the great outlaw had been lowered into the grave, within the dooryard of the old homestead, he sought her out and requested an interview. After the purpose had been explained, she said:

"I hope you will do Jesse and me justice. There has been so much written about him that is untrue and shameful, that I would really like to see a book in which he was spoken of with truth."

She was assured that what she might say would be given to the world precisely as it left her lips, and she appeared satisfied.

"In the first place," said Mrs. Samuels, "I have been accused of ignorance, and my first husband has been spoken of as a man of inferior attainments. I would have it known, sir, that I came from Woodford County, Kentucky, and that there is no better blood in this country than ours. There is a royal red coursing through my veins," and here she drew herself up proudly.

"Did you believe that it was really Jesse who had been shot and killed, when you heard the news?" was then asked her.

"I feared so, yes;" and she sobbed convulsively, "I knew it was my boy. I knew he was in St. Joe, though it has been published that I denied this, and I was at once sure that base treachery had made him the victim of its bloody hand."

"To whom, Mrs. Samuels, do you ascribe the killing—that is, who incited it?"

"O! to Crittenden and Sheriff Timberlake. Timberlake and Commissioner Craig of Kansas City, also, have been working together in pursuit of my boy for over a year. That traitor Ford was only a tool in their cunning hands. He is only a boy, and they moulded his nature until he was ready to undertake an assassination none of the others dared attempt."

"Do you believe that Jesse ever suspected him?"

"Well, he didn't have any too much confidence in Bob, but he trusted him for Charley's sake. Why, Jesse sheltered and fed and clothed them both. He gave them money, and was more than a brother in kindness to them. Oh! the miserable traitors! It was only three weeks ago today that Charley Ford was here. I cooked for him with this one hand. (Here she dramatically held up her remaining hand and shook it as if in an appeal to vengeance on the murderer of her son.) I did all I could for him, and when he went away, I went out to the gate with him and said: 'Charley, something tells my heart there is danger lurking around Jesse. You will always be true to him, won't you? He would not look me in the eyes, but he raised his hand to heaven and said: 'I call on God to witness that I will protect him with the last drop of my blood.' And then he rode off and the next thing I heard from him was that they had murdered my poor sainted boy."

"Mrs. Samuels, was there, in your opinion, any motive of revenge in this killing of Jesse?"

She broke out impetuously—"What makes you call it 'killing,' why don't you say 'murder,' as it is? No, I do not think there was any such motive. Money was all they wanted. Blood-money it is, and it will stain their hands, as the crime has stained their treacherous souls. May God Almighty judge them and my poor boy. I would rather be in his place than in theirs."

"Has Jesse ever been accused of crimes he did not commit?"

"Accused of them? Oh, my God. He has never been guilty of

one-third the charges laid at his door. Every time a bank was robbed or a train was stopped they said, 'Oh that's Jesse James, Jesse James,' when he often was hundreds of miles away and knew nothing about the matter until afterwards. Jesse was driven to do what he did. They forced it on him by hunting him down like a dog and refusing him mercy. He would have been a good man if they had left him alone."

"What do you believe of Jesse's hereafter, Mrs. Samuels?"

"Jesse's heart was all right. The last time he was here, only a little over three weeks ago, he kissed me as he went away, and said 'Good-bye, mother. If I don't see you again on earth I will meet you in heaven.' And I believe that we will surely see each other there."

"Had you ever looked for such an end as this for your son?"

"Naturally, I had expected that someday he would die from a bullet. But I thought it would be fighting like a brave man. So he would if it hadn't been for this vile treachery which shot him from behind when he was unarmed. They did not even dare fire at his back when he had his revolvers by his side. They were cowards as well as traitors. No three men that ever lived could have captured my Jesse face to face. He was too quick for them, and he never missed a shot since he was a boy."

"Will Frank seek to avenge Jesse's death?"

"That is not for me to say, I would not take away the vengeance of God—but Frank is a man who knows no fear, and who loved his brother. What he will do I do not know, but I do know I would not choose to be in the places of the men who instigated this foul assassination," and with these words and a significant and bitter smile the outlaw's mother turned away.

AUTOGRAPH LETTER BY JESSE JAMES.

The only letter Jesse James ever wrote over the signature of Thomas Howard, was addressed to Mr. J. D. Calhoun, of the Lincoln, (Neb.) *Journal*. At great trouble and expense the original manuscript of this letter has been secured exclusively by the publishers of this authentic history; and the exact fac-simile of it here given is one of the most interesting relics of his extraordinary career ever given to the public.

Mr. J. D. Calhoun
Lincoln Neb
    Dear Sir
        I have noticed that you have 160 acres of land advertised for sale in Franklin co. Neb please write at once and let me know the lowest cash price that will buy your land. give me a full description of the land &c.
    I want to Purchase a farm of that size provided I can find one to suit. I will not buy a farm unless the

Land is now.
I will start on a trip in about 6 days to northern Kan & western Nebraska and if the description of your R.R. land is write one. I will look at it & if it suits me. I will buy it from the advertisement in Liveral Journal I suppose your land can be* made a good farm for Stock & growing please answer at once
Respectfully,
Tho. Howard
no 1318 Lafayett St
St. Joseph
Mo

(March 2nd 82.)

THE YOUNGER BROTHERS

CHAPTER 1

The Younger Family

Whom the Gods love die young. The happiest of the Youngers was Richard, the eldest son of his parents, who died in 1860, at the outset of a manhood, full of promise and upon the threshold of the tragic and lurid strife which was about to call into play, many of the best and the worst, the noblest and the most fiendish traits of human nature. The vendetta of the irrepressible conflict had really begun in the border counties of Kansas and Missouri years before. Richard Younger was almost the only member of that ill-fated family who escaped draining to its very dregs, the bitter cup of evil passion and final desolation.

Thomas Coleman Younger, by all odds the foremost of the Brothers whose daring exploits and thrilling adventures fill so large a page in the story of guerrilla warfare and border brigandage, was born in Jackson county, Missouri, on the 15th of January, 1844. John Younger who died in mutual death with one of Pinkerton's men in March, 1874, was born in 1846. Bruce Younger comes next, in 1848, James in 1850, and Robert in December, 1853. Bruce did not live to play a conspicuous part in the stirring events which have given to the family a continental fame.

A life sentence in the Minnesota state prison at Stillwater, came to the three surviving brothers, as the penalty of failure and overmastering fate in the attempt upon the Northfield hank. In the seclusion of those prison walls, Coleman, James and Robert Younger, have ample leisure to reflect upon the events of their stormy career; with the lights now before them, their lives, if they were to be lived over again, would doubtless be lived differently; but whatever regrets there may be for the past, no word that has ever come from Stillwater, indicates that these men feel the remorse which torments conscience-stricken

HENRY W. YOUNGER.
(Father of the Bandit Brothers.)

Mrs. H. W. YOUNGER.
(Mother of the Younger Brothers.)

Cole Younger.

Bob Younger.

Jim Younger.

criminals Their lawless deeds were primarily the natural outcome of lawless times and monstrous wrongs, against which the law stretched forth no protection. Outlawry made the war between them and society perpetual. Under such circumstances a wise man submits or flees; a proud man fights on to the end.

Kentucky was the birthplace of Henry Washington Younger, but early in life he moved to Missouri, and planted his vine and fig tree in Jackson county.

Here some years later, in 1830, when the vine had spread its branches, and the fig tree had begun to bear fruit, he married Miss Beesheba Fristoe, who proved a loving wife and a faithful helpmate. Besides the sons whose names have already been given, eight daughters were born of this union, making a happy family of fourteen children, all of whom, except three grew up to manhood and womanhood.

The father of the Younger Brothers was a thrifty man, and a good citizen. He reared his family as a country gentleman's family should be reared, giving his sons the best educational advantages that were to be had in that part of the state, and fitting his daughters to become the wives of men of wealth and standing m the community. He was something of a politician, too, for he was thrice elected to the Missouri Legislature, and was for eight years Judge of the Jackson County Court. A good business man was Henry Washington Younger, striving successfully as he did, to lay by something comfortable for the rainy days, and have enough besides to give the boys a fair start in the world. Besides the fine farm of six hundred acres in Jackson County, he owned another estate near Harrisonville, in Cass County, whither he moved in 1858, and began a profitable business as a stock-raiser and trader. Two country stores and a livery stable at Harrisonville, were also among his ventures. One hundred thousand dollars was a very large sum of money in western Missouri twenty years ago, and yet so successful a man was Henry W. Younger in the peaceful pursuits of business, that his estates and belongings at the time of his death, were estimated to be worth more than one hundred thousand dollars.

As far as can be learned, it was the possession of wealth, more than anything else, which caused Henry W. Younger, though a Union man, to become the chosen victim of the Kansas Jayhawkers on the outbreak of the war in 1861. In one of Jennison's first raids into the Missouri Counties along the border, that freebooter carried off many valuable vehicles and forty head of blooded horses from the Younger stable at Harrisonville, inflicting a loss of $20,000 upon the owner.

From that time forward, the property of the Youngers was steadily wasted and consumed by foraging parties of Jayhawkers and Red Legs from Kansas.

Their atrocities culminated in the summer of 1862, in the assassination and robbery of Henry W. Younger, five miles from Independence, Missouri. The Jayhawkers had learned that the successful man of business, would on a certain day receive a large sum of money at Independence, the proceeds of a sale of cattle. He went in his buggy at the appointed time, and on his return, was halted by a party of about a dozen Jayhawkers lying in wait, murdered as he sat in the vehicle, and his rifled body left lying in the road. Four hundred dollars was all that the robbers got as their reward for this hideous crime, their victim having taken the precaution to conceal a much larger sum in a belt which he carried buckled around his person beneath his clothing, and which was not discovered until the body was being prepared for burial by the family of the murdered man.

The pitiless rain of sorrow and adversity which had now begun to descend upon the head of the widowed mother of the Younger Brothers, abated nothing of its fury during the remainder of her tortured life. Her sons were driven one after another to the black flag of Quantrell's avengers, where their terrible prowess and remorseless deeds doubly inflamed the hatred of wolfish enemies, against the noncombatant members of the family, and added brimstone to the fires of persecution. The vine and fig tree that had grown so luxuriant in the happy springtime, shed their leaves as in a winter's blast, and were consumed as by the breath of a volcano.

Schoolboy Days and Country Home of the Younger Boys.

Her daughters were torn from her side and their mangled bodies brought back dead from the ruins of the prison, which an infuriated mob tore down over their heads. Taking refuge at last in the little home that remained to her in Cass County, twenty-two wolves in Federal uniform pursued her thither on the 9th of February, 1863, and demanded the secret of Coleman Younger's hiding place. Threats failing to extort a secret which the poor woman did not possess, the soldiers compelled her to set fire to her own house with her own hands, and when the last timber was consumed, the homeless widow was permitted to totter three miles through the snow to a neighbour's house for shelter.

It was this atrocity which sent James Younger, then a lad of only fourteen years, into Quantrell's band in search of vengeance. It was about this time, too, that the seeds were developed of that fatal consumption, which terminated her blighted life in May, 1870. From the ashes of her Cass County home, she shortly after found a refuge under the roof of her son-in-law, Lycurgus Jones, in Clay County. When the war was over, Coleman Younger went to Texas for the purpose of preparing there a new home for his mother, but her health was never strong enough to bear the fatigues of a journey thither.

It has already been stated that the father of the Younger Brothers was a Union man, who fell a victim, as did so many other peaceable citizens and Union men, to the hyena-like rapacity of the Jayhawkers. Under paternal guidance and with the paternal example before his eyes, Coleman Younger remained at his Cass County home until the autumn of 1861, when a body of Missouri militia, under command of Neugent, were stationed at Harrisonville. Among Neugent's officers was a valiant militia captain named Irvin Walley.

Coleman Younger, then a lad of some seventeen or eighteen summers, was frequently a guest at social parties in the village where the militiamen were also entertained. Nothing disturbed the smooth current of village pleasure until cupid, and cupid's minion, jealousy, began to make trouble among the young revellers. The story goes, that at one of these parties, given at the house of Colonel McKee, Mss Younger declined to dance with Captain Walley. The maiden was coy, perhaps because she did not like the captain, perhaps because she liked another better; but whatever the cause of the refusal, it ruffled the militiaman's temper not a little. Nor was his mood made more genial by the interest which the *belle* of the evening seemed to take in Coleman Younger, who monopolised most of her time and attention, much to the chagrin of the captain.

Walley manifested an inclination to provoke a quarrel with the lad before the party broke up, and was finally heard to remark that "soldiers would stand no chance until they took that pesky Younger boy out." Likely enough, there were other grounds of ill will between the Youngers and Captain Walley, lying behind these petty social rivalries. At any rate, Coleman Younger withdrew from the gathering, and upon reaching home, told his father what had happened, saying he feared they had not heard the last of the affair, as Captain Walley seemed determined to provoke a difficulty. The old gentleman advised him to go down to the Jackson County farm and raise a crop, thinking by this course to remove the lad from the enmity of the militiaman, and keep him out of trouble.

The advice was promptly acted upon, but not an hour to soon, for on the following night, Walley with a party of his men went down to Mr. Younger's house, and made some violent demonstrations, threatening to "show Cole Younger how the dancing went." But Cole Younger was already on his way to Jackson County, and the demonstration passed off without immediate results. The militiamen, however, were ready enough to take up any pretext which gave them an excuse to embark in foraging enterprises against wealthy or well-to-do citizens. Cole Younger was not permitted to pursue his bucolic avocations very long before he learned that Captain Walley, with his militia, was on the way from Harrisonville to Jackson county for the purpose of "capturing Cole Younger, a noted bushwhacker."

Being unarmed and inexperienced in war, the lad took refuge for a few weeks among his relatives while his father endeavoured to pacify Walley and settle the pretended difficulty between him and Cole. When these efforts at pacification failed, the old gentleman advised that the boy had better go to school, a proposition to which Cole assented. Arrangements to that end were at once begun, and the usual outfit prepared. Upon mentioning his plan to a friend in Kansas City, Mr. Younger was surprised to learn that his intentions had been anticipated, that he was closely watched and that it would be unsafe to attempt to remove Cole from the neighbourhood. The militiamen were determined to drive the boy to desperation, in order to gain a pretext for robbing the father. On being informed of the facts, Cole Younger cut the whole matter short with the words: "It is all right, I will fight them awhile then."

CHAPTER 2

With Quantrell

It was about the 1st of January, 1862, that Cole Younger found his way into Quantrell's camp. The life upon which the high-spirited youth now entered was a moving kaleidoscope of dashing adventure, bold deeds and hair-breadth escapes. The band was composed mainly of young men who, like their leader, had some foul wrong to redress or some frightful vengeance to wreak. But the border war was not as hideous as it has sometimes been depicted in the desire to produce a startling effect. Though fighting often outside the rules of war, Quantrell and his men were all under the same oath to the Confederacy as that which bound their fellow soldiers belonging to regular commands.

The "terrible black oath" attributed to the guerrillas is ascertained to be in reality a fervid bit of fiction, and as such cannot hold a place in a work which seeks to present this stirring page of American history with fidelity to historic truth. A valued and highly interesting letter from Cole Younger to the publishers of this volume conclusively refutes the slander which would fasten that fiendish objurgation upon him and his comrades. The following is so much of the letter as space will admit the reproduction of here. The scathing criticism in which he indulges concerning the inaccuracy of two other works on guerrilla history is omitted as foreign to the purpose and dignity of this work. It, however, effectually disposes of the "black oath:"

Stillwater, Minn., May 1st, 1881.

My Dear Sir: Your letter of April 25, was delivered to me a few days ago by Warden Reed, and I must say I was somewhat surprised and amused. My dear sir, I know nothing concerning the subject you refer to. The "Black Oath" is a myth originating in the brain of some irresponsible, badly-informed and reckless chronicler. It was all new to me, and had no existence in fact. I had nothing to do with either of those histories.

★★★★★★

The idea has gotten abroad that the Guerillas of Missouri were not recognised by the Confederates as Confederate soldiers. That is false. They took the same oath that was administered to all Confederate soldiers, and were recognised as such by all the generals in the Trans-Mississippi Department. The Confederate War Department refused to give Quantrell a commission as colonel of partisan rangers independent of the generals in command of the different departments West of the Mississippi; but they recognized him as captain with authority to recruit as many companies for the Confederate service as he could.

★★★★★★

Now, as for myself. I took the same oath and it was administered by the same officers that swore all of Col. Up. Hayes' men in. Quantrell and all of his men took the same oath. I was personally recognised by nearly all the generals in the Trans-Mississippi Department—as a guerrilla, it is true, but as an officer of the Confederate Army at the same time.

The generals that I met with were as follows: In the fall of 1863, I reported to Gen. Henry E. McCullough, at Barnum, Texas, in command of Northern Texas. He recognised my papers as correct, and all my orders on the Commissary and Quartermaster's Departments were signed by me as Captain C. S. A., and duly honoured. I was recognised by Gen. Dick Taylor, while operating in his department in the same way.

★★★★★★

I drew pay as a confederate officer from August, 1862, up to the time I went on the Western trip. I was recognised by Gen. Marmaduke and Gen. Shelby as a confederate officer. In February, 1864, Gen. Marmaduke sent to Gen. Shelby for an officer and forty of the best-mounted and best-armed men he had. I was the officer detailed and, after selecting the men, reported in person to Gen. Marmaduke, at his headquarters at Warren, Arkansas. He was alone in his tent when I entered. After looking at me closely—as I was a beardless boy, I suppose he was wondering if I would fill the bill—he told me what he wanted. It was to go on a scouting expedition to find out the plans of the Federals at Little Rock, who, he had information, intended a movement against Camden.

******

I carried out the orders, returned to Camden and told Gen. Shelby, I thought all the Federals were asleep in Little Rock.

T. C. Younger.

Cole Younger made his mark as the possessor of rare courage and other soldierly qualities in the first fight in which Quantrell's men were engaged after he joined them. The command, returning from an expedition into Kansas, stopped for a night at the house of John Flannery, in Jackson county. The house was surrounded by a body of Federals under Captain Peabody, who aroused the inmates by beating on the door, and then demanded an unconditional surrender. In Quantrell's dictionary there was no such word as surrender. He promised to return an answer in ten minutes, and when the time was up, having disposed his men to the best advantage, peremptorily refused to surrender, and accompanied the refusal with a murderous volley of buckshot.

A hot fight ensued, which lasted for nearly two hours, when the Jayhawkers finding it impossible to dislodge the guerrillas in any other way, set fire to the house at the rear of the ell, a point that was not covered by the guns of the inmates. When the flames began to invade the rooms, Cole Younger was called down from the attic window in the loft where he had been doing effective work, and the fire-trapped guerrillas got ready for a sortie. Dummies, made of pillows, with hats placed upon them, were set in the windows, and when the fire of the beleaguers had been drawn by this means, the guerrillas rushed from the burning building, and as they emerged into the open air every man discharged his gun into the face of the enemy, broke through their line and escaped. Cole Younger, who acted with the most remarkable coolness and bravery throughout this fight, became separated from his companions in the sortie, and was pursued by twelve cavalrymen whom he kept in check by once and again raising his empty gun at them as he fled through the timber.

A month later Cole Younger with Quantrell and twenty of his men, was sleeping at the farm house of Major Tate in Jackson County. At midnight a shot from the sentinel at the gate announced the approach of two hundred cavalrymen, and a few minutes later a lieutenant was kicking the door with a demand for unconditional surrender. Quantrell crept to the door and placing the officer by the sound of his voice, sent a bullet crashing through the panel. The lieutenant fell with a death wound in his chest, and a fierce interchange of volleys began. A truce was called in order to allow Major Tate and his family to retire to the barn, and then the combat was renewed, with Cole Younger, Quantrell and six others firing from the upper story, while the lower floor was occupied by George Shepherd and the rest of the force.

After three terrible hours, the cavalrymen again resorted to the torch which was applied to the rear of the ell, as at Flannery's; and again, the guerrillas made their sortie with loaded weapons, broke through the line of their besiegers with a volley and escaped. The cavalrymen lost twenty men killed, and nearly forty wounded. The Guerrillas lost their horses and one man killed. They got a remount the next afternoon in a skirmish with thirteen cavalrymen, from whom they captured as many horses as they needed.

Bright and early on the morning of February 26, 1862, Quantrell and his fifty men lying in a strongly fortified camp on Indian Creek, in Jackson County, were surprised by a shell which came crashing through the timber and exploded overhead. The guerrillas were not many minutes in finding out that the shell was a messenger from a party of two hundred Jayhawkers under Col. Buell, who had brought a couple of cannon along and had completely surrounded their camp during the night. The guerrillas were in a bad fix and held a very earnest council of war, at which Cole Younger called attention to the fact that inside the Jayhawkers' lines there was a farmhouse with spacious stock yards filled with cattle. Cole's plan for getting out of the scrape was to hold the Jayhawkers in check until night, and then under cover of darkness to stampede those cattle right through the enemy's lines, draw their fire and slip out of the trap while the Jayhawkers were pouring murderous volleys into the steers.

A lively fight was kept up all day, and when the night settled down black and cloudy. Cole Younger, with three trusty companions, slipped out from the camp and started a lively commotion in the barnyard. The Jayhawkers were thrown into confusion, and fled to arms with the cry that the guerrillas were upon them. When morning dawned, Quantrell's men were in the rear of their besiegers, and Cole Younger led a sudden charge upon the surprised artillerymen, who surrendered their batteries without resistance. Three hundred cavalrymen under Jennison approaching at this instant, were mistaken by Buell's men for Confederates, and the wildest disorder ensued. Before Quantrell let up on the demoralised Jayhawkers, he had killed and wounded a hundred of them, captured scores of horses, twelve hundred rounds of ammunition and a couple of ten-pound guns. His loss was eight men. So much for Cole Younger's brilliant piece of backwoods strategy.

After the fight at Flannery's, Cole Younger took refuge for a couple of days at the house of Mr. Jerry Blythe, a relative, until he could find out the whereabouts of his comrades. The Jayhawkers learned that Cole was there and seventy-five of them at once set out to capture him. When the Jayhawkers got to Blythe's house, Cole Younger wasn't there; but before they left the house the armed men brutally murdered a little son of Mr. Blythe, scarcely more than twelve years old. Cole had by this time rejoined Quantrell's men, who were already on the track of the Jayhawkers, and learning what had been done, a terrible vengeance was prepared for the murderers.

As the band rode into Blue Cut on their return, the guerrillas opened fire on them, front and rear, and from the embankments which overhung the road on both sides. They were taken completely by surprise, and scarcely a man of them escaped. Cole Younger killed ten of them with his own hand. As one of the Jayhawkers dashed out in front of the cut, Cole grabbed his horse by the bridle, drew his revolver and shot the rider dead.

About a year later, Cole Younger with twenty-five men was ordered to ambuscade a body of fifty cavalrymen under Captain Long, who would have to pass through Blue Cut on their way from Harrisonville to Independence. Captain Long was an old friend of Cole, but riding with the cavalrymen was a man named Shoat, whom Cole suspected of being a spy, and was therefore very anxious to kill him. Having posted his men at the cut, the young guerrilla ordered them to take every care not to hurt Captain Long, but at all hazards to kill Shoat.

Fifteen minutes of hard fighting after the cavalrymen rode into the ambush, sufficed to route them with a loss of twenty-seven killed and wounded, and ten prisoners, among whom was Captain Long, whose horse was shot from under him by Cole. After chasing Shoat and bringing him down at the second shot from his heavy pistol. Cole rode back to Captain Long, and greeted him cordially as if the two had just met, after a long separation, under the happiest auspices and unbroken friendship. Some time was spent in friendly conversation, and then Captain Long and his fellow prisoners were released on parole.

Unfortunately, such instances of magnanimity on the part of the guerrillas, are offset by many bloody deeds which the very nature of the warfare waged between them and the Jayhawkers, perhaps made unavoidable. The barbarities practiced upon the Younger family, the murder of Cole's father, the atrocity which compelled his mother to fire her own house with her own hand in the dead of winter, the cruel arrest and cowardly murder of three of his sisters and several of his female relatives, in the Kansas City jail, filled him with a burning thirst for vengeance which frequently wreaked itself in deeds which find no sanction outside the rules of war approved by savages.

CHAPTER 3

The Guerrillas Disband

The border warfare increased in bitterness as the participants in it became inured to slaughter, and men who had begun by being valorous, ended by being bloodthirsty. The ranks of the guerrillas were gradually decimated by the overpowering force of numbers, and in September, 1863, shortly after the sacking of Lawrence, Quantrell's men abandoned their old stamping ground and rode off to the south. Coleman Younger reported to Kirby Smith, and with a command of fifty horsemen, did some effective service in Louisiana, attacking small convoys and capturing supply trains. Early in 1865, he went with some sort of a commission from the Confederate government, to raise a company in California. He had some adventures with hostile Apache Indians, who were encountered on the way, but he had hardly reached his destination, when the surrender at Appomattox put an end to the war.

James Younger went with Quantrell to Kentucky, in the fall of 1864, was taken prisoner in the fight in which Quantrell was mortally wounded, and was sent to the military prison at Alton, Illinois, where he was kept until the summer of 1866. Upon his release, he returned to the Jackson County farm, where his mother and his younger brothers, John and Robert, were then living. Cole returned from California about the same time, and thus in the fall of 1866, eighteen months after the close of the war, we find all of the Younger boys back at the old family homestead, going to work making rails, mending fences and repairing the ravages of war about the farm.

But as the Kansas border war began before Sumter, so it continued after Appomattox. The Jayhawkers had not abandoned the saddle, and vigilance committees were still moving about for the purpose of driving obnoxious characters from the country. The memory of the sanguinary deeds committed on both sides during the conflict, was perhaps too bitter to die out for many years, and moderation was hardly to be expected of the victorious party, when their old enemies were comparatively at their mercy. All the offices of profit and authority, under the semi-military government, which succeeded the war in the border counties, were held either by Jayhawkers, or by members of Neugent's old Missouri State Militia Regiment. These men cherished a deadly hatred for the remnants of Quantrell's men individually and collectively, and they did not hesitate to use their authority for the purpose of gratifying their personal revenge.

The ex-guerrillas were one after another murdered in their homes, or thrown into loathsome prisons. At length one of these men who had an impliicable hatred against Cole Younger, and who was at the time acting as deputy sheriff, organized a posse of swashbucklers, and set out for the Younger homestead to capture and possibly to murder Cole. The band created a reign of terror as they passed through the little town of Lee's Summit, where they seized one of the ex-guerrillas named George Wigginton, and after subjecting him to the most shameful treatment, carried him along with them as a guide and decoy.

Arriving at the house of the Youngers, the posse found that Cole had eluded them, and after compelling the family to provide them with supper, they took John Younger, then a mere boy, out to the barn, tied a rope around his neck, threw the other end over a rafter and told the lad that his only hope for life was in telling the whereabouts of his elder brothers, Cole and Jim. Three times was he strung up, and three times he refused to betray his brothers. The fourth time he was left dangling in the air until the rope had cut into his flesh, and respiration had almost ceased.

Weak and scarcely able to stand, the ruffians compelled the lad to accompany their march for some distance, accelerating his speed by blows with the butts of their muskets. He crawled back home the next morning, half dead, to find his mother's end hastened by the agonising suspense of the night. It did not take many demonstrations of this kind to convince the Younger Brothers that it was impossible for them to live in safety at their old home, and accordingly Cole, James and John departed for Texas, intending, it is said, to remove the rest of the family thither, as soon as a suitable home could be provided in the Lone Star State.

When the Younger Brothers left their Jackson County home for the last time, they were to all intents and purposes outlaws, and their movements from that time onward, until their death or capture are enveloped in mystery, or marked by violent offences against law, life and property. The full pardon which was granted to the Jayhawkers, for all crimes and excesses committed under colour of military service, was never extended to members of the old guerrilla bands who returned to Missouri after the war was over. Efforts were made in good faith by friends of the Jameses and Youngers, to put them once more at peace with society and the law; but nothing came of it, and the proscribed men, hunted and waylaid at every turn, settled permanently down into the life of *desperadoes*.

From their Texas cattle ranch, the Youngers returned frequently to their old haunts, brought back by the semi-annual cattle drive, or by sheer restlessness of spirit. In just how many of the bank robberies, train robberies and highway robberies, with which their names are connected, they really had a hand, will probably never be known. Doubtless, at times other desperate men have taken advantage of their outlawry, to pillage and murder in their names. Every highway robbery in the West about which there was a deed of boldness or dash, was placed to their account and added at once to their fame and infamy. As a full record of these robberies is given in another part of this volume, it is needless to recount them here.

But there are enough well authenticated incidents in the later career of the Youngers, to fill a spacious volume. John Younger, in 1866, when only fourteen years of age, had occasion to go up to Independence to get a pistol repaired. After the job was finished, and while John was standing in front of the public square, a man named Gillcreas came along, and learning that John was a veritable brother of Cole Younger, began a violent tirade of abuse which he ended with a kick.

"If you do that again I will kill you," said John. The kick was repeated, and Gillcreas fell dead, with a bullet through his heart. The coroner's jury which investigated the affair, found that John acted in self-defence, and the grand jury declined to review the verdict. Again, while clerking in a store at Dallas, Texas, John Younger was frolicking with some companions in a bar room one night. There was present, the usual bar room, butt, an old codger with whom everybody took liberties, and by way of a prank, John laid a wager to brush the old fellows nose with a pistol bullet without hitting him. The ball was fired, swerved a little out of its aim, and John's target was the next instant hopping about the room with a bloody proboscis.

The Outlaws, Safe in their Backwoods Retreat, Enjoying Themselves.

Partly by way of carrying out the joke, perhaps, for the man was not really hurt, some of the crowd persuaded him to swear out a warrant against John for attempt to kill; and before the joke was ended, John Younger had actually killed the sheriff attempting to arrest' him, and had his own arm almost severed from the shoulder by a charge of buckshot. He made his way to Missouri, and thence to the home of his uncle in California, but his restless disposition soon brought him back.

The robbery of a train at Gad's Hill, on the Iron Mountain Railroad, about the 1st of March, 1874, created wild excitement throughout eastern Missouri. Large rewards were offered by the railroad and express companies for the capture of the robbers, and bands of armed men went out in every direction in pursuit. Two of Pinkerton's best detectives, Capt. Allen, *alias* Lull, and Boyle, *alias* James Wright, were sent to St. Clair County, in search of John and James Younger, who were supposed to be in that region, and who were of course suspected of having had a hand in the Gad's Hill exploit. The detectives reconnoitred around Osceola for a week, and having engaged the services of an ex-deputy sheriff named Edwin B. Daniels, the trio set out for Chalk Level, in the guise of cattle dealers. On the 16th of March, two of the party stopped at the house of Mr. Theodore Snuffer, inquired about the road to the widow Simmon's house and rode on, but not by the road, to the widow Simmon's.

John and James Younger were in the house eating their dinners, while the detectives were talking at the gate, and their quick intuition saw through the disguise of the "cattle dealers" almost at a glance. They at once saddled their horses and followed the men, for it was ever the policy of the Younger Brothers, as well as of the James Boys, to make war to the death, upon all detectives caught following their trail. Both the brothers were heavily armed, John alone having four revolvers in his belt, and a shot gun across the pommel of his saddle.

When the Youngers came up with these men, Wright drew his pistol, but quickly concluding that prudence was the better part of valour, put spurs to his horse and fled, his pace being accelerated by a shot which knocked the hat from his head without doing any other injury. Daniels and Allen stopped for a fatal parley. John Younger's shot gun was levelled quick as thought, and both the men were forced to drop their heavy pistols to the ground. The gun was kept levelled while the detectives were closely questioned. But Allen was too quick for the outlaw.

Suddenly drawing a small Smith and Wesson pistol, he shot John Younger in the neck. With his life's blood gushing from the wound, John Younger returned the lire, disabled his assailant and finally gave him a mortal wound before he himself dropped out of the saddle, never to mount again. Daniels was also killed, but whether by John or James Younger, has never been clearly ascertained.

After this tragedy, James Younger went to Boone county, Arkansas, where he remained until the summer. Cole and Bob Younger then joined him, and a series of exciting adventures with bands of men hunting for horse thieves followed.

CHAPTER 4

Northfield and Stillwater

The career of the Younger Brothers now draws to a close. In all their wanderings, the old home in Jackson county held its attraction for them, and ever and anon they returned to the scenes so full of sad and happy memories. It was from their secret haunt in Jackson county, that the brothers, almost the last survivors of a family whom the war found happy, prosperous and full of promise, set out about the middle of August, 1876, on one of their roving trips to Texas. The curse of the wanderer and the outlaw was upon them. To make their peace with the law and with the world had long since become impossible, and perhaps the inclination so to do had long since passed away. They had not proceeded far on their journey, when they fell in with the James Boys and others, outlaws like themselves, ever ready for any adventure which promised excitement or profit. The expedition against the bank at Northfield, Minnesota, resulted from this meeting.

It is said that Cole Younger did not approve the plan, that he thought the enterprise of doubtful success, that "the game was not worth the ammunition." Nevertheless, the Texas outfit was sold and the Youngers, Cole, James and Robert, went with the rest by railroad to Minnesota. In the desperate street fight which followed the abortive attempt upon the bank, Robert Younger received a painful wound in the right elbow, and in the moment of flight, Jim Younger who had an ugly wound in the mouth and had lost his horse, was borne from the scene by his brother Cole. Jim Younger's wound was the greatest drawback to the outlaws in making their escape, as it not only left an unmistakable trail of blood by which their course was easily tracked, but made him a burden on his comrades who were less severely hurt, and greatly retarded their movements.

It is even asserted that Jesse James proposed to Cole Younger, that the only way for the hotly pursued bandits to make good their escape, would be to end Jim Younger's suffering with a pistol bullet.

"Jim cannot live," Jesse James is reported to have said. "He is almost dead now, and to attempt to carry him, will only result in certain death to the whole party."

To this proposition. Cole and Bob Younger indignantly replied that they would stay by their brother until he died, and then carry his dead body as long as their strength made it possible. Shortly after this Frank and Jesse James separated from the rest of the band, and finally got away to Mexico, while Clell Miller and the Youngers made their way as best they could, with the whole country up in arms against them. Cole and Bob Younger staid manfully by their sorely wounded brother, carried him over streams and through swamps, until their own wounds made further flight impossible.

Two weeks after the attempt upon the Northfield bank, Clell Miller and the Youngers were hunted into a small patch of timber, which was quickly surrounded by 150 armed men, who began firing into the woods to drive the robbers out. But even this terrible fusillade had no effect upon them. Weary, foot-sore, and with festering wounds, the outlaws stood desperately at bay, determined to sell their lives and liberty as dearly as possible. Then sheriff McDonald called for volunteers to go into the brush and stir them up. Before this party of seven men had advanced fifty yards into the brush, Clell Miller rose in front of them and levelled a revolver, which exploded at the same instant with the sheriff's rifle.

The sheriff was not hit, but Clell turned and dropped dead after running a few yards. It was the turn of the Younger Brothers next. They rose to their feet for their last encounter and opened fire, as the sheriff's men approached. One of the posse was wounded, another had his watch shattered into a thousand pieces by a ball from the Youngers, while yet a third owed his life to a pipe in his vest pocket, which broke the force of a well-directed pistol ball. The fire of the assailants, however, brought Cole and Jim Younger again to the ground, groaning with the pain of broken bones.

The Youngers retreated a little, and soon found themselves exposed to the fire of the men on the further outskirts of the woods. Hemmed in on every side, and encompassed by a girdle of fire, the Brothers again retreated to within twenty yards of the advancing posse with whom they had just fought. Cole and Jim Younger were by this time utterly disabled, but Bob, with one arm shattered and dangling by his side, grasped his revolver with his left hand and fired repeatedly at his assailants, aiming first at one end of the line, then at the other, and again at the centre, a fresh revolver being handed him as fast as the one he held was exhausted.

But his aim was unsteady, and seeing that the contest was without shadow of hope, he called a truce as the Boys "were all shot to pieces," threw down his pistol, and the famous Younger Brothers who had faced death in a thousand forms, were at last captured, more dead than alive. In this fight, and in the pursuit which preceded it. Cole Younger was wounded eleven times, which, added to previous ones, makes a total of twenty wounds which the hardy outlaw bears upon his person. Jim Younger was wounded four times in the Northfield affair, and six times in all. Bob Younger was never wounded before the Northfield adventure, where he received three shots, one of which shattered his right elbow, leaving him a stiffened arm and hand for life.

But though thus riddled with bullets, in a way that would have been the death of any man of less iron nerve, not one of the Younger Brothers was mortally hurt. After the capture, they were taken to Madelia, where their wounds were dressed, the best surgical attention given them, and wonderful kindness shown them by the citizens. Jim's wounds were looked upon as hopeless, but a constitution of steel aided by good nursing, brought him through the crisis. People who visited them were surprised to find the terrible Younger Brothers looking so little like the *desperadoes* their deeds had proved them to be. Tall, handsome, gentlemanly in bearing, demeanour and language, they made a most favourable impression on everyone who met or conversed with them. Still they had engaged in desperate work, and expected nothing but that they must abide by the consequences.

The grand jury returned four indictments against the Youngers, one of which charged Cole Younger with the murder of a Norwegian who was killed in the streets of Northfield, and two witnesses were ready to swear that they saw Cole fire the fatal shot. The penalty of murder in the first degree was death, if the prisoners should be convicted on trial after entering a plea of "not guilty." Accordingly, when the District Court met at Faribault, on the 7th of November, they entered a plea of "guilty." The judge ordering them to stand up, pronounced the sentence that each of the prisoners be confined in the state penitentiary at Stillwater, for the period of their natural lives. When these words were uttered, Miss Retta, the young and beautiful sister of the outlaws, who had come to visit them in their suffering, almost fainted away, and then falling upon Cole's neck, gave utterance to such heart-rending grief that everyone in the courtroom was moved to tears.

True to the teachings and the pledge of the outlaws, the Younger Brothers in their prison life, sturdily refuse to utter a word that might compromise a comrade, or betray the secrets of their dark and strange career. Upon indifferent matters concerning themselves alone, and upon topics that have become historical, they talk freely, intelligently and interestingly enough. But beyond that, their mouths are sealed beyond the power of the most ingenious questioning, or even "all the tortures cunning mankind can inflict" to open them.

In September, 1880, Col. George Gaston of Kansas City, turned aside from a tour of the Minnesota, lakes to visit, in their prison at Stillwater, the Younger Brothers, whom he had known before the war. Describing his interview with the incarcerated bandits, after the preliminary introduction to the prison authorities. Col. Gaston proceeds as follows:

"There was a man at the top of the steps to receive us, another official with the conventional bunch of keys. 'Come this way,' said he, and we followed him into a square room with walls and ceilings of stone. There were chairs and we sat down. A door at one side opened, and three men walked in. They were Cole, Jim and Bob Younger. They took chairs opposite and directly facing us. They wore the prison garb, and their faces were shaven and their hair cropped close. They looked so genteel despite their striped clothing, that my nervousness disappeared at once. I told them who I was, and whence I came, and introduced my wife.

"They were very courteous, and bowed and said they were glad to see me. Jim hitched back his chair, and addressing my wife, said laughingly: 'It is so long since we have been permitted to converse with anybody, that I don't know as we can talk.' Then followed a desultory conversation. Cole said his health was poor, he complained of suffering from the effects of the wound in his head, received at the time of his capture. The rifle ball entered near the right ear and lodged under the left ear, and has never been removed. Jim was shot in the mouth, but there are now no signs of the wound. Bob had his jaw broken, but he too has entirely recovered, and is the handsomest one in the trio. He is the youngest; I remember him as a boy. He has developed into a robust, fine looking young man.

"It was really very touching," continues Col. Gaston, "to hear them talk of the past and the present. Cole told of his army life; how at the age of nineteen, he had been promoted to a captaincy in the Confederate Army. He spoke of the murder of his father, and of his career since the close of the war. 'My exploits in the army were exaggerated,' said he, 'just as my exploits as an outlaw have been exaggerated. In one instance, I have been too highly praised, and in the other, grossly wronged.'

"I learned from their own lips the story of their prison life; Cole Younger is a changed man. I found him positively entertaining. He converses with a correctness, fluency and grace that are charming. None of the brothers are compelled to do very much work; they spend a great deal of their time reading in their cells. Jim is reading law books, and Bob is studying medicine; Cole seems to have developed a theological turn of mind. These three men are great favourites in the prison; they are looked up to by their companions, as a sort of demi-gods, creatures immeasurably above the ordinary inmates of the penitentiary.

"The most dreadful feature of their lives is the fact, that though they occupy adjoining cells, they are not permitted to converse with each other. It is only once a month that they can meet and talk to one another, and then only for a few moments. They told me that they prayed earnestly every night, that the month might pass quickly. It was touching beyond expression, to hear Cole speak of his early days. His misspent life he charges to the faults of his early training. He says he was taught to be ruled by his passions, and his passions alone. And as he talked in this vein, the tears came into his eyes and I felt that he was indeed a penitent man.

"He inquired after his old army friends, and I told him what I knew of them and their whereabouts. In the course of our conversation, the James Boys were mentioned.

"Do you believe Jesse is dead?' I asked.

"Cole straightened up, glanced quick as a lightning flash at his brothers on either side of him, and replied. 'He is, if George Shepherd says he is.' I asked him what he meant, and he answered: 'There are sometimes two things alike in the world, and Jesse James and George Shepherd were as near alike as they could be, in character, I mean. Both are quick, nervous and brave.'"

It is, however, pretty well established, that Jesse James is alive and well, despite his encounter with George Shepherd. Several persons who know Jesse well, assert that they saw him frequently in the mining regions of Colorado, as recently as December, 1880.

If a desperate assault upon the Stillwater prison gave fair promise of releasing the Youngers and restoring them to liberty and safety, there are doubtless some hundreds of their old comrades and friends yet living, who would not turn back from any danger that might be encountered in such an enterprise. But though some movement of the kind was once talked about, the manifest madness of the attempt, caused the idea to be abandoned before the plan ever assumed definite shape.

Looking upon the Youngers as victims of war, rather as ordinary outlaws, it has been suggested by their friends, that political influences might in some way be brought to bear to secure their pardon, a plan which might be more feasible if their offences were confined to any one commonwealth. It is known that Jesse James at one time looked upon the pardon of the Youngers from the Minnesota penitentiary, as not beyond the range of possibilities, and that he made some efforts to enlist political influence in their behalf.

The only attempt that has ever been made to rescue the brothers, was as clumsy in its conception, as it was abortive in its outcome. In the latter part of 1877, two ex-guerrillas who were ardent admirers of the Youngers, met in western Missouri, and after discussing the situation, reached the conclusion that if they were once on the inside of the same prison with the redoubtable brothers, the five of them could, by a bold push, make their way out. They accordingly proceeded to Minnesota, where one of them stole a watch and was sentenced to the Stillwater penitentiary, for a year. The other committed some petty larceny, and got only a short term in the county jail. The one who was sent to the penitentiary, found no means of communicating with the Youngers, got never a sight of them in fact, and had not even the poor consolation of revealing to them the kindly scheme which had made him for a time the partner of their captivity.

ALSO FROM LEONAUR
AVAILABLE IN SOFTCOVER OR HARDCOVER WITH DUST JACKET

THE FALL OF THE MOGHUL EMPIRE OF HINDUSTAN *by H. G. Keene*—By the beginning of the nineteenth century, as British and Indian armies under Lake and Wellesley dominated the scene, a little over half a century of conflict brought the Moghul Empire to its knees.

LADY SALE'S AFGHANISTAN *by Florentia Sale*—An Indomitable Victorian Lady's Account of the Retreat from Kabul During the First Afghan War.

THE CAMPAIGN OF MAGENTA AND SOLFERINO 1859 *by Harold Carmichael Wylly*—The Decisive Conflict for the Unification of Italy.

FRENCH'S CAVALRY CAMPAIGN *by J. G. Maydon*—A Special Correspondent's View of British Army Mounted Troops During the Boer War.

CAVALRY AT WATERLOO *by Sir Evelyn Wood*—British Mounted Troops During the Campaign of 1815.

THE SUBALTERN *by George Robert Gleig*—The Experiences of an Officer of the 85th Light Infantry During the Peninsular War.

NAPOLEON AT BAY, 1814 *by F. Loraine Petre*—The Campaigns to the Fall of the First Empire.

NAPOLEON AND THE CAMPAIGN OF 1806 *by Colonel Vachée*—The Napoleonic Method of Organisation and Command to the Battles of Jena & Auerstädt.

THE COMPLETE ADVENTURES IN THE CONNAUGHT RANGERS *by William Grattan*—The 88th Regiment during the Napoleonic Wars by a Serving Officer.

BUGLER AND OFFICER OF THE RIFLES *by William Green & Harry Smith*—With the 95th (Rifles) during the Peninsular & Waterloo Campaigns of the Napoleonic Wars.

NAPOLEONIC WAR STORIES *by Sir Arthur Quiller-Couch*—Tales of soldiers, spies, battles & sieges from the Peninsular & Waterloo campaigns.

CAPTAIN OF THE 95TH (RIFLES) *by Jonathan Leach*—An officer of Wellington's sharpshooters during the Peninsular, South of France and Waterloo campaigns of the Napoleonic wars.

RIFLEMAN COSTELLO *by Edward Costello*—The adventures of a soldier of the 95th (Rifles) in the Peninsular & Waterloo Campaigns of the Napoleonic wars.

AVAILABLE ONLINE AT **www.leonaur.com**
AND FROM ALL GOOD BOOK STORES

ALSO FROM LEONAUR
AVAILABLE IN SOFTCOVER OR HARDCOVER WITH DUST JACKET

THE 9TH—THE KING'S (LIVERPOOL REGIMENT) IN THE GREAT WAR 1914 - 1918 *by Enos H. G. Roberts*—Mersey to mud—war and Liverpool men.

THE GAMBARDIER *by Mark Severn*—The experiences of a battery of Heavy artillery on the Western Front during the First World War.

FROM MESSINES TO THIRD YPRES *by Thomas Floyd*—A personal account of the First World War on the Western front by a 2/5th Lancashire Fusilier.

THE IRISH GUARDS IN THE GREAT WAR - VOLUME 1 *by Rudyard Kipling*—Edited and Compiled from Their Diaries and Papers—The First Battalion.

THE IRISH GUARDS IN THE GREAT WAR - VOLUME 1 *by Rudyard Kipling*—Edited and Compiled from Their Diaries and Papers—The Second Battalion.

ARMOURED CARS IN EDEN *by K. Roosevelt*—An American President's son serving in Rolls Royce armoured cars with the British in Mesopotamia & with the American Artillery in France during the First World War.

CHASSEUR OF 1914 *by Marcel Dupont*—Experiences of the twilight of the French Light Cavalry by a young officer during the early battles of the great war in Europe.

TROOP HORSE & TRENCH *by R.A. Lloyd*—The experiences of a British Lifeguardsman of the household cavalry fighting on the western front during the First World War 1914-18.

THE EAST AFRICAN MOUNTED RIFLES *by C.J. Wilson*—Experiences of the campaign in the East African bush during the First World War.

THE LONG PATROL *by George Berrie*—A Novel of Light Horsemen from Gallipoli to the Palestine campaign of the First World War.

THE FIGHTING CAMELIERS *by Frank Reid*—The exploits of the Imperial Camel Corps in the desert and Palestine campaigns of the First World War.

STEEL CHARIOTS IN THE DESERT *by S. C. Rolls*—The first world war experiences of a Rolls Royce armoured car driver with the Duke of Westminster in Libya and in Arabia with T.E. Lawrence.

WITH THE IMPERIAL CAMEL CORPS IN THE GREAT WAR *by Geoffrey Inchbald*—The story of a serving officer with the British 2nd battalion against the Senussi and during the Palestine campaign.

AVAILABLE ONLINE AT **www.leonaur.com**
AND FROM ALL GOOD BOOK STORES

ALSO FROM LEONAUR
AVAILABLE IN SOFTCOVER OR HARDCOVER WITH DUST JACKET

ESCAPE FROM THE FRENCH by *Edward Boys*—A Young Royal Navy Midshipman's Adventures During the Napoleonic War.

THE VOYAGE OF H.M.S. PANDORA by *Edward Edwards R. N. & George Hamilton, edited by Basil Thomson*—In Pursuit of the Mutineers of the Bounty in the South Seas—1790-1791.

MEDUSA by *J. B. Henry Savigny and Alexander Correard and Charlotte-Adélaïde Dard*—Narrative of a Voyage to Senegal in 1816 & The Sufferings of the Picard Family After the Shipwreck of the Medusa.

THE SEA WAR OF 1812 VOLUME 1 by *A. T. Mahan*—A History of the Maritime Conflict.

THE SEA WAR OF 1812 VOLUME 2 by *A. T. Mahan*—A History of the Maritime Conflict.

WETHERELL OF H. M. S. HUSSAR by *John Wetherell*—The Recollections of an Ordinary Seaman of the Royal Navy During the Napoleonic Wars.

THE NAVAL BRIGADE IN NATAL by *C. R. N. Burne*—With the Guns of H. M. S. Terrible & H. M. S. Tartar during the Boer War 1899-1900.

THE VOYAGE OF H. M. S. BOUNTY by *William Bligh*—The True Story of an 18th Century Voyage of Exploration and Mutiny.

SHIPWRECK! by *William Gilly*—The Royal Navy's Disasters at Sea 1793-1849.

KING'S CUTTERS AND SMUGGLERS: 1700-1855 by *E. Keble Chatterton*—A unique period of maritime history-from the beginning of the eighteenth to the middle of the nineteenth century when British seamen risked all to smuggle valuable goods from wool to tea and spirits from and to the Continent.

CONFEDERATE BLOCKADE RUNNER by *John Wilkinson*—The Personal Recollections of an Officer of the Confederate Navy.

NAVAL BATTLES OF THE NAPOLEONIC WARS by *W. H. Fitchett*—Cape St. Vincent, the Nile, Cadiz, Copenhagen, Trafalgar & Others.

PRISONERS OF THE RED DESERT by *R. S. Gwatkin-Williams*—The Adventures of the Crew of the Tara During the First World War.

U-BOAT WAR 1914-1918 by *James B. Connolly/Karl von Schenk*—Two Contrasting Accounts from Both Sides of the Conflict at Sea D uring the Great War.

AVAILABLE ONLINE AT **www.leonaur.com**
AND FROM ALL GOOD BOOK STORES

www.ingramcontent.com/pod-product-compliance
Lightning Source LLC
Chambersburg PA
CBHW031617160426
43196CB00006B/163